| Biblical Refigurations

Disability and Isaiah's Suffering Servant

BIBLICAL REFIGURATIONS

General Editors: James Crossley and Francesca Stavrakopoulou

This innovative series offers new perspectives on the textual, cultural, and interpretative contexts of particular biblical characters, inviting readers to take a fresh look at the methodologies of Biblical Studies. Individual volumes employ different critical methods including social-scientific criticism, critical theory, historical criticism, reception history, postcolonialism, and gender studies, while subjects include both prominent and lesser known figures from the Hebrew Bible and the New Testament.

DISABILITY AND ISALAH'S SUFFERING SERVANT

JEREMY SCHIPPER

OXFORD

UNIVERSITY PRESS

OXFORD

UNIVERSITY PRESS

Great Clarendon Street, Oxford OX2 6DP

Oxford University Press is a department of the University of Oxford.
It furthers the University's objective of excellence in research, scholarship,
and education by publishing worldwide in

Oxford New York

Auckland Cape Town Dar es Salaam Hong Kong Karachi
Kuala Lumpur Madrid Melbourne Mexico City Nairobi
New Delhi Shanghai Taipei Toronto

With offices in

Argentina Austria Brazil Chile Czech Republic France Greece
Guatemala Hungary Italy Japan Poland Portugal Singapore
South Korea Switzerland Thailand Turkey Ukraine Vietnam

Oxford is a registered trade mark of Oxford University Press
in the UK and in certain other countries

Published in the United States
by Oxford University Press Inc., New York

© Jeremy Schipper 2011

British Library Cataloguing in Publication Data

Data available

Library of Congress Cataloguing in Publication Data

Data available

Typeset by SPI Publisher Services, Pondicherry, India
Printed in Great Britain
on acid-free paper by
MPG Books Group, Bodmin and King's Lynn

ISBN 978–0–19–959485–6 (hbk)
      978–0–19–959486–3 (pbk)

1 3 5 7 9 10 8 6 4 2

Contents

Abbreviations

AB	Anchor Bible
ABD	*Anchor Bible Dictionary.* Edited by D. N. Freedman. 6 vols. New York, 1992
ACCS	Ancient Christian Commentary on Scripture
AJT	*American Journal of Theology*
ANET	*Ancient Near Eastern Texts Relating to the Old Testament.* Edited by J. B. Prichard. 3d edn. Princeton, 1969
ArBib	The Aramaic Bible
BASOR	*Bulletin of the American Schools of Oriental Research*
BibInt	*Biblical Interpretation: A Journal of Contemporary Approaches*
BJRL	*Bulletin of the John Rylands University Library of Manchester*
BZ	*Biblische Zeitschrift*
BWANT	Beiträge zur Wissenschaft vom Alten und Neuen Testament
BZAW	Beihefte zur Zeitschrift für die alttestamentliche Wissenschaft
ConBOT	Coniectanae biblica: Old Testament Series
COS	*The Context of Scripture.* Edited by W. W. Hallo. 3 vols. Leiden, 1997–
CBQ	*Catholic Biblical Quarterly*
EvT	*Evangelische Theologie*
FAT	Forschungen zum Alten Testament
HSM	Harvard Semitic Studies
IDB	*The Interpreter's Dictionary of the Bible.* Edited by G. A. Buttrick. 4 vols. Nashville, 1962
ICC	International Critical Commentary
JAOS	*Journal of the American Oriental Society*
JBL	*Journal of Biblical Literature*
JHS	*Journal of Hebrew Scriptures*
JSOTSup	Journal for the Study of the Old Testament: Supplement Series

KJV	King James Version
LHBOTS	Library of Hebrew Bible/Old Testament Studies
NIB	*The New Interpreter's Bible*
NICOT	New International Commentary on the Old Testament
NIV	New International Version
NovTSup	Novem Testamentum Supplements
NRSV	New Revised Standard Version
NovT	*Novum Testamentum*
OTL	Old Testament Library
PRSt	*Perspectives in Religious Studies*
RA	*Revue d'assyriologie et d'archéologie orientale*
RelArts	Religion and the Arts
RevExp	*Review and Expositor*
RevQ	*Revue de Qumram*
RHPR	*Revue d'historie et de philosophie religieuses*
SAA	State Archives of Assyria
SBLDS	Society of Biblical Literature Dissertation Series
SBLSymS	Society of Biblical Literature Symposium Series
VT	*Vetus Testamentum*
VTSup	Vetus Testamentum Supplements
WBC	Word Biblical Commentary
ZAW	*Zeitschrift für die altestamentliche Wissenschaft*

Preface

In her important book *Biblical Corpora: Representations of Disability in Hebrew Biblical Literature*, Rebecca Raphael comments that 'disability critiques of standard commentaries are an imperative for future research'. This book serves as a response to this observation. More specifically, I intend this book to refine some aspects on my earlier book, *Disability Studies and the Hebrew Bible*, which focused on how disability imagery plays an important role in how the Hebrew Bible, particularly Samuel–Kings, articulates and organizes various ideological positions. Since then, I have become more aware that the ubiquitous use of disability imagery in the Hebrew Bible does not translate into the presence of people with disabilities in the Hebrew Bible. Isaiah 52:13–53:12 provides an ideal text for a discussion of how disability imagery eclipses persons with disabilities in the history of biblical interpretation.

In his annotations to Isaiah in the *Jewish Study Bible*, however, Benjamin D. Sommer characterizes this text as 'One of the most difficult and contested passages in the Bible, [it has] attracted an enormous amount of attention from ancient, medieval, and modern scholars.' For someone like me who does not specialize in Isaiah, much less prophetic literature, Sommer's statement makes writing even a short monograph on this passage an exceptionally daunting task. Luckily, the wonderful assistance that I received from a variety of very talented people greatly improved my first attempt at a serious study of prophetic literature and the history of its interpretation.

The Center for the Humanities at Temple University (CHAT) provided tremendous support for this book in a variety of ways. From 2007 to 2009, CHAT sponsored a faculty reading group, 'Disabilities Studies across the Humanities', which drew faculty and staff from Temple's departments of English, Religion, Education, and the Institute on Disabilities. The group of friends that I made through this reading group, especially Ann Keefer, Josh Lukin, Carol Marfisi, and Michael L. Dorn, influenced my thinking about disability and allowed me to refine many of the ideas reflected in this book. CHAT also awarded me a faculty fellowship during the 2009–10 academic year and Temple University granted me a Summer Research Award in 2010. The fellowship and the award provided both the time and resources necessary to complete this book. I am also grateful to the Louisville Institute for awarding me a Sabbatical Grant for Researchers in 2011.

I worked out many of the arguments in the book in a number of invited lectures and talks. The idea for this book began as a presentation at the Chatlos Bible Conference at New York Theological Seminary in October 2008. I would like to thank Jin Hee Han for his invitation to this very enjoyable conference. From the spring of 2009 to the spring of 2010, I developed several lectures on disability and the Hebrew Bible for Temple's 'Mosaic' classes as part of a grant entitled 'Ensuring Higher Education for All' awarded to Temple's Institute on Disabilities by the United States Department of Education. The materials from these lectures greatly inform my arguments in Chapter 1 of this book. I would like to thank David T. Mitchell for the invitation to work on this grant. I also presented parts of this book in February 2010 as a participant in the CHAT Distinguished Faculty Lectures series. This project benefited greatly from the opportunity to present portions from it to the Disability Studies Forum at the University of Notre Dame in April 2010. I greatly appreciate the invitation from Candida Moss as well as her graciousness as a host during my visit to Notre Dame. Candida read most of my manuscript in one form or another. She provided valuable critiques and timely encouragement. I have learned a lot from her. Finally, I appreciated the invitation to present portions of this book to the 'Biblical Hermeneutics: Aesthetics and the Bible' task force of the Catholic Biblical Association of America during their annual meeting in August 2010.

I would also like to thank Hector Avalos, Joel S. Baden, J. Blake Couey, Stephen L. Cook, Christopher B. Hays, Jeremy M. Hutton, Alan Lenzi, G. Brooke Lester, Mark Leuchter, Patrick D. Miller, Dennis T. Olson, David Tabb Stewart, J. Ross Wagner, and Brittany E. Wilson for their various roles in helping to refine and improve my thinking about Isaiah 53 through conversations, emails, readings, and bibliographic recommendations. Although it was a course requirement, I would like to thank my students in my Spring 2010 graduate seminar, 'Topics in Biblical Studies: The Body and the Bible' for reading a version of this manuscript and participating in a series of helpful discussions of it throughout the semester. I am very grateful to my excellent graduate research assistant Kin Cheung for improving the manuscript in countless ways as we prepared for publication. I appreciate that the Department of Religion, currently chaired by Terry Rey, and the College of Liberal Arts provided the financial support for such a high quality research assistant. Of course, this book would not have come about without the enthusiastic and much appreciated support of my editor at Oxford University Press, Tom Perridge, and the series editors, Francesca Stavrakopoulou and James Crossley.

Unlike the history of scholarship on Isaiah 52:13–53:12, this book is relatively short. Since this book often focuses on what suffering servant scholarship has neglected in its treatment of this passage, it seems only fair to state upfront that I was not able to engage or include all of the scholarship worthy of discussion because of the space restrictions for volumes in this series (60,000 words). Readers should not assume that I do not appreciate or am unaware of a particular article or book just because I did not reference or discuss it here.

All biblical translations in this book come from the New Revised Standard Version and follow its versification, although I modify the transitions at several points when necessary. In order to make this book clearer to readers without knowledge of biblical languages, I use a simplified system of Hebrew and Greek transliterations that usually follows the 'general-purpose style' transliteration system in *The SBL Handbook of Style*. To further help with the clarity of the book, I often transliterate the root of a word rather than copy its exact form in the Masoretic text. All abbreviations follow *The SBL Handbook of Style*.

It is a great honour to dedicate this book to Nyasha Junior. I do so under no illusion that it matches the high standards she sets for her own remarkable scholarship. It is not my place to judge the quality of this book. This dedication does not mean that this is my best work, although I hope it is received as such. Rather, this dedication reflects an association. Regardless of its critical reception, I am prouder of this book than anything else I have published and I associate what I am most proud of in my life with Nyasha. Nothing in this world gives me more pride than my relationship with her. Everyday.

Jeremy Schipper
Philadelphia, Pennsylvania

Introduction

Disabling Progress in Suffering Servant Scholarship

> Rather than accepting disability and accommodating it as an expected part of every life course, we are stunned and alienated when it appears.... The visibly disabled body intrudes on our routine visual landscape and compels our attention, often obscuring the personhood of its bearer.
>
> Rosemarie Garland-Thomson, *Staring: How We Look*

> [T]here were many who were astonished at him—so marred was his appearance, unlike human semblance, and his form unlike that of mortals.
>
> Isaiah 52:14

Isaiah's 'Suffering Servant' (Isa 52:13–53:12) has captured the imagination of readers since very early in the history of biblical interpretation. Although many interpreters have focused on uncovering this unnamed servant's historical identity, when we read Isaiah 53 closely,[1] we discover that the passage focuses much more on the servant's suffering than on his historical identity. Nevertheless, scholars rarely appreciate how much our interpretation and identification of the servant depends on the ways we imagine his so-called suffering. Most interpreters understand the servant as an otherwise able-bodied person who suffers. By contrast, this book will show that Isaiah 53 describes the servant with language and imagery typically associated with disability in the Hebrew Bible and other ancient Near Eastern literature. We will trace both the disappearance of the servant's disability from the interpretative history of Isaiah 53 and the scholarly creation of the able-bodied suffering servant.

As we will discover, many scholars acknowledge the fact that Isaiah 53 describes the servant as having a disability, but few stop to consider the implications of his disability for how we interpret the servant. Instead, scholarly discussions of the servant's suffering usually revolve around the theological issue of vicarious suffering.[2] This approach finds the so-called meaning of the servant's suffering primarily in the potentially redemptive impact that it has on others. Unfortunately, this type of interpretation can easily slip into yet another instance of the able-bodied using persons with disabilities as resources for their own medical, literary, aesthetic, scientific, ethical, or theological development.

To cite just one example from outside biblical scholarship, those working in disability studies have frequently examined how characters with disabilities in Victorian literature often function as melodramatic instruments of moral instruction for able-bodied characters and the readers.[3] Framing the disability imagery in Isaiah 53 within this literary or cultural context would demand a fresh approach to the servant's so-called suffering. Too often, we interpret disability as an individual tragedy isolated from the ubiquitous exploitation that saturates disability's appearance in art and literature.[4] While we are not dismissive of theological interpretations of Isaiah 53 themselves, a corrective in light of disability studies would enhance our analysis, theological or otherwise, of this important text. Thus, we aim to show that the servant's so-called suffering in Isaiah 53 helps to poetically describe his disability as a social and political experience as opposed to simply an individual tragedy or data for a medical diagnosis.

Our proposal contrasts sharply with many interpretations in which disability imagery in Isaiah 53 functions as a powerful literary trope expressing the suffering and struggles of a presumably able-bodied person or community instead of experiences of people with disabilities. Over the centuries, scholars have used many interpretative strategies that allow the disability imagery in Isaiah 53 to retain its literary power without having to describe a figure with disabilities. This situation contributes to the appearance (or illusion) of a Hebrew Bible that uses disability as a rich literary trope while disavowing the presence of figures or characters with chronic disabilities.

To develop our thesis, this book engages the history of biblical scholarship, broadly defined, on Isaiah 53. Somewhere in their treatment of this passage, most recent critical commentaries on Isaiah make the observation that the literature written on Isaiah 53 is enormous. Thus, we do not offer an exhaustive survey of the scholarship on this biblical chapter because several fine surveys of the history of scholarship already exist.[5] Instead, we use representative examples of scholarship that provide an overall sense of the methods and strategies that scholars use to interpret the servant in Isaiah 53. As a starting point, our introduction provides a translation of Isaiah 53 and a brief discussion of its figures, sources, and structure. We conclude with some thoughts on why this book discusses the servant within the context of disability studies followed by a brief overview of the forthcoming chapters.

A translation of Isaiah 53 (52:13–53:12)

52:13 See, my servant shall prosper; he shall be exalted and lifted up, and shall be very high.

52:14 Just as there were many who were astonished at him—so marred was his appearance, unlike human semblance, and his form unlike that of mortals.

52:15 so he shall startle many nations;[6] kings shall shut their mouths because of him; for that which had not been told them they shall see, and that which they had not heard they shall contemplate.

53:1 Who has believed what we have heard? And to whom has the arm of the LORD been revealed?

53:2 For he grew up before him like a young plant, and like a root out of dry ground; he had no form or majesty that we should look at him, nothing in his appearance that we should desire him.

53:3 He was despised and withdrew from humanity;[7] a man of sufferings and acquainted with diseases; and like someone who hides their faces from us,[8] he was despised and we held him of no account.

53:4 Surely he has borne our diseases and carried our suffering; yet we accounted him plagued,[9] struck down by God, and afflicted.

53:5 But he was made profane[10] for our transgressions, crushed for our iniquities; upon him was the punishment that made us whole, and by his bruises we are healed.

53:6 All we like sheep have gone astray; we have all turned to our own way, and the LORD has laid on him the iniquity of us all.

53:7 He was oppressed, and he was afflicted, yet he did not open his mouth; like a lamb that is led to the slaughter, and like a sheep who is mute before its shearers, so he did not open his mouth.

53:8 Without restraint and without justice,[11] he was taken away. Who cared about his dwelling[12] because he was excluded from the land of the living, plagued for the transgression of my people?

53:9 They prepared his grave with the wicked and his tomb with the rich, although he had done no violence, and there was no deceit in his mouth.

53:10 The LORD was delighted to crush him, to make him diseased.[13] When you make his life an offering for sin, he shall see his offspring, and shall prolong his days; through him the will of the LORD shall prosper.

53:11 Out of the injustice of his life, he shall see light; he shall find satisfaction through his knowledge. The righteous one, my servant, shall make many righteous, and he shall bear their iniquities.

53:12 Therefore I will allot him a portion with the great, and he shall divide the spoil with the strong; because he poured out himself to death, and was numbered with the transgressors; yet he bore the sin of many, and made intercession for the transgressors.

The figures in Isaiah 53

Isaiah 53 does not identify any of its speakers. Instead, the passage refers to the speakers with pronouns, such as 'I' or 'we'. As David J. A. Clines has shown, the use of pronouns rather than proper names has allowed for numerous identifications of the speakers throughout the history of interpretation.[14] While we touch on various scholars' identifications of the speakers throughout our study, we do not try to settle the issue of their identity ourselves. The servant himself never speaks in this passage. Since our book focuses on the depiction of the servant, who is speaking concerns us less than what they (both the speakers in our passage and, more important, the scholars analysing Isaiah 53) say about the servant. It seems sufficient to observe that the imagined speakers recount the treatment of the servant with language and imagery that appear elsewhere in the Hebrew Bible to describe persons with disabilities.

As we will discuss in Chapter 4, scholars also debate whether the servant in Isaiah 53 represents an individual person or a collective reference to Israel or Zion based on the use of the term 'servant' elsewhere in Isaiah. Although most other references to a servant in the surrounding chapters seem to refer to Israel collectively (e.g. Isa 41:8; 43:10; 44:1–2, 21; 45:4; 49:3), many scholars question whether Isaiah 53 comes from the same source as these other references to a servant. Some scholars argue that the servant in Isaiah 53 referred to an individual originally, but that later expansions of the chapter that lead up to its present form continually reinterpreted the servant as a collective reference to exiled Israel or Zion.[15] Very little textual evidence exists, however, to support such speculations about the development of Isaiah 53 through multiple versions or redactions during various historical periods. In fact, there are so many differences between the Hebrew, Greek, Aramaic, and other ancient manuscripts of Isaiah 53 that it seems nearly impossible to recover the original text to begin with—much less speculate about how it developed through multiple but hypothetical editions or redactions.[16]

All we can say for certain regarding the servant's identity is that he is a figure in a poem that currently appears in Isaiah 53. Beyond that statement, it is a matter of speculation whether we identify the servant as a typological figure (see Chapter 3), a reference to a historical person, or a collective reference to a community. Through the history of his interpretation, scholars have gradually transformed this poetic figure into an able-bodied, more fully developed character or a historical person. In contrast, while we interpret Isaiah 53 as a description of the servant's social experience of disability, we will not speculate or fill in any back story for the servant that assumes that he has a life independent of this biblical passage. Isaiah 53 is a poem and not a diagnostic text or a biography of a person who existed outside of the poem. Poetic depictions of an experience of disability do not need to provide clear or developed descriptions of either the figure or the disability in order for readers to recognize it as describing a figure with disabilities. As we shall find in the forthcoming chapters, the disappearance of the servant with disabilities from Isaiah 53 and the creation of the suffering servant from bits and pieces of various passages throughout Isaiah 40–55 results primarily from attempts to create typological connections or a historical back story for the servant that does not appear anywhere in our passage.

Sources and structure of Isaiah 53

Most scholars believe that the book of Isaiah comes from multiple sources usually identified chronologically as First Isaiah (roughly Isaiah 1–23, 28–33), Second Isaiah (roughly Isaiah 34–55), Third Isaiah (roughly Isaiah 56–66), and the Isaianic Apocalypse (roughly Isaiah 24–7).[17] Although they debate whether Isaiah 53 comes from Second Isaiah, Third Isaiah, or another author or editor,[18] most believe that this passage comes from a time after the destruction of Jerusalem by the Babylonians in 587 BCE. For our purposes, it is not essential to determine the exact time period beyond 587 BCE to which Isaiah 53 belongs.

Instead, we should simply note that Isaiah 53 contains a number of the themes and images that appear throughout the Isaianic tradition (i.e. the material that currently makes up the book of Isaiah). Although the description of the servant's experience of disability in Isaiah 53 is unique, Isaiah 53 probably alludes to Isa 1:5–6; 2:12–14; 6:1–11; 11:1–10; 42:1–9, 18–23; 49:1–13; 50:4–11 as well as several other biblical texts outside of Isaiah (Lamentations 3; Jer 11:19–22; Ps 91:15–16).[19] In the mid-twentieth century, scholars also argued for numerous parallels, some more convincing than others, between Isaiah 53 and other Mesopotamian texts and traditions such as Tammuz liturgies.[20] Attention to the use of these themes and images elsewhere in Isaiah and other ancient Near Eastern literature may help us better understand how our passage depicts the servant.

Throughout this book, we discuss 52:13–53:12 as if it represents a unified passage even if it does not follow the traditional chapter divisions between Isaiah 52 and 53. Both the opening and closing verses (52:13; 53:11b–12) refer to the 'servant' specifically, whereas the material before and after these verses (52:12 and 54:1) deal with subjects other than the servant. Frequently, scholars have proposed that this passage is a composite text made up of two or more originally independent sources. Some scholars have argued that 52:13–15 and 53:1–12 come from different sources because of the supposedly different genre of these verses.[21] The majority scholarly opinion, however, holds that the passage follows a three-part structure with a divine speech or oracle as the introduction and conclusion of the text (52:13–15 and 53:11b–12) and a psalm about the servant as the main body of the passage (53:1–11a).[22]

An editor may have inserted the psalm in the middle of two divine speeches, but the ancient manuscripts of Isaiah 53 provide no hard evidence to support this theory of an inserted psalm. The best textual evidence for this idea comes from a biblical manuscript from the Dead Sea Scrolls. This manuscript begins a new line at 53:1 (1QIsa[a]). Nonetheless, another manuscript from the Dead Sea Scrolls treats 52:13–53:12 as a single unit (1QIsa[b]). Even if the inserted psalm theory were correct, descriptions of the servant's disability still appear in both the divine speech (52:14) and the psalm (53:2). We could speculate that the similar vocabulary in 52:14 and 53:2 used to describe his disability ('form' and 'appearance') reflects a later editor's attempt to unify two independent texts and that the divine speech did not originally describe the otherwise exalted servant as having a disability. Nevertheless, since no extant ancient manuscript supports such speculation about the editorial process, we have no good reason to believe that the text(s) that eventually became Isaiah 53 ever described the servant without a disability. As we discover throughout this book, the removal of the servant's disability through scholarly theories about our passage's editorial history represents just one of the many reading strategies that allow us to imagine the servant as able-bodied. Thus, it is imperative to situate such reading strategies for Isaiah 53 within the cultural history of disability.

The suffering servant and the cultural history of disability

In my first book on disability and the Hebrew Bible, I wrote that as an adult with cerebral palsy I can pass as an able-bodied white male most of the time.[23] In the few years since that book, my teaching responsibilities have allowed me to spend much more time in front of large groups of people. Having had the opportunity to reflect on my public appearance in a new perspective and discuss it with a variety of people, I have become far less confident that I ever could pass as able-bodied for any sustained amount of time even if my cerebral palsy does not yet limit major life activities. This realization led me to re-evaluate my strategies for interpreting disability in the Hebrew Bible and to consider how the pressure to pass as able-bodied influences scholarship. The ability to pass as able-bodied represents a major form of most people's socialization, regardless of how they self-identify. While many people with disabilities are painfully aware of the pressure to pass on a daily basis, this issue has received little attention within disability scholarship,[24] and virtually no attention within biblical scholarship interested in disability.

When my first book came out in 2006, most of the biblical scholarship of disability or disease focused on medicine or diagnosis rather than disability as a cultural product or social experience. There was very little scholarship in print that considered disability as a literary trope that biblical authors and editors used to articulate various theological and ideological viewpoints. In part, my first book tried to show that certain texts use disability along with more well-known tropes such as kingship or Zion to articulate and organize various perspectives on ancient Israelite identity. Since then, important monographs by other Hebrew Bible scholars, such as Saul Olyan and Rebecca Raphael, have expanded the study of disability as a literary device or analytic tool that conveys various forms of social organization and representation. Their commendable work includes many texts that my first book did not focus on.[25] Overall, recent work of disability, including my own, has shown that the Hebrew Bible is full of disability imagery that requires further critical enquiry.

Yet, while disability imagery is ubiquitous in the Hebrew Bible, characters with disabilities are not. The presence of the former does not guarantee the presence of the latter. For example, most of the disability imagery in the prophetic literature describes the moral or physical state of otherwise able-bodied people. The divorce of disability imagery from lived experience can create the dangerous impression of a biblical world full of imagery of disability but free of people with disabilities. Intentionally or not, biblical scholarship tends to reinforce this impression in its treatment of prominent biblical characters. In the New Testament, Jesus or his followers frequently remove disability through healings. By contrast, the Hebrew Bible contains relatively few healings of specific characters.

Thus, less obvious ways to distance disability from seemingly deserving characters emerge within the history of the Hebrew Bible's interpretation. As we discover in Chapter 1, many scholars explain how Moses is ineloquent rather than disabled or assume that Jacob is injured rather than disabled or associate the blindness of Isaac, Eli, and others with advanced age rather than disability. This allows such characters to pass as able-bodied people who follow the normal or at least expected life cycle.

While we explain away disabilities in specific characters, we celebrate the rhetorical contributions that disability imagery makes to the literary artistry of biblical prose and poetry. Since Isaiah 53 does not simply use disability imagery, but describes the experience of a figure with disabilities, its rich interpretative history provides a wonderful example of this dynamic at work. We rely on people with disabilities for their poignant imagery, but deny descriptions or documentations of their experience. Outside biblical studies, disability scholars have shown that this situation appears as a regrettable constant in the cultural history of disability more generally.[26] Although disability scholars have tested this thesis mostly on disability in the modern era, the history of scholarship on the servant in Isaiah 53 is similarly marked by the exegetical recruitment of disability imagery and the disavowal of a figure with disabilities. Studying this tendency in suffering servant scholarship within the context of disability studies not only furthers our understanding of the book of Isaiah, but makes a substantive contribution to the writing of a cultural history of disability as well.

Before explaining how our argument will unfold over the following chapters, we should note that we have not framed our treatment of the servant within the context of disability studies to claim a privileged insight into Isaiah 53 based on an appeal to a personal experience of disability. In fact, while an author's personal experience influences any interpretation, disability scholarship on the Bible should not rely on personal experiences as *evidence* for our interpretations. Instead, our interpretative conclusions should rely on arguments that any competent scholar could produce regardless of her or his relationship to people with disabilities.

Certainly, there are many critical issues in so-called suffering servant research that we cannot discuss given the size of this book.

The issues of the servant's disability and his assumed able-bodied status, however, seem especially critical for understanding how scholars have imagined and identified the servant through his interpretative afterlife. The way that we interpret his physical condition remains an important, but frequently neglected and unstated, critical issue for any historical, literary, or theological scholarship on the servant. This issue reflects more than simply a unique perspective arising from the personal experiences of a scholar with disabilities.

Overview of forthcoming chapters

Chapter 1 examines a variety of methodological issues that will influence our study of the servant throughout this book. First, we consider how our concept of disability may change according to the particular type of language we use. Disability studies emphasizes that what we understand as disability depends on the type of language that we use to approach this subject (e.g. medical, legal, religious, military, social scientific, cultic, political, and so on). When we talk about disability we are usually referring to something more than a simple medical diagnosis or objective biological description of an individual. This chapter begins by discussing different models for disability used within disability studies, including the medical model, social model, and cultural model. Second, it explores various factors involved in how we determine what counts as a disability beyond a medical definition. These factors include age, legal standing, and differentiations between permanent disabilities and temporary or fatal injuries. Additionally, we discuss the tendency to interpret disability imagery as metaphors for almost any condition or situation other than the lived experience of persons with disabilities. These interpretations assume that if a text does not describe the experience of disability in a literal or diagnostic fashion, then it must be describing something other than a figure with disabilities. Such assumptions allow us to divorce the imagery of disability from the lived experience of disability. This chapter helps explain what we mean when we refer to the servant as a figure with disabilities throughout this book.

When Bernhard Duhm proposed his influential theory of four distinct 'servant songs' within Isaiah in 1892, he identified the servant in Isaiah 53 as a person with a skin anomaly. Yet, while his 'servant songs' proposal has greatly influenced biblical criticism for more than a century, scholars have largely rejected his identification of the servant as having a skin anomaly. Nevertheless, compelling evidence exists that Isaiah 53 describes the servant with the language of disability, be it a skin anomaly or another condition. Through a close reading of descriptions of the servant in Isaiah 53, Chapter 2 begins by arguing that his description uses imagery that typically describes the social and political experiences of people with disabilities in other biblical and ancient Near Eastern contexts. Second, we find that Isaiah 53 does not simply describe the servant's disability as data for a medical diagnosis or as a tragic biological condition isolated in the individual. Rather, it constructs his disability as a lived experience with a complex constellation of social, political, and theological dimensions. Third, we examine reading strategies that have allowed scholars to interpret the servant as an otherwise able-bodied figure who either suffers an injury, dies, recovers from his disability or injury, or is imprisoned. Such strategies allow scholars to imagine the servant's suffering as related to almost anything but a disability.

Chapter 3 examines early translations of Isaiah 53 and other scriptural references to the suffering servant that depict the servant not as a figure with disabilities but as an otherwise able-bodied figure who suffers. First, this chapter examines how ancient versions of Isaiah 53 from the Dead Sea Scrolls as well as Greek, Aramaic, and Latin translations render the disability imagery. These ancient versions tend to downplay or even remove the servant's disability. Second, the chapter examines typological interpretative strategies common in later scriptural references to Isaiah 53. These typologies, in which two or more characters or figures are interpreted as examples that reflect a particular character type or profile, involve the servant but tend not to include his disability. Rather, they invoke the servant as a messianic figure or as an otherwise able-bodied figure who suffers or dies. Certain texts even connect the servant to a figure who heals disabilities rather than has disabilities.

Chapter 4 explores how post-biblical scholarly exegetical practices often reinforce the notion of the servant as an able-bodied sufferer rather than a figure with disabilities. This chapter shows how the search for the servant's historical identity often reconfigures the servant as a figure or group not usually understood as having a disability. With the arrival of modern biblical criticism, discovering the historical identity of the servant became one of the most popular interests among biblical scholars. Chapter 4 begins by showing that, like Duhm, a minority of interpreters throughout history have focused on the disability imagery in order to connect the servant to a person with disabilities. Second, we discover that more recent scholars have downplayed disability as a prominent clue to the servant's historical identity. Instead, they locate his identity among characters traditionally understood as able-bodied or as healed by God. Third, we turn to scholars who prefer to identify the servant with the personification of a collective group rather than identifying the servant with one particular individual. For some, the servant's experience becomes Israel's collective experience of exile. Throughout prophetic literature, we find disability imagery used to describe the experience of exile rather than the experience of disability. These passages appropriate the imagery of disability to describe the suffering and hardships of the presumably able-bodied in exile. Often, the collective identification of the servant results in an interpretation of the servant's disability as describing the experience of exile rather than disability. Read together, Chapters 3 and 4 trace the transformation of the servant from a figure with disabilities in a biblical poem to a typological figure to a historically identifiable and usually able-bodied person or group.

After a summary of the key points of the book, the conclusion will reflect on the tendency within scholarship to restore the servant to among the ranks of the able-bodied even if little textual support exists for such an interpretive move. We examine the consequences of appropriating disability imagery as a literary trope that articulates the experiences of able-bodied sufferers. While we may appreciate this creative reapplication of the servant's experience to wider circles, it remains important to contextualize this process within the cultural history of disability, a history with an uneasy relationship with how, as with other minority groups, dominant groups have exploited disabled bodies as sources of medical, moral, scientific, and theological enquiry.

1

Disabling Methodology in Hebrew Bible Studies

[D]isability seldom has been explored as a condition or experience in its own right; disability's psychological and bodily variations have been used to metaphorize nearly every social conflict outside its own ignoble predicament in culture.

David T. Mitchell and Sharon L. Snyder, 'Disability Studies and the Double Bind of Representation', in *The Body and Physical Difference: Discourses on Disability*

[The prophet in Isa 42:18–19] carries the metaphor to the point of absurdity when he calls the people 'a blind servant' and 'a deaf messenger'. To begin the scene like this is to be sure of the listeners' attention. A blind servant is useless, a deaf messenger ineligible. Everyone must realize that from his or her own experience.

Klaus Baltzer, *Deutero-Isaiah: A Commentary on Isaiah 40–55*

Recently, biblical scholars have shown an increased interest in how ancient Near Eastern literature, including the Hebrew Bible, uses disability as an analytic tool for social and political organization and interpretation, similar to gender or ethnicity.[1] Informed by the burgeoning field of disability studies, this scholarship demonstrates that when we discuss disability, we usually imply more than a medical diagnosis or objective description of a particular physical or cognitive trait. Thus, we should pay close attention to the particular language or contexts that a given passage uses to discuss disability.

This chapter examines a variety of methodological issues that will influence our study of the servant throughout this book. First, we consider how our concept of disability may change according to the particular type of language we use to approach this subject. We discuss different models for disability used within disability studies, including the medical, social, and cultural models. Second, we explore various factors involved in how we determine what counts as a disability beyond a medical definition, including age, legal standing, injury, and metaphorical uses. This chapter helps explain what we mean when we refer to the servant as a figure with disabilities throughout this book.

Defining disability according to various models

Biblical Hebrew has no word equivalent to the English word 'disability'. The Hebrew word *mum*, usually translated as 'blemish' in the NRSV, refers to many conditions that we may consider a disability, such as blindness or lameness (cf. Lev 21:16–23). Yet *mum* does not cover every trait that we may consider a disability. The Bible does not use the word *mum* for conditions such as deafness, muteness, or skin anomalies, even though these conditions are sometimes paired with other conditions that qualify as a *mum* (e.g. the pairing of 'blind' and 'deaf' in Lev 19:14; Isa 29:18; 35:5; 43:8).[2] Nevertheless, this does not mean that the concept of disability would not have made sense to people in ancient Israel. As Rebecca Raphael observes, biblical Hebrew does not have a word equivalent to the English word 'religion' either. Yet studies of ancient Israelite religion abound within biblical scholarship.[3] Furthermore, the Hebrew Bible frequently groups together words for certain physical traits such as 'lame', 'blind', or 'deaf' (Exod 4:11; 2 Sam 5:8; Jer 31:8; Mal 1:8). This grouping suggests that ancient Israelites did not understand these particular conditions as isolated occurrences, but as belonging to a larger conceptual category.[4] Exactly what qualifies as markers of this category, however, could change. For example, not every culture would necessarily understand cerebral palsy and anorexia as belonging to a common conceptual category. Understandings of the concept of disability may differ according to their particular social and cultural location.

Medical model of disability. Different understandings of disability according to location do not factor into what some disability scholars refer to as the 'medical model' of disability. This model understands disability as an anomalous condition isolated in an individual's body and in need of diagnosis and correction or cure. The medical model approaches disability as exclusively a medical condition that must be cured by doctors or overcome by the individual through lifestyle changes. It positions disability as a pathological condition even in cases when, as with attempts to pathologize certain races, genders, or sexual orientations, no solid scientific or medical basis exists to do so.[5] In many ways, the focus on a cure or correction uncritically reflects and reinforces the immense social pressure to pass cosmetically as able-bodied regardless of whether this is the healthiest choice for the individual. This focus overlooks the fact that, although a disease may result in a disability, a healthy person with a disability is not an oxymoron.[6]

Adherents to the medical model may consider social factors as aiding in the diagnosis of a disability but not as contributing to the definition of disability. The medical model portrays disability as the result of an anomalous body unrelated to a society's political, educational, religious, architectural, and other structures. Thus, when persons with disabilities appear to navigate these structures like able-bodied people do, we often congratulate them for 'overcoming' their disability as if the difficulty lay solely in the individual body and not at all in their experience of society's larger structures. Yet we would not claim that racism, homophobia, or sexism operates on the individual level alone and has nothing to do with larger social and political structures. It would seem absurd to argue that we could resolve these issues if individuals could just overcome their minority status and act like a white, heterosexual man. Instead, or at least ideally, we critically examine the social and political structures that contribute to racism, homophobia, and sexism. Unfortunately, we rarely do this with disability.

Furthermore, the Hebrew Bible rarely discusses disability within a medical context that aims to diagnose a particular condition based on symptoms appearing in an individual body. While certain extant Babylonian and Assyrian 'diagnostic texts' approach disability as a medical issue,[7] the Hebrew Bible tends to discuss disability as a social, political, cultic, sexual, moral, theological, or military issue, to name just a few examples.

Social model of disability. In contrast to the medical model's definition of disability, the 'social model' of disability distinguishes between 'impairments' and 'disabilities'. The social model enjoys popularity among disability scholars working primarily in the social sciences in the United Kingdom.[8] According to this model, the term 'impairment' describes a particular physical, emotional, or cognitive trait that results in the inability of the mind or body to function as expected. Although a person may acquire impairments through a disease or illness, impairments are not necessarily related to a disease. Since impairments can also result from an injury or a congenital condition; they do not necessarily represent pathological or contagious conditions.

Distinct from impairment, the social model defines the term 'disability' as socially created discrimination against people with impairments. For example, a wheelchair user's restricted mobility may not result from his or her impairment alone but also from a lack of access ramps into some buildings. Likewise, diminished eyesight or hearing in young people qualifies as an impairment. Yet, as Lennard Davis observes, we tend not to understand eyeglasses as a marker of disability among young people, whereas visible hearing aids often mark a young person as a person with a disability.[9] In this sense, the label of disability does not come from any intrinsic property of the impairment itself. Rather, it comes from the perceived frequency or rarity of the impairment within a particular society. Such designations probably tell us more about our social norms than they do about an individual's body. Defining disability as a social construction does not mean advocates of this model resist advances in medicine or support technology. After all, deciding what counts as an impairment requires the diagnostic work usually associated with the medical model.[10] Instead, distinguishing between disability and impairment implies that, as with race or sexual orientation, we should not confuse impairment with pathology.

The social model has received criticism, however, because it defines disability primarily as a social construction. Critics of the social model emphasize that disability is a real, lived social experience that describes how many people with impairments experience the world. Disability is not simply an abstract concept of discrimination that has no concrete point of contact with the limitations of individuals' actual bodies. Jenny Morris notes 'a tendency within the Social Model of disability to deny the experience of our own bodies, insisting that our physical differences and restrictions are entirely socially created'.[11] For example, while it is a contributing factor, social discrimination is not the only factor that restricts a wheelchair user's mobility. The provision of access ramps does not mean that a wheelchair user can now walk. Likewise, despite the social meanings that we assign to eyeglasses or hearing aids, this does not suggest that visual or hearing impairments are entirely social constructions that do not actually exist in the individual body. In this sense, disability differs from racism, sexism, or homophobia in that we cannot identify the restrictions that disable people as prohibitions against otherwise able-bodied persons.[12]

Furthermore, certain factors blur the line between impairment and disability. If we define impairment as a trait that inhibits the mind or body from functioning as expected, we assume a set of socially determined expectations for how minds or bodies should function. In that sense, impairments are defined partially by some socially accepted notion of reasonable expectations. Moreover, we could ask whether conditions such as anorexia qualify as impairments or disabilities. With anorexia, it seems hard to distinguish neatly between the products of an individual's particular biological condition and (internalized) socially constructed discrimination.[13]

This difficulty increases when we try to draw a neat line between impairment and disability in ancient Near Eastern cultures because we have very limited understandings of or access to either the biological conditions of individuals or their larger social norms. In many cases, we can only make an educated guess regarding the particular impairment described in an ancient Near Eastern text or the types of meanings such cultures assigned to these particular impairments. Often, we cannot pinpoint an impairment precisely enough to separate it from any accompanying social discrimination. Nevertheless, we do not have to diagnose an impairment precisely in order to identify ancient Near Eastern descriptions of the social experience of persons with impairments. Likewise, we can identify these descriptions without completely understanding the process of disability's social construction reflected in these descriptions.

Cultural model of disability. Rather than defining disability as socially constructed discrimination against persons with impairments, we define the term 'disability' in this book as *the social experience of persons with certain impairments.* This definition of disability reflects the influence of the 'cultural model' of disability, which has gained popularity among many North American disability scholars working primarily in the humanities.[14] How an individual or community, regardless of whether they self-identify as disabled, articulates or narrates these social experiences depends on the type(s) of language that they use. As suggested earlier, when we discuss disability we may use a combination of social, political, medical, sexual, religious, scientific, athletic, legal, environmental, cartoonish, and military language, to name just a few examples.

As we will find in the following chapter, Isaiah 53 does not diagnose the servant's impairments. Rather than describing the servant's disability as an abnormal medical condition in need of diagnosis and treatment, Isaiah 53 describes the servant's social and political experience of living with impairments. In this sense, it is appropriate to refer to the servant as a figure with disabilities based on our 'cultural model' definition. We must study carefully the depiction of this experience of disability in order to understand the nature of the servant's so-called suffering.

Focusing on disability as a social experience has important implications for how we study disability in the Hebrew Bible. First, it reminds us that the medical model is not always the dominant model for conceptualizing disability. This holds true not only in the contemporary industrialized world, but even more so within the world of ancient Near Eastern literature. As Raphael suggests, theological frameworks or discourses rather than medical ones denominate understandings of disability in the Hebrew Bible.[15] We will discover in the next chapter that Raphael's suggestion helps us understand how Isaiah 53 approaches disability. Yet a tendency exists in biblical scholarship to assume that the medical model popular within the contemporary industrialized world represents the normative and universal meaning of disability.[16] Many scholars assume that Isaiah

53 does not depict the servant as a figure with disabilities because the text does not offer a precise medical diagnosis of his condition. Yet this assumption understands disability only through a medical model that biblical texts rarely use.

Second, analysing how we articulate disability entails analysing how we articulate able-bodiedness instead of assuming that able-bodiedness represents the unstated natural order of things. In questioning the (false) dichotomy between disability as abnormal and able-bodied as normal, this approach foregrounds another important assumption that many of us bring to reading the Hebrew Bible. Since the Hebrew Bible does not describe the vast majority of characters physically, we tend to imagine these characters as able-bodied by default. Yet, if by normal we mean the majority or typical, we should note that the most commonly described types of bodies in the Hebrew Bible are those that do not function as expected due to age, injuries, diseases, or other impairments.[17]

For some, that the Hebrew Bible includes descriptions of disability implies that otherwise undescribed characters are able-bodied, assuming that able-bodied represents the body's normal state of existence. Robert McRuer comments on this tendency when he notes that while 'homosexuality and disability clearly share a pathologized past . . . Able-bodiedness, even more than heterosexuality, still largely masquerades as a nonidentity, as the natural order of things.'[18] Yet, like disability, 'able-bodied' is a marker of bodily difference and not the default normal state of human existence from which disability deviates.[19]

In fact, we spend most of the early and later years of a 'normal' life cycle without what we usually understand as able-bodied capabilities. Martha Nussbaum observes, 'As the life span increases, the relative independence that many people sometimes enjoy looks more and more like a temporary condition . . . Even in our prime, many of us encounter shorter or longer periods of extreme dependency on others—after surgery or a severe injury, or during a period of depression or acute mental stress.'[20] The aging process of a person who would otherwise identify himself or herself as able-bodied creates problems for the notion that disability represents an abnormal state. To emphasize this point, some disability scholars and activists refer to people who identify themselves as non-disabled as TABS, which stands for 'temporarily able-bodied'.[21] In this sense, the line between disability and able-bodied is not absolute and obvious. A variety of factors beyond a person's biological condition influences how we distinguish between disability and able-bodied.

What counts as disability imagery?

A major complication with analysing the ways that a text articulates disability as a social experience is determining whether certain language and imagery represents disability or some other state or condition. Deciding what counts as disability remains difficult enough in some contemporary literature, but even more so when the text comes from a very different time and culture. In the following sections, we examine some of the factors that complicate a textual study of disability. In the process, we address several issues that obscure the servant's status as disabled and allow readers to imagine him as able-bodied more by default than by textual evidence.

Defining disability according to age. We rarely determine whether a person has a disability by a medical diagnosis alone. We also consider our social expectations for a person of his or her age. If a person uses a walking stick in his or her sixties or seventies, we might consider the walking stick as a sign of advanced age, a natural point in the aging process. If another person uses an identical walking stick in his or her twenties or thirties, we might consider the same walking stick as a sign of disability, an anomaly within the expected life cycle. Often, we measure a cognitive impairment in adulthood through a comparison with an able-bodied child. We may say that he or she has the cognitive capacity of an (able-bodied) six-year-old. In a 2008 book, Tobin Siebers noted that there are nearly 50 million people with disabilities in the United States. Yet he observed that this number does not include 'the elderly, many of whom cannot climb stairs or open doors with ease, nor children, whose physical and mental abilities fit uncomfortably in the adult world. The disabled represent a minority that potentially includes anyone at anytime.'[22] Whether we consider a person disabled depends largely on the point in life and how suddenly he or she acquires an impairment. If an impairment develops slowly over a long period of time, we might consider it a natural by-product of aging. On the other hand, if one acquires it rapidly through an accident or injury, we might consider the same impairment a disability.[23]

In the Hebrew Bible, infertility, or barrenness, provides a prime example of the complicated relationship between age and disability. Infertility is the most frequently discussed disability affecting women in the Hebrew Bible (e.g. Gen 11:30; 16:2; 20:18; 25:21; 29:31; Exod 23:26; Deut 7:14; Judg 13:2–3; 1 Sam 1:5).[24] A number of ancient Near Eastern texts, such as the Sumerian myth of Enki and Ninmah (*COS* 1.159: 518) or a rabbinic commentary on Isaac's birth in Gen 21:2 (*Gen. Rab.* 53:8), include infertility within their discussions of other disabilities such as blindness, lameness, or certain cognitive disabilities.[25] These texts suggest that infertility qualified as a disability in those cultures.

The Hebrew Bible describes infertility more as a social experience than a biological anomaly.[26] For example, 1 Sam 1:2–20 focuses on Hannah's experience of infertility. Since Peninnah, Hannah's sister wife, had many children, she 'used to provoke Hannah severely, to irritate her, because the LORD had closed her womb. So it went on year by year; as often as she went up to the house of the LORD, she used to provoke her. Therefore Hannah wept and would not eat' (vv. 5–6). The following verses portray this social dynamic as making Hannah's 'heart sad' (v. 8), she is 'deeply distressed' (v. 10), in a state of 'misery' (v. 11) and 'deeply troubled' (v. 15). We should note that none of these descriptions are inherent properties of infertility as a medical condition. The passage describes her experience of infertility and not the causes of her infertility. It describes her infertility not as an impairment alone but as a disability. Like 1 Samuel 1, we will find that Isaiah 53 focuses more on the servant's social and political experience of impairments than on the specific nature of the impairments themselves.

Hannah's experience as depicted in this passage would explain why we could label her as disabled by our cultural model definition. Nevertheless, this passage does not explain how the characters in the story would have induced her infertility. They would probably not identify her as infertile as a result of biological cause or medical examination. She would not have undergone medical tests at a fertility clinic as we might do in a contemporary industrialized society. Although the text provides a theological reason for her condition, namely that the LORD closed her womb (1 Sam 1:5–6; cf. Gen 16:2; 20:18), it does not explain explicitly how the characters would have realized that she was infertile. Assuming she had inter- course on a routine basis, they would have had to induce her divinely caused infertility from the amount of time that passed without conception. In this sense, her age would have played a large role in determining her infertility. While the Hebrew Bible does not usually mention the age of an infertile woman, Gen 18:11 reports that, 'Abraham and Sarah were already old and well advanced in years, and Sarah was past the age of childbearing' (NIV). Cases of infertility in the Hebrew Bible highlight the fact that certain biblical characters did not qualify as disabled because of a medical diagnosis or a clear intrinsic difference from able-bodied characters. Rather, disability could be determined by social expectations for a person of a particular age.

Certainly, just like disability, what one society considers elderly might differ considerably from what another society considers elderly. The language and images that the art and literature of a particular culture associates with the aging process may not be universally recognized across all cultures. In fact, one of the difficulties for biblical scholars in studying disability is determining whether ancient audiences would have associated particular motifs with disabilities or advanced age. Would certain images have represented disability or old age or both for these audiences? For example, 1 Kgs 1:1 states, 'King David was old and advanced in years; and although they covered him with clothes, he could not get warm.' We could ask if this verse depicts David primarily as elderly or disabled. Along similar lines, Isaac (Gen 27:1), Jacob (Gen 48:10), Eli (1 Sam 4:15), and Ahijah (1 Kgs 14:4) all have visual impairments in old age.[27] Ancient audi- ences may have considered visual impairments as a natural and expected by-product of the aging process and therefore understood the imagery as indicating advanced age instead of disability. After all, none of these passages imply that these characters experienced any social discrimination due to their visual impairment.[28] Moreover, the number of euphemisms for blindness in ancient Near Eastern texts may suggest that it was a frequent, even 'normal', experience in those cultures.[29] Retaining one's eyesight late in life may have represented the exception rather than the rule. Deuteronomy 34:7 depicts Moses' keen eyesight at the time of his death at age 120 as extraordinary.[30] The cultural distance between modern biblical scholars and the ancient Near East makes it difficult to determine what language and images would have counted as disability imagery for ancient audiences.

Legal definitions of disability. The relationship between disability and age may not seem very important for our study of Isaiah 53. After all, the passage provides no indication of the imagined age of the servant. It focuses much more on the servant's relationship to a larger community. If his description contains a social component, we could consider whether the passage depicts the servant's disability in legal terms. Nevertheless, we still must consider age even if we define disability according to the law rather than medicine. In the United States, part of the legal definition of 'disability' according to the Americans with Disabilities Act of 1990 (ADA) includes 'a physical or mental impairment that substantially limits one or more of the major life activities of such individual'.[31] One of the 'major life activities' that the ADA focuses on is employment. The United States' economic system places a high value on employment since it plays an important role in the country's financial structures.

Yet a medical or biological definition of what it means to be a living human being does not include employment. We would not speak of employment as a 'major life activity' as we would speak of breathing as a major life activity. Unlike breathing, we do not expect to engage in employment our entire lives. Ideally, small children should not have to find employment and a person should retire by at least his or her seventies or eighties. We expect employment to be a 'major life activity' roughly between a person's twenties and sixties in our society. Thus, if a person uses a walking stick and this limits the type of job that he or she can perform during his or her twenties through sixties, we might consider this person disabled. If he or she uses a walking stick after the age in which employment is socially expected of him or her as a 'major life activity', then the walking stick may not signify a disability as much as his or her 'normal' elderly status.

Appealing to a legal definition of disability, however, may not help us understand what would have counted as a disability in ancient

Near Eastern contexts.[32] To our knowledge, no extant legal code from the Bible or other ancient Near Eastern literature provides a legal definition of disability. At most, we have a few statements that provide very general protections for people with disabilities. For example, Lev 19:14 states, 'You shall not revile the deaf or put a stumbling block before the blind.' Deuteronomy 27:18 declares, 'Cursed be anyone who misleads a blind person on the road.' Likewise, in chapter 25 of the Egyptian *Instruction of Amenemope*, one reads, 'Do not laugh at a blind man, Nor tease a dwarf, Nor cause hardship for the lame.'[33] An Assyrian text mentions the practice of giving bread to the deaf.[34] Nonetheless, these examples hardly suggest that persons with disabilities enjoyed a protected legal status or that people in the ancient Near East ever conceived of persons with disabilities as a legally defined group that deserved special protections.

Defining disabilities versus injuries. The writing style in the Hebrew Bible is extremely terse. For example, Genesis 1 narrates the creation of the entire heavens and earth in just thirty-one verses with minimal physical description. Regarding physical descriptions of specific characters, the Hebrew Bible may describe them as hairy (Gen 27:11), fat (Judg 3:17), tall (1 Sam 9:2; 16:7; 17:4–7), beautiful (1 Sam 16:12; 17:42; Prov 11:22; Song 1:8; 2:10, 13; 5:9; 6:1), and so on, but such occasional descriptions lack sufficient detail to assist us in picturing a biblical character's appearance. This writing style suggests that when the text mentions a disability it does not intend to aid us in diagnosing the condition (unlike other ancient Near Eastern diagnostic texts[35]). Thus, it becomes very difficult to determine whether certain descriptions signal an acquired disability or a temporary injury.

We should not assume that ancient Near Eastern audiences would share our assumption that a character's injury is temporary unless the text informs us otherwise. For example, in one of the rare instances in which the Hebrew Bible describes an injured body following a non-fatal accident, it associates the injury with an acquired disability. According to 2 Sam 4:4, 'Saul's son Jonathan had a son who was crippled in his feet. He was five years old ... His nurse picked him up and fled; and, in her haste to flee, it happened that he fell and became lame. His name was Mephibosheth.' Mephibosheth's accident leads to an acquired disability as the text indicates repeatedly during stories of his adult life (2 Sam 9:3, 13; 19:26).[36] Considering the medical technology available at the time, ancient Near Eastern audiences may have associated serious non-fatal injuries with acquired disabilities instead of temporary conditions from which a full recovery was the expected norm (cf. Exod 21:18-19; Code of Hammurabi 206 [*ANET*, 175]; The Hittite Laws 10 [*ANET*, 189]).[37] Imagining the undescribed body after injury as able-bodied by default may represent a relatively modern reading convention. The description of Mephibosheth may represent the rule rather than the exception in the ancient Near East.

The descriptive economy of biblical prose introduces other complications in distinguishing disability from injury. Often, the text makes only one mention of a character's impairment. For example, Jacob sustains a hip injury during a wrestling match (Gen 32:25). After Gen 32:31 notes that Jacob limped away because of this injury, there is no further discussion of his hip or mobility.[38] Following Genesis 32, Jacob's body remains undescribed until Gen 48:1–10. In this passage, he loses his health and eyesight in old age, but this might mark Jacob as elderly rather than disabled for many of us. Thus, we have no way to determine if he made a full recovery from his hip injury in Genesis 32. We do not know if his condition signals a temporary injury to an otherwise able-bodied person or a permanent disability.[39] An assumption that Jacob recovered because the text does not indicate otherwise presupposes that able-bodied is normal by default. This assumption, however, comes from textual silence rather than textual evidence. Again, we do not know that ancient audiences shared this assumption.

The wide semantic range of certain Hebrew words further complicates matters. For example, the Hebrew Bible uses forms related to the word *ḥlh* for a variety of conditions, including temporary and fatal injuries and illnesses, emotional distress, impairments, and disabilities. As with the English word 'sick', *ḥlh* can refer to anything from a minor cough to lung cancer.[40] Isaiah 53 uses forms related to this word repeatedly when describing the servant's so-called suffering (vv. 3, 4, 10). The NRSV translates Isa 53:10a as 'it was the will of the LORD to crush the servant with pain (*ḥlh*)'. In light of other biblical uses of *ḥlh*, we could understand the servant's 'pain' as emotional grief or concern for others (1 Sam 22:8; Amos 6:6), as lovesickness or lust (2 Sam 13:2), as a fatal or near fatal illness (1 Kgs 14:1 and 2 Kgs 20:1 respectively), as a chronic disability or disease (1 Kgs 15:23; 2 Chr 16:12), as wounds sustained through human violence (2 Kgs 8:29), as a severe injury due to an accident (1 Kgs 1:2), as a symbol of iniquity (Isa 33:24), and so on. Working with such vague vocabulary alone, we cannot know whether the text describes the servant as a figure with a disability or an otherwise able-bodied figure who sustains severe if not fatal injuries. Deciding whether the description signals injury or disability makes a big difference in how interpreters have imagined the nature of his so-called suffering. Nevertheless, scholars often opt for injury over disability when interpreting *ḥlh* in Isaiah 53. For example, when commenting on Isaiah 53, Roger N. Whybray writes, '[*Ḥlh* does not] necessarily refer to organic or other naturally caused diseases. [A form of *ḥlh*] is used in 2 Kings 1:2 of injuries caused by a fall. [It is] entirely suitable to describe injuries due to ill treatment.'[41]

Impairments as metaphors. Similar to the word *ḥlh*, many words or images used for impairments could signify some condition or circumstance other than the social experience of disability. We can use the English word 'lame' to describe a mobility impairment or some failed or ineffective effort or circumstance. Similar to the English word 'weak', the Hebrew word *dal* could describe physical weakness (Gen 41:19) but often refers to undesirable social or economic conditions (Exod 30:15; Lev 14:21; Ruth 3:10). Thus, when a word or phrase could represent a disability, frequently interpreters have the option to decide that it represents some other condition. Often, biblical scholars have exercised this option.

Moses' speech difficulty in Exodus provides a good example of the scholarly tendency to choose an idiomatic interpretation of impairment language when textual evidence for both an idiomatic and non-idiomatic reading exists. In Exod 4:10, Moses explains that he is not a 'man of words' because he is literally 'heavy of mouth and heavy of tongue'. Many interpreters read this reference to his heavy mouth and tongue as an idiom for general ineloquence rather than a physical disability.[42] This interpretation finds support when Moses describes his speech difficulty as a case of 'uncircumcised lips' in 6:12

and 6:30. Describing something other than the genitals as 'uncircum-cised' does not have to refer to a physical impairment. Jeremiah 6:10 connects 'uncircumcised ears' with the inability to hear the prophetic word, Lev 26:41 connects an 'uncircumcised heart' with iniquity (cf. Jer 9:26; Ezek 44:7, 9), and Lev 19:23 discusses the 'uncircumcised fruit' of newly planted trees.

In these other examples, however, the uncircumcised item never symbolizes ineloquence. Furthermore, interpreting Moses' 'heaviness of mouth' as an idiom for ineloquence disregards the use of the phrase 'if a man's mouth is heavy...' in ancient Near Eastern medical texts that offer diagnoses for various impairments.[43] It also disregards the repeated appearances of physical impairments in the verses surround-ing Exod 4:10. In 4:6–7, Moses contracts a skin anomaly temporarily, and in 4:11, God responds to Moses' objection that he has a heavy mouth and tongue by asking rhetorically, 'Who gives a mouth to humans? Who makes them mute or deaf, seeing or blind? Is it not I, the LORD?' Nonetheless, despite the immediate context of 4:10 and the fact that cognate languages use a similar phrase in contexts that describe physical impairments, scholars tend to choose an idiomatic interpretation rather than imagine Moses as having a physical disability.

When the option for reading an impairment as symbolic exists, scholars have found it hard to resist. This holds especially true for Isaiah 40–55 since these chapters use such imagery quite frequently. As Raphael observes, 'Most of the imagery is metaphorical and not about actual disabled persons. Quite a lot of Isaiah's blind and deaf people have Normal eyes and ears.'[44] Readers of this portion of Isaiah may become accustomed to the use of such imagery to describe presumably able-bodied people. For example, Isa 42:18 commands the deaf to listen and the blind to see but does not suggest a healing of an impaired audience. 'Listen, you that are deaf; and you that are blind, look up and see! Who is blind but my servant, or deaf like my messenger whom I send? Who is blind like my dedicated one, or blind like the servant of the LORD?' (Isa 42:18–19). In these verses, the similes involving deafness and blindness and a servant or messen-ger reinforce a metaphorical interpretation.

By the point that we reach Isaiah 53, we may hardly even stop to consider that the imagery may describe the experience of disability rather than the moral or physical condition of the otherwise able-bodied. For example, John N. Oswalt writes, 'Was the Servant [in Isaiah 53] literally a sick man?... this does not seem likely. If all the images of suffering are taken literally, we end up with a composite picture that is unintelligible... [Instead, t]he point is that because he does not fit the stereotype of the arm of the Lord he will be treated as though he were ill; he will experience what the ill experience: avoidance.'[45] We may take Oswalt's position as representative of several other scholars.[46] This argument assumes that if the poetic imagery in Isaiah 53 does not allow us to envision the disability precisely, then it must be describing something other than disability. This argument shows how quickly scholars can move from the recognition that the disability imagery is not literal to the conclusion that it must not describe a figure with disabilities.

Against such arguments, we should note that biblical poetry rarely describes any physical appearance literally. For example, the poetry of the Song of Songs describes a beautiful woman as follows: 'Your eyes are doves behind your veil. Your hair is like a flock of goats, moving down the slopes of Gilead. Your teeth are like a flock of shorn ewes that have come up from the washing, all of which bear twins, and not one among them is bereaved. Your lips are like a crimson thread, and your mouth is lovely. Your cheeks are like halves of a pomegranate behind your veil' (4:1b–3).[47] As Oswalt observes regarding Isaiah 53, if we take all the images of beauty in this passage literally we end up with a composite picture that is unintelligible. Nonetheless, few, if any, readers would conclude that this passage must not describe a beautiful woman simply because it describes her beauty with fruit and animal comparisons instead of a more literal image.

In poetry, we recognize descriptions of beauty without precise, clinical, language. Likewise, we should not deny the presence of disability because the poetry lacks precise, clinical, language. That approach assumes a medical model that understands disability through our ability to diagnose it. Yet the medical model ranks among the least poetic approaches to disability. It is hardly an appropriate model for analysing disability imagery in biblical poetry. Instead ancient Near Eastern poetry often uses a composite picture to depict disease or disability. For example, the narrator in the Mesopotamian 'Poem of the Righteous Sufferer' describes his illness or disability as follows: '[Demons] churned up my bowels, they tw [isted] my entrails(?), Coughing and hacking infected my lungs, They infected(?) my limbs, made my flesh pasty... Paralysis has fallen upon my flesh. Stiffness has seized my arms, Debility has fallen upon my loins' (*COS* 1.153: 489).[48] This composite picture becomes unintelligible only if we use it for primarily diagnostic purposes.

Oswalt does not approach 'illness' through a medical model alone. Although probably unintentionally, he acknowledges that Isaiah 53 uses imagery of 'illness' to depict a social experience ('avoidance'). Similarly, William L. Holladay writes that the last half of v. 3 'repeats the theme of rejection, for people treat [the servant] *as if* he were a leper (read Lev. 13:45–46 on this matter)'.[49] Although Holladay does not discuss the possibility that the servant may have a disability, he connects the description in v. 3 to the social experience of a person with a skin anomaly. Likewise, Isaiah 53 concentrates on the servant's experience of disability in terms of his social interactions. The servant endures oppression and isolation from the community. In this sense, our passage constructs disability closer to the social or cultural models than to the medical model.

Moreover, both Oswalt and Holladay imply that the passage appropriates certain social experiences of those who are ill or have a disability to articulate the social experience of the presumably able-bodied servant. Oswalt argues that the servant was not a 'sick man'. Holladay's use of '*as if* he were a leper' implies that the passage compares the servant's experience to that of a person with a skin anomaly without suggesting that the servant himself has a skin anomaly. In other words, the passage recruits one group's experience of oppression to serve as a metaphor for the experience of another group, but denies the text describes a member of the first group. Interpreting the imagery of disability as a literary trope to describe the presumably able-bodied contributes to the erasure of figures and characters with disabilities from the biblical record.

All description, including the poetry of Isaiah 53, is metaphorical on some level. The presence of metaphor in the disability imagery of our passage does not signal the absence of disability in the servant's description. Throughout this book, we will find that there is not a convincing reason to interpret the imagery in Isaiah 53 as primarily describing something other than an experience of disability. Appeals to the metaphorical quality of this passage are no exception. Nevertheless, many interpreters assume that the poetic use of disability imagery in the description of the servant must describe something other than a figure with disabilities. This assumption ignores the fact that poetic descriptions of figures with disabilities appear in the subsequent chapters: an infertile woman in Isaiah 54 and a eunuch in Isaiah 56. We should not dismiss the idea that Isaiah 53 describes a figure with disabilities simply because the language is poetic rather than precise and clinical. If Psalms 6, 38, 41, or 'The Poem of the Righteous Sufferer' provide any indication, poetry serves as a common means of describing disease and disability in ancient Near Eastern literature.

Conclusions

Regarding disability and the Hebrew Bible, scholars have not spent nearly as much time considering what counts as disability imagery in relation to age or injury as they have developing the symbolic potential of disability as a literary trope for the experiences of the able-bodied. Moreover, scholars have spent so much energy looking for symbolic clues for the servant's identity that we assume too quickly that the imagery, including the physical descriptions, must symbolize something other than disability. As we will find throughout this book, this situation has had a significant impact on how interpreters have imagined the servant in Isaiah 53.

The Servant as a Figure with Disabilities

[T]he vocabulary of 'leprosy' is most likely present here, though it is conceivable that the author is using it in a metaphorical sense to describe the Servant's condition.

Michael L. Barré, 'Textual and Rhetorical-critical Observations on the Last Servant Song (Isaiah 52:13–53:12)', *CBQ* 62 (2000)

It would be presumptuous at best, foolhardy at worst, to venture a new interpretation of the Servant Song in Isa 52:13–53:12. So I propose instead to do the next best thing—to revive an old one.

Alan Cooper, 'The Suffering Servant and Job: A View from the Sixteenth Century', *'As Those Who are Taught': The Reception of Isaiah from the LXX to the SBL*

Isaiah 53 is one of the most familiar prophetic passages in the Hebrew Bible. Many people may recognize it from reading the Hebrew Bible or from the repeated references to it in the New Testament (which we discuss in Chapter 3) or from its use in artistic classics such as Handel's *Messiah*.[1] Yet very few people recognize it as a biblical passage about a figure with disabilities. Generally speaking, familiarity with this passage does not come from its repeated use of imagery involving disability.

In Chapter 1, we defined disability as a social and political experience of impairment. In this chapter, we argue that Isaiah 53 depicts the servant as a figure with disabilities. Whether the servant represents a known or unknown historical or fictional figure is immaterial for our argument that he is a figure with disabilities in a poem. Nor does it matter for our purposes that we cannot diagnose his disability precisely. Scholars such as Bernhard Duhm have made strong cases for diagnosing him as having some type of skin anomaly. Yet, even if we find Duhm's specific diagnosis unconvincing, we should not overlook the idea, as some scholars have, that the text describes an experience of disability. Focusing on social experience rather than medical diagnosis allows us to understand more clearly the experience that the passage describes and the nature of the servant's so-called suffering.

We begin this chapter with a brief review of Duhm's theory of the 'servant songs' and his identification of the servant as a person with a skin anomaly. Second, we discover that the various images of disability in Isaiah 53 emphasize the servant's social experience rather than providing evidence for a medical diagnosis. Third, we examine reading strategies that have allowed scholars to interpret the servant as an otherwise able-bodied figure who either suffers an injury, dies, recovers from his disability or injury, or is imprisoned. Although we find very little support within our passage for any of these four options, by analysing such arguments we begin to uncover why interpreters understand the servant as an able-bodied sufferer. This chapter will set up this book's larger point that, in effect, we have slowly removed the servant with disabilities from Isaiah 53 and replaced him with an able-bodied suffering servant.

Bernhard Duhm, the servant songs, and the servant with disabilities

In 1875, Duhm proposed a theory that Isaiah 53 belongs to a set of four texts within Isaiah that Duhm called the 'servant songs' (Isa 42:1–4; 49:1–6; 50:4–11; 52:13–53:12).[2] Duhm argued that Isaiah 40–55 did not originally contain these four passages and that the text would read rather seamlessly if they were not included. Duhm identified the servant in Isaiah 53 as an otherwise anonymous 'teacher of the law' who had leprosy.[3] The NRSV translates the Hebrew word *sara'at* as 'leprosy' with the footnote that it is a 'term for several skin diseases; precise meaning unknown'. The current scholarly consensus, however, cautions against identifying *sara'at* with leprosy or Hansen's

Disease. Rather, *sara'at* may refer to a range of skin lesions and anomalies in humans. According to Lev 13:47–58 and 14:34–45, *sara'at* can also appear in fabrics and on walls of houses. Thus, we should not identify *sara'at* simply as leprosy.[4] Throughout this book, we refer to cases of *sara'at* in humans as 'skin anomalies' instead of 'leprosy' or 'skin diseases'. Following our definition of disability discussed in the previous chapter, skin anomalies could qualify as disabilities without implying that these conditions were necessarily contagious.

Instead of *sara'at*, Isaiah 53 uses a more general Hebrew word for sickness or diseases (*ḥlh*). Yet our passage also describes the servant as 'plagued' in both vv. 4 and 8. The same word for 'plagued' appears in various noun and verb forms sixty-one times in Leviticus 13–14. Most of these uses in Leviticus refer to a skin anomaly of some sort. Although the word *sara'at* does not appear in Isaiah 53, Duhm suggests that the images of the servant as 'profaned' and 'crushed' in 53:5, 10 were descriptions of the effects of his skin anomaly. To support this idea, he noted that the idiomatic use of the word 'stricken' (Isa 53:4, 8) refers to the effects of skin anomalies elsewhere in the Bible. For example, Lev 13:22 uses the same Hebrew word as Isa 53:8, 'If an anomaly spreads in the skin, the priest shall pronounce him unclean; it is diseased (literally: "stricken").' Moreover, the last half of 53:8 uses the words 'excluded' and 'stricken' to describe the servant's experience. The only other place in the Hebrew Bible where these two words appear together is 2 Chr 26:20–21. This passage describes how the LORD 'struck' King Uzziah with a skin anomaly and how the king was 'excluded' from the community. '[King Uzziah] had a skin anomaly in his forehead. They hurried him out, and he himself hurried to get out, because the LORD had struck him. King Uzziah had a skin anomaly to the day of his death, and having a skin anomaly, he lived in a separate house, for he was excluded from the house of the LORD.' For Duhm, the use of the same words to describe both the story of Uzziah's skin anomaly and the experience of the servant provides further support to the idea that Isaiah 53 describes the experience of someone with a skin anomaly. According to Duhm, this unknown 'teacher of the law' was not killed by human hands. Rather, his skin anomaly caused his death.[5]

Many scholars have questioned whether Duhm's four 'servant songs' ever existed independent of Isaiah 40–55 because these texts may not exhibit the same literary genre. Scholars also disagree over the number of servant songs present in Isaiah 40–66 or which verses belong to each individual servant song. For example, many scholars argue that Isa 61:1–4 represents a servant song (cf. Luke 4:18–19) or that the servant song in Isaiah 42 extends beyond v. 6 to include the references to a servant in 42:18–20. Furthermore, that the servant songs contain several similarities in vocabulary and imagery with several passages throughout the rest of Isaiah leads many scholars to doubt Duhm's theory that the servant songs originated independent of their present context.[6] Moreover, no scholarly consensus exists that the servant in Isaiah 53 is the same servant as in Duhm's other three servant songs. In fact, since shortly after Duhm's theory appeared, other scholars have suggested that Isaiah 53 came from a different source than the previous servant songs.[7]

For the purposes of this book, we will not interpret Isaiah 53 as one of the so-called 'servant songs'. Instead, we interpret it simply as a poem describing a servant with disabilities. Our approach focuses on the descriptions of the servant found within Isaiah 53 rather than a reconstruction of his supposed experience by piecing it together from several of the servant songs or other biblical texts. The cogency of Duhm's servant song theory does not concern us as much as his connection between the servant in Isaiah 53 and a figure with disabilities. Duhm's servant songs theory has been incredibly influential within scholarly circles over the last century or so. Yet his identification of the servant as someone with a skin anomaly has enjoyed very little popularity.

Ironically, the theory that Isaiah 53 is one of several servant songs has contributed to the dismissal of Duhm's argument that the servant had a skin anomaly. While Duhm used Isaiah 53 to identify the servant throughout the four servant songs as a figure with a skin anomaly, his servant song theory has allowed scholars to place the servant's description in Isaiah 53 in the context of other servant song passages that discuss suffering but not disability. For example, Karl Budde agrees with Duhm that Isa 53:3–4 describe the servant as having a skin anomaly. Yet Budde downplays the importance of this description for interpreting the servant's suffering because, as Duhm himself acknowledges, the servant discusses his suffering in Isa 50:6 without any reference to a skin anomaly.[8] As we observe later in this chapter, the tendency to interpret the servant in Isaiah 53 against the backdrop of the other servant songs allows scholars to imagine the servant in Isaiah 53 as injured (50:6) or imprisoned (42:7; 61:1; cf. 49:9) by humans rather than as having a disability. In contrast, while we cannot be certain of its diagnosis, good evidence exists to support the suggestion that Isaiah 53 describes the servant as having some type of disability.

Even though we cannot diagnose the servant's condition precisely, Isaiah 53 makes it very clear that the LORD 'struck' the servant in v. 4. This verse reinforces the idea that the servant's condition was brought on by God, not humans. This idea fits with certain ancient Near Eastern notions that disabilities and diseases were brought on by divinity. Ancient Near Eastern literature often views disease and disability as the product of divine causation, whereas in the modern industrial world we often look for medical and biological causes for diseases and disabilities located within the individual body. Rather than approaching disease and disability through a 'medical' model, ancient Near Eastern literature employs a 'theological' model, as we observed in Chapter 1.[9] In v. 4, the people attribute the servant's condition to the fact that he was 'stricken, plagued by God, and afflicted'. According to v. 10, 'The LORD was delighted to crush him, to make him diseased.' Elsewhere in the Hebrew Bible, God 'strikes' Pharaoh's house with plagues (Gen 12:17), the Philistines with tumours (1 Sam 5:9; 6:9), and King Uzziah with a skin anomaly (2 Kgs 15:5). Additionally, the satan 'strikes' Job with skin anomalies (Job 2:5). This notion that a divine being controls impairment and disease appears in the burning bush story as well. After God causes and then heals a skin anomaly on Moses' hand, Moses complains that he has a speech impediment. In Exod 4:11, the LORD responds, 'Who gives speech to humans? Who makes them mute or deaf, seeing or blind? Is it not I, the LORD'? Against the backdrop of these other biblical texts, the physical conditions that Isaiah 53 describes as divinely caused afflictions seem to depict the servant as having a disease or disability of some sort. The 'striking' of the servant does not indicate that other humans injured or wounded him.

Outside the Hebrew Bible, many Mesopotamian texts concerning human illnesses present both chronic and temporary illnesses as under the direct control of a divine 'sender/controller'.[10] Mesopotamian texts refer to various diseases as 'the touch' (Akkadian: *lapātu*) of a god, in the sense of a divine being afflicting someone with a disease.[11] Likewise, various illnesses result from 'the hand' of a particular deity according to certain biblical texts as well as Mesopotamian diagnostic texts.[12] For example, the Akkadian text 'The Poem of the Righteous Sufferer' (*COS* 1.153: 490–1) includes a lengthy but non-specific description of the narrator's disease or illnesses. The narrator attributes his condition to some type of ghost or demon. Moreover, the narrator connects his condition with his social experience of isolation and rejection by others.[13] When read in the context of biblical and other ancient Near Eastern texts, Isaiah 53 appears to describe the servant as having an unspecified disability.

While we cannot claim for certain that the servant had a skin anomaly, Joseph Blenkinsopp comes to a reasonable conclusion when he writes, 'That the servant had contracted leprosy was assumed by Jerome (Vulg. 53:4 *leprosum*) and taken up by Duhm...This is a hypothesis that is certainly plausible but can be neither proved nor disproved.'[14] Since we cannot prove Duhm's hypothesis that the servant had a skin anomaly, many scholars have not pursued the idea that the servant has a disability. This situation, however, may show the influence of the medical model by assuming that we must focus discussions of disability on diagnosis. Yet 53:3 uses plural forms for the words 'sufferings' and 'diseases' in the phrase 'a man of sufferings and acquainted with diseases'. The use of plural forms suggests that our passage does not describe one disability precisely as if intended to aid in diagnostic attempts. Instead, as we find in our next section, Isaiah 53 focuses on how the servant's physical condition relates to his social experience without providing a medical description of an anomalous body.

The servant's disability as a social experience

We begin this section by reviewing further connections between the descriptions of the servant and characters with skin anomalies elsewhere in biblical and other ancient Near Eastern literature. These connections do not necessarily support Duhm's hypothesis that the servant had a skin anomaly. Instead, they suggest that Isaiah 53 focuses on the servant's disability as a social experience regardless of how we diagnose his condition. After reviewing these connections, we turn to imagery in the passage that describes a disability without necessarily connecting it to a skin anomaly. To claim, as we do, that the servant has a disability is not a diagnosis but a comment on the description of his social experience of impairment. Moreover, to claim that he does not have a skin anomaly does not mean that he does not have a disability.

Skin anomalies as a social experience. Isaiah 53:3 states that the servant 'was despised and withdrew from humanity; a man of sufferings and acquainted with diseases and like someone who hides his face from us'. This description leads some scholars to suggest that our passage describes an unfortunate social expectation of a person with a skin anomaly in ancient Near Eastern literature.[15] John F. A. Sawyer writes, 'The first part [of Isaiah 53] depicts the suffering as physical and social, like that of a leper, "despised and rejected by men". The Hebrew word for "men" is an unusual form and connotes "men of standing" (cf. Prov. 8:4), stressing the social implications of the disease.'[16] Regarding social implications, actions such as hiding one's face from others correspond with ancient Near Eastern 'skin anomaly' curses that speak of the exclusion of people with skin anomalies (Akkadian: *saharšuppû*) from the temple.[17]

A Babylonian omen text describes a person with a skin anomaly as 'rejected by his god (and) he is rejected by humanity'. Another prayer explains impairments (including, but not limited to, skin anomalies) as a punishment for entering a temple while in a state of impurity (a term which we will explain below).[18] In the Mesopotamian text 'Gilgamesh, Enkidu, and the Netherworld', those with skin anomalies were isolated even in the netherworld. When Gilgamesh asks Enkidu about the fate of persons with skin anomalies in the netherworld, Enkidu informs him that they reside outside the city, with separated food.

Likewise, we find the social isolation of people with skin anomalies called for in other passages from Leviticus and Numbers. According to Lev 13:46, a person with a skin anomaly 'shall live alone; his dwelling shall be outside the camp' (cf. 2 Kgs 15:5).[19] In Num 5:2, the Israelites are instructed to 'remove from the camp everyone with a skin anomaly'. When Miriam contracts a skin anomaly in Numbers 12, Aaron compares her skin to the skin of a dead baby and she is 'shut out' of the Israelite camp for seven days (12:10–15). Moreover, Aaron interprets Miriam's skin anomaly that results in her isolation as punishment for not only herself but others as well (v. 11; cf. Isa 53:4–6).[20]

As the story of King Azariah, also called Uzziah, indicates, even kings could undergo isolation if they had a skin anomaly. 'The LORD struck the king, so that he had a skin anomaly to the day of his death, and lived in a separate house. Jotham the king's son was in charge of the palace, governing the people of the land' (2 Kgs 15:5; cf. 2 Chr 26:16–23). In Isa 38:11, Hezekiah faces potential exclusion from the 'land of the living'. His physical condition includes a 'boil' (38:21), a word which indicates a skin anomaly elsewhere in the Hebrew Bible (Lev 13:20; cf. Exod 9:9–11; Job 2:7), although we cannot be sure of this diagnosis. Along these lines, a rabbinic tradition interprets Hezekiah's condition as a skin anomaly that caused his skin to peel off as a divine punishment because he 'peeled off' the gold of Solomon's temple and gave it to the Assyrians (2 Kgs 18:16).[21]

The social isolation of those with skin anomalies may also help us understand the phrase in Isa 53:8 that the servant was 'excluded from the land of the living'. A very similar verbal form of the word 'living' appears in 2 Kgs 5:7a when the Syrian king requests that the Israelite king cure Naaman's skin anomaly. The Israelite king responds, 'Am I God, to give death and *give life* that this man sends word to me *to cure a man of his skin anomaly* (emphasis added)'? Here, 'life' refers to the absence of a skin anomaly rather than the act of bringing a dead person to life.[22] In this sense, the exclusion from among the living in 53:8 may refer to the isolation of those with skin anomalies. It may build on the perceived connections between skin anomalies and death that we found in the story of Miriam's skin anomaly. Who cares where the servant dwells, as long as he does not dwell among us, in the land of the living? Isaiah 53, however, condemns this treatment of the servant as oppression and a miscarriage of justice (vv. 4, 8–9).

The isolation of people with skin anomalies did not result from a notion that people with skin anomalies were sinful (a moral model of disability). These commands for the isolation of persons with skin anomalies operate under more of a cultural model of disability. Rather than focusing on sinfulness, biblical texts present this isolation as a social experience connected to Israelite practices concerning ritual purity and impurity. Impurity prohibits a person from participating in certain religious or cultic practices. Generally, scholars distinguish between ritual and moral impurity, sometimes called tolerated and forbidden impurities respectively. Ritual impurity refers to impurity contracted through circumstances expected throughout the typical life cycle, such as death, sickness, menstruation, sex activity, and so on. By contrast, moral impurity results from often, but not always, avoidable wrongdoings or pollutions of certain sacred spaces. The Hebrew Bible presents skin anomalies as a ritual or tolerable impurity rather than a moral or forbidden impurity.

Thus, although skin anomalies can be a form of punishment for sin in the Hebrew Bible (2 Kgs 5:20–7; 2 Chr 26:16–21), having a skin anomaly is a ritual impurity but not a sin. Only the mishandling or disregard of required rituals in cases of a skin anomaly constitutes a sin.[23] This distinction between ritual and moral impurity highlights the injustice of associating the servant with the wicked and transgressors. Despite the fact that the servant commits no moral offence, he is grouped with these parties largely on account of his physical condition (vv. 8, 12). The passage decries this treatment as an act of oppression.

Nor is a medical model appropriate for understanding the isolation of people with skin anomalies in the Hebrew Bible. Ritual purity requirements in the Hebrew Bible did not always apply to non-Israelites. Thus, besides an aesthetic objection, a concern over the contagiousness of their condition would provide the only plausible reason to isolate non-Israelites with skin anomalies. In 2 Kings 5, however, the Syrian general Naaman has a skin anomaly, but still leads his troops and interacts with his family, his king, and even the Israelite prophet Elisha. Thus, people with skin anomalies were not isolated because their condition was considered medically contagious. After citing the case of Naaman, Jacob Milgrom writes,

To be sure, had [Naaman] been Israelite he would have been banished like Miriam (Num 12:14–16), the four outcasts (2 Kgs 7:3–10), and Uzziah

(2 Kgs 15:5). But this only proves that Israelites bearing [skin anomalies] were not banished for hygienic reasons. In fact, Leviticus confirms the idea that [a skin anomaly] was not considered a [contagious] disease: furniture removed from the house before a priest's examination cannot be declared impure (14:36).... [Likewise, the rabbis] declare that [skin anomaly] rules are not applicable to non-Jews and their homes in the Holy Land (*m. Neg.* 3:1) and to all houses outside the Holy Land (*m. Neg.* 12:1). In short, we are dealing with ritual, not pathology.... The conclusion is inescapable: [skin anomaly] rules are grounded not in medicine but in ritual.[24]

Skin anomalies were understood as a ritual or cultic contaminant that could render sacred Israelite spaces impure. The inspection of skin anomalies by priests (Leviticus 13–14) was not meant to provide a medical diagnosis, but to determine a person's status as ritually pure or impure in regard to cultic participation. In this sense, skin anomalies are understood as a social or cultic issue and not simply a medical condition.

Other disability imagery in Isaiah 53 as a social experience. The imagery in Isaiah 53 that does not necessarily suggest a skin anomaly still focuses heavily on the servant's disability as a social experience. The passage begins with a description of the servant in 52:14. 'Just as there were many who were astonished at him—so marred was his appearance, beyond human semblance, and his form beyond that of mortals' (cf. Isa 49:7). Elsewhere, biblical authors use Hebrew words such as 'appearance' (*mr'h*) and 'form' (*t'r*) to describe humans and animals physically. For example, Genesis uses these words to describe Rachel's beauty (29:17) and Joseph's good looks (39:6; cf. the cows in 41:18–19). Yet Isa 52:14 describes the servant's appearance and form as 'marred'. The prophet Malachi uses a similar form of this word 'marred' to describe animals that are physically 'lame and diseased'. In Mal 1:13–14, the prophet declares, 'You bring what has been taken by violence or is lame or diseased (*hlh*), and this you bring as your offering!... Cursed be the cheat who has a male in the flock and vows to give it, and yet sacrifices to the Lord what is marred.' Likewise, Lev 22:25 prohibits the sacrifice of animals that 'are marred, with a blemish (*mum*) in them'. Thus, the imagery used to describe the servant by Isaiah as 'marred in appearance' can connote an unspecified physical disability or disease. While the imagery does not focus on the exact nature of his disability, it clearly focuses on his social experience. As the passage continues, we discover that Isaiah 53 frames the servant's disability or disease primarily as a social and political experience and not just a physical description.

As in 52:14, Isaiah 53 uses the words 'appearance' and 'form' again in v. 2. The passage foregrounds the social dimensions of the servant's experience of disability in v. 2 by insisting that others saw his physical appearance as extremely undesirable. 'He had no form or majesty that we should look at him, nothing in his appearance that we should desire him.' The following verses explain his perceived unattractive appearance as the result of an impairment of some sort (vv. 3–4).

David J. A. Clines interprets the comparison in 53:2 of the servant to 'a young plant, and like a root out of dry ground' as an image of stunted growth.[25] Although stunted growth may not qualify as a disability, it would qualify as a stigmatizing physical feature, especially if we identify v. 2 as the reaction of the shocked kings mentioned in 52:15. A short or even average stature was a disqualifying feature for candidates for the throne in other ancient Near Eastern texts such as the Ugaritic Baal Cycle.[26] Moreover, the association of ground that is 'dry' (*syb*) with disability imagery appears elsewhere in Isaianic passages that come from the same time period as Isaiah 53. In a utopian vision, Isa 35:1 declares that 'The wilderness and the dry land (*syb*) shall be glad.' The following verses continue this vision of transformation by promising that 'Then the eyes of the blind shall be opened, and the ears of the deaf unstopped; then the lame shall leap like a deer, and the tongue of the speechless sing for joy' (35:5–6a). The connection between dry ground and disability as conditions in need of transformation in Isaiah 35 may explain the association of the servant with both dry ground and disability in Isa 53:2.

With our focus on social experience in mind, we should note that John H. Walton discusses an intriguing possible source of influence on Isaiah 53. Citing the imagery in 52:13–14, Walton draws parallels between a Hittite and Assyrian ritual which involves the elevation to kingship of a person with a cognitive impairment in order to take on the suffering of the real king and Isaiah 53's exaltation of a person with a physical disability in order to take on the punishment of the people (cf. vv. 4–6). In the mid-twentieth century, scholars began to investigate parallels between Isaiah 53 and this Mesopotamian 'substitute king ritual'.[27] This ritual sought to save a king from harm when an omen seemed to threaten him. It involved the enthronement of a substitute king in the hope that the negative effects of the omen would fall upon the substitute and the real king would remain unharmed. One Assyrian text describes the substitute as a 'simpleton' or 'halfwit' (Akkadian: s*aklu*). Walton understands the use of the word *saklu* as suggesting a person with a cognitive impairment.[28] If the substitute king ritual influenced the description of the servant and his suffering for others, this possible parallel may shed light on why Isaiah 53 describes the servant as a figure with disabilities. Also, it draws attention to Isaiah 53's focus on disability as a social experience.

The examples reviewed in this section do not provide decisive evidence for a specific disability, be it a skin anomaly or some other condition. Nevertheless, they show that when we interpret the disability imagery in Isaiah 53 as a social experience rather than through a medical model, the portrayal of the servant as a figure with disabilities becomes clearer. Yet the influence of the medical model is not the only reason that scholars have rejected Duhm's idea that the servant had a disability. Rather than a figure with a disability, scholars have also tended to interpret the servant as an able-bodied victim who suffers either temporary or fatal injuries.

Was an able-bodied servant injured?

As we discussed in Chapter 1, an injury may result in an acquired disability. This was likely a common occurrence in ancient Israel. We should distinguish, however, between an acquired disability and a fatal injury. When scholars interpret the servant as injured, they tend to understand his injury as resulting in death rather than an acquired disability. In other words, scholars portray the servant as a (fatally) injured able-bodied figure instead of one who acquires a disability through injury.

In part, this portrayal may reflect the scholarly tendency to interpret Isaiah 53 as one of Duhm's servant songs. Some of Duhm's other servant songs describe a physical injury caused by humans. For example, in Isa 50:6, a servant states, 'I gave my back to those who struck me, and my cheeks to those who pulled out the beard; I did not hide my face from insult and spitting.' By contrast, Isaiah 53 does not contain any explicit description of a physical injury caused by humans.[29] We may interpret the servant in Isaiah 53 as primarily injured by humans rather than disabled by divinity only if we read this chapter against the backdrop of the servant song in Isaiah 50. This interpretative move becomes clear in Claus Westermann's comment that in 52:14 'the last servant song takes up the central part of 50:4–9'.[30] Intentionally or not, scholars who argue for injury by humans as the context of the servant's suffering may be reading Duhm's other servant songs into Isaiah 53.

The servant's condition does not appear to result from humanly inflicted injuries in Isaiah 53. In his 1999 presidential address to the Catholic Biblical Association of America, Michael L. Barré observed that

> [T]here is not a single term in [Isa 52:13–53:6] that refers to any affliction of the Servant clearly brought about by human agency. Rather, the vocabulary is consistent in alluding to physical afflictions traditionally ascribed to the gods in ancient Near Eastern literature.... By comparison, what the Servant suffers at the hands of fellow human beings [in 53:7–12] consists almost exclusively of being arrested, being taken away from his home(land?) by juridical decree, and being classified with sinners.[31]

For Barré, the servant's physical condition does not result from human torture or attack on an otherwise able-bodied individual. The first part of the passage does not describe the suffering of an able-bodied person. Instead, it describes physical conditions brought on by a divine being. The so-called 'suffering' that the servant endures at the hands of other humans focuses on an oppressive social experience of living with disabilities as depicted in the later part of the passage. In this sense, our passage portrays disability as a social and political reality and not simply a medical condition. The servant's suffering arises from an unjust interaction of a figure with impairments with his social environment (53:8, 10).

Nevertheless, scholars have claimed repeatedly that the context of Isaiah 53 implies physical injury rather than disability. For example, Roger N. Whybray writes, 'The words and phrases used in the poem to describe his sufferings were not, *or at least not primarily*, due to sickness but to physical ill treatment.'[32] Whybray's textual support for this claim remains unconvincing. He interprets, 'stricken by God' in

v. 4 as a superlative for 'horribly beaten' by humans.[33] Yet this interpretation prefers an idiosyncratic reading of 'stricken by God' over the usual biblical association of God 'striking' an individual or group with a disease or disability that we discussed earlier. We can only justify Whybray's claim if we read the descriptions of the servant's physical condition in the first parts of the passage as the result of the oppressive treatment by humans described in 53:8–9. Yet, the fact that Isaiah 53 connects the specific physical descriptions throughout the passage to a divine causation calls this interpretation into question.

As we discussed in the previous chapter, determining whether the servant had an injury or disability is complicated by the fact that *hlh* has a wide semantic range that includes injury, illness, disease, and disability. Although Isaiah 53 uses forms of *hlh* to describe the servant's condition throughout the passage, many scholars have decided not to associate this repeated use of *hlh* with a disability or disease. For example, regarding 53:3, John Goldingay and David Payne write, 'In parallelism with *mak'ōbôt* ["suffering"] is *hōli* ["disease"], which commonly means "illness"... But the context speaks more explicitly of harm from other people than of disease. The noun and the verb *hālāh* do occasionally mean "wound" (significantly 1.5) and this would thus fit well. But more often the noun denotes "weakness".'[34] Contrary to this interpretation, the context in which *hlh* appears in regard to the servant suggests a disability more than a physical injury afflicted by humans. Even if the passage uses *hlh* as a metaphor for the condition of others in v. 4 (cf. Isa 33:24) and speaks metaphorically of their 'healing' in v. 5, it does not mean that *hlh* is primarily a metaphor for something other than the servant's disability in vv. 3 or 10.[35] An early Greek translation known as the Septuagint (LXX) reflects this important distinction. In v. 4, it uses a Greek word meaning 'sin' (*amartia*) to translate *hlh* when it does not refer to the servant: 'he bears our sins' instead of 'he has borne our diseases'. Yet the same translation uses Greek words meaning 'sickness' and 'disease' to translate *hlh* when it refers to the servant in vv. 3 and 10.[36] Furthermore, Goldingay and Payne admit that *hōli*, which is a form related to *hlh*, commonly means illness. Thus, we should only opt for another meaning, such as wound or injury, if the context clearly suggests these alternative meanings. The context of Isaiah 53, however, does not clearly suggest such meanings.

None of the physical descriptions in Isaiah 53 suggests that his condition results from injuries inflicted by humans. The servant is not presented as an otherwise able-bodied figure who suffers physical abuse or injury. Instead, he suffers socially oppressive conditions as a by-product of living with his impairments. As Barré implies, the later portion of Isaiah 53 documents this social experience of disability.

Was an able-bodied servant killed?

The servant seems alive and well in 53:10–11. Yet many interpreters argue that vv. 7–9 focus on the servant's death. This allows us to imagine the servant as an otherwise able-bodied figure who dies rather than one who lives with disabilities. Two main reasons support the argument that the (able-bodied) servant dies. First, there are references to his grave, death, and his exclusion from the land of the living in vv. 8–9, 12. Second, some scholars have connected the language in vv. 7 and 10 to the ritual sacrifices in Leviticus and Numbers.

Possible references to the servant's death. Although v. 8 states that the servant is 'excluded from the land of the living', this verse does not describe the murder or execution of the servant by humans. Instead, it may describe the isolation experienced by some ancient Israelites with skin anomalies or other disabilities. The word 'living' in the phrase 'excluded from the land of the living' (v. 8) refers to healthy or able-bodied people and not simply the living. The phrase 'land of the living' also appears in Isa 38:11. The larger context of Isaiah 38 concerns a restoration to health of the diseased (*ḥlh*) King Hezekiah. In 38:16, a verbal form of this word 'living' refers to this type of restoration when Hezekiah says, 'Oh, restore me to health and make me live!' (cf. 'the living' in 38:19). Thus, 'the land of the living' in Isa 53:8 may refer to the community of healthy or able-bodied people. Gillis Gerleman observes that the Hebrew Bible also applies the phrase 'land of the living' to the land of Israel.[37] Similarly, Whybray understands 'land of the living' in Ezek 32:23–7, 32 as a reference to human society or communities more generally (cf. Ps 116:9).

Whybray also notes that Isa 53:8 uses the verb 'excluded' rather than 'cut off' from the land of the living.[38] As Jan Alberto Soggin has shown, whereas 'cut off from the land of the living' can refer to killing or the death penalty (cf. Jer 11:19), 'excluded from the land of the living' can refer to a state of separation.[39] Thus, some scholars interpret Isa 53:8 as indicating that the servant was removed from Israelite, or even human, society rather than killed. As we discussed earlier, this type of isolation from the community seems in keeping with how other Hebrew Bible and ancient Near Eastern texts portray the social experience of people with skin anomalies and other disabilities.

Isaiah 53:9 could imply the servant's death when it states, 'They prepared his grave with the wicked and his tomb with the rich.' Yet the preparation of his grave does not mean that he occupied it. Furthermore, scholars have compared this verse to a line from the Mesopotamian 'The Poem of the Righteous Sufferer'.[40] After describing his disability or illness for several lines, the narrator of this poem states, 'My grave was open, my funerary goods ready. Before I died, lamentation for me was done' (*COS* 1.153: 489). As with Isa 53:9, this poem states that others prepared the narrator's grave and not that they killed or buried him. Like 'The Poem of the Righteous Sufferer', Isaiah 53 mentions the preparation of the servant's grave after several verses that describe a divinely induced disease or disability. In this sense, the reference to the servant's grave fits with a description of the servant's physical condition more than a description of his death due to humanly inflicted injuries.

We should also note that v. 10 states that the servant will 'see his offspring, and shall prolong his days'. Elsewhere, the Hebrew Bible connects the ability to see one's offspring for several generations with a long and fulfilled life (Gen 50:23; Job 42:16; cf. Adad-guppi's claim to see her 'great-great grandchildren' [*ANET*, 561]).[41] This description of the servant depicts him as living to an old age rather than meeting an untimely death.

Finally, we could interpret the phrase 'he poured out himself to death' in v. 12 as a reference to his death. Yet it probably means that the servant risked his life. In Ps 141:8, the NRSV translates an almost identical Hebrew phrase as 'leave me defenceless'. This implies that the phrase may refer to a life-threatening situation rather than death. The LXX's translation of Isa 53:8–9 supports the former option. In this Greek version, the servant 'is led to death' (v. 8), but God 'turns over the wicked instead of [the servant's] grave and the rich instead of his death' (v. 9; author's translation).

The servant as ritual sacrifice. Isaiah 53:7 compares the servant to 'a lamb that is led to the slaughter' and 'a sheep who is mute before its shearers'. For some scholars, the comparison to a slaughtered lamb implies that the servant died by human hands. Yet scholars rarely, if ever, suggest that the comparison to a mute sheep implies that the servant has a speech impairment even though similar forms of the Hebrew word translated as 'mute' describe Ezekiel's speech impairment (cf. Ezek 3:26; 24:17; 33:22). Instead, since 53:10 refers to the servant as 'an offering for sin' ('*šm*), some understand the passage as comparing the servant's death to the ritual sacrifice of a goat or lamb as a 'sin/guilt offering' ('*šm*) in Lev 5:18–19 or the scapegoat in Lev 10:17 and 16:22.[42] While the NRSV's translation of 52:15 as 'so he shall startle many nations' comes from a Greek version of Isaiah 53, translations such as the KJV come from Hebrew and other Greek versions that read 'so shall he sprinkle many nations'.[43] Some scholars note that the verb 'sprinkle' refers to the sprinkling of animal blood in texts involving ritual sacrifices (Lev 4:6, 17; 5:9; 6:20; cf. Exod 29:21). In this sense, the servant dies as a sacrificial lamb on behalf of others.

Leviticus 5:15, 18, and 25 repeatedly require that the animal used for the ritual sacrifice be 'without blemish' (*tamim*), a term that refers to the animal's physical condition (cf. Lev 22:21). This allows interpreters to compare the servant to the unblemished or physically fit animal that dies a sacrificial death in ritual texts from the Pentateuch while downplaying the more immediate comparisons involving disabilities that run throughout Isaiah 53. It ignores the fact that Isa 52:14 describes the servant as 'marred' (Hebrew root *šht*) which would render him unfit to serve as a ritual sacrifice according to Lev 22:25. Similarly, Malachi decries the use of 'diseased' (*ḥlh*) or 'marred' (*šht*) animals for ritual sacrifice (Mal 1:13–14). In fact, Mal 1: 12 describes the sacrificial food from such animals as 'despised', which is the exact same Hebrew word used twice to describe the servant in 53: 3 (cf. Mal 1: 7). Moreover, Mal 1:12 claims that such sacrifices 'profane' the name of the LORD, which is the same word used to describe the servant in 53:5.

Regarding 52:15, one would not 'sprinkle' the blood of something marred (52:14) because such disfigurement renders it unfit for sacrifice. It is possible that the 'sprinkling' in 52:15 could refer to the servant's blood spilled through violence. This is how the word is used in its only other appearance in the book of Isaiah (63:3; cf. 2 Kgs 9:33). Yet, a more probable explanation is that the servant's physical appearance 'startles' many nations rather than sprinkles them. When compared with the ritual requirements in Leviticus and Malachi, the vocabulary used to describe the servant throughout Isaiah 53 depicts him as physically unfit for sacrifice rather than as an unblemished offering.

Furthermore, the word for 'slaughter' (*tbh*) in the phrase 'a lamb that is led to the slaughter' (53:7) never appears in Leviticus or Numbers. The Bible never uses this word in the context of a ritual sacrifice or death performed by a priest. Instead, this type of slaughtering of an animal refers to work of a cook or butcher killing for food (Gen 43:16; Exod 22:1 [21:37 in Hebrew]; Deut 28:31; 1 Sam 25:11; cf. 1 Sam 9:23–24).[44] Other texts extend this image metaphorically to the wartime slaughtering of humans as a divine punishment (Isa 34:2; 65:12; Jer 25:34; Lam 2:21; Ezek 21:10, 15, 28 [21:15, 20, 33 in Hebrew]), but this metaphor does not invoke imagery of a ritual sacrifice performed by priests.[45] The closest parallel to the image of a slaughtered lamb in 53:7 does not come from a text involving ritual sacrifice. In Jer 11:19, the prophet claims, 'But I was like a gentle lamb led to the slaughter. And I did not know it was against me that they devised schemes, saying, "Let us destroy the tree with its fruit, let us cut him off from the land of the living, so that his name will no longer be remembered"' (cf. Ps 44:22; Prov 7:22). Rather than suggesting a ritual sacrifice, the lamb imagery expresses how Jeremiah's opponents deceived the prophet. Moreover, both Fredrick Hägglund and Bernd Janowski argue that the language of 'an offering for sin' (*'šm*) in 53:10 does not reflect the sacrificial language of Leviticus or Numbers.[46] Instead, Janowski compares our passage's use of *'šm* to its use in 1 Sam 6:3 and other texts outside Leviticus and Numbers.[47]

The use of *'šm* in 1 Sam 6:3 associates this offering with imagery of impairment and ritually impure animals rather than the sacrificial death of an unblemished animal. In 1 Sam 5:9, the LORD 'strikes' (cf. Isa 53:4, 8) the Philistines with tumors. In 1 Sam 6:3, the

Philistines are told, 'If you send away the ark of the God of Israel, do not send it empty, but by all means return him a guilt offering (*'šm*). Then you will be healed (*rp'*) and will be ransomed; will not his hand then turn from you'? As part of their guilt offering, the Philistines create five golden models or images of both their tumors and of the mice (*'kbr*) that 'mar' (a verbal form of *šht*) the Philistines' land (1 Sam 6:5, 11; cf. Isa 52:14). Leviticus 11:29 lists mice (*'kbr*) as ritually impure animals (cf. Isa 66:17). In other words, representations of the Philistines' impairments and ritually impure animals serve as an offering to heal them. Similarly, the servant, who is described as 'marred' (a noun form of *šht* in Isa 52:14) and as if he is ritually impure throughout Isaiah 53, serves as the offering in the phrase, 'When you make his life an offering for sin (*'šm*)' (53:10). Moreover, 53:5 states that 'by [the servant's] bruises we are healed (*rp'*; cf. 1 Sam 6:3)'.

If we want compare the servant to an animal because 53:10 refers to him as an *'šm*, we should remember that an *'šm* could involve a golden image of a ritually impure animal as well as an unblemished, sacrificed, animal. Although the parallels between Isaiah 53 and 1 Samuel 6 are not exact,[48] the similarities between these passages show that the ritually pure, unblemished, sacrificial lamb required in Leviticus is not the only animal associated with an *'šm*. Together, the imagery in Isaiah 53 that repeatedly describes the servant as unfit for sacrifice (cf. Malachi 1), the lack of the word 'slaughter' in instructions for ritual sacrifices, the lamb imagery in Jer 11:19, and the *'šm* imagery in 1 Samuel 6 all discourage comparisons between the servant and a ritually sacrificed animal.

Did an able-bodied servant recover?

As with Isa 52:13, Isa 53:10–12 emphasize that the servant will ultimately enjoy a place of divine honour. For some interpreters, these verses imply the servant's return to at least an able-bodied state, if not a reference to his resurrection.[49] According to such interpretations, the servant, identified as 'righteous' in v. 11, experiences a divine healing and is once again able-bodied by the end of Isaiah 53. We suspect, however, an assumed connection between righteousness and physical restoration influences such interpretations more than clear evidence from the text. We will begin this section by demonstrating that Isaiah 53 does not make this connection. Then, we examine how scholars assume a physical restoration by assigning Isaiah 53 to a particular genre rather than basing their claim on clear textual evidence.

The pious person with disabilities. Elsewhere in the Isaianic tradition pious persons with disabilities receive divine rewards without becoming able-bodied. For example, Isa 56:4–5 allows the pious eunuch to enter the temple: 'For thus says the LORD: To the eunuchs who keep my sabbaths, who choose the things that please me and hold fast my covenant, I will give, in my house and within my walls, a monument and a name better than sons and daughters; I will give them an everlasting name that shall not be cut off.' Genital damage would qualify a eunuch as a person with a disability by our definition of disability. Saul M. Olyan discusses eunuchs within the context of disability.[50] He interprets Isaiah 56 as a critical response to Deut 23:1, which bans people with genital damage from sacred spaces. Olyan writes,

> Isa 56:3–7 does not envision the normalization of the eunuch through efforts by Yhwh to mitigate any marginalizing effects of his physical disability.... Rather, it is the cultic proscription of the eunuch, based on a broad reading of Deut 23:2 (Eng. 1), that is to be eliminated in the future utopia, allowing the eunuch to participate fully in the rites of Yhwh's temple...it is not the eunuch's disability per se that Yhwh addresses, but rather the ban of his entry into the temple and participation in its rites.[51]

Isaiah 56:3–7 decries the eunuch's removal from the community as an incident of unjustified oppression. Although some scholars suggest that Isaiah 53 and 56 come from different authors, they portray experiences of figures with disabilities as unacceptable social oppression in a similar manner. Furthermore, in both cases, the disability is neither healed nor removed. These texts do not approach issues of disability through a medical model. Instead, they critique the oppressive social circumstances experienced by the figure with disabilities. Both Isa 53:10–12 and 56:4–5 promise that the pious figure with disabilities will enjoy a position of privilege in the future with no indication that his physical condition will change.[52] In contrast to 'The Poem of the Righteous Sufferer', these texts contain no divinely induced removal of or recovery from a disease or disability. Instead,

Isa 53:10–12 has more in common with Job 42:7–17. Like Isa 53:10–12, this passage affirms Job's righteousness and claims that he will be honoured with a divine reward. Like the servant in Isa 53:10, Job lives to 'see' multiple generations of his children (Job 42:16). Like the servant, Job's community discovers that Job does not suffer because of his own sins but ultimately intercedes on their behalf (Job 42:7–9; Isa 53:4–5).[53] Yet the Bible does not claim that Job undergoes a physical healing of the skin anomaly that he acquires in Job 2:5.[54] To assume that divine honour and reward must include the removal of a disability suggests that we cannot imagine a person having both a disability and a high quality of life. Since, unlike the New Testament, the Hebrew Bible rarely focuses on the healing of disabilities,[55] this assumption may tell us more about our own biases than about the text itself.

Healing through genre. Scholars frequently supply a recovery that does not actually appear in the text by interpreting our passage according to the conventions of certain genres of biblical poetry. The study of ancient Near Eastern literary genres has served as a standard tool of analysis within biblical scholarship for well over a century. This approach suggests that if we can determine the genre or type of speech reflected in a given passage, then we can better understand how the text uses its language or images. Yet this interpretative strategy may also lead to the removal of the servant's disability by interpreting the disability imagery as a stock feature of a genre rather than a description of a figure with disabilities. While scholars have expressed a wide variety of opinions regarding the exact genre that Isaiah 53 reflects,[56] many compare it to a genre of biblical poetry that they call 'the individual song of thanksgiving'. Thus, Isaiah 53 becomes an example of a genre that celebrates the recovery of the able-bodied instead of recounting the servant's experience of disability.

Roughly a century ago, Hermann Gunkel isolated the formal properties of the individual song of thanksgiving. For Gunkel, examples of this genre usually contain the following elements: 1) an introduction in which the individual says that he or she will thank God. 2) A narration of the individual's trouble. In this narration, the individual often recounts the former trouble that he or she faced, how he or she petitioned the LORD, and how the LORD delivered him or her from the trouble. 3) A proclamation, usually to others, of the LORD's deliverance. Gunkel thought that an ancient Israelite would have used this genre of psalms in a religious or cultic worship setting. The individual would have praised God and recounted his or her experience of divine deliverance to the congregation, sometimes accompanied by a sacrifice.[57]

Gunkel saw this genre reflected in Psalms 18, 30, 32, 34, 40, 41, 66, 92, 116, 118, 138 as well as other biblical texts such as Isaiah 38, Jonah 2, or Job 33.[58] Several of these texts mention some type of physical disability or illness as the source of trouble. Gunkel proposed that 'extreme illness' was the most frequent cause of distress addressed by these texts.[59] For example, in Ps 32:3–4, the individual states, 'While I kept silence, my body wasted away through my groaning all day long. For day and night your hand was heavy upon me; my strength was dried up as by the heat of summer.' In Ps 41:3, he or she declares, 'The LORD sustains them on their sickbed; in their illness you heal all their infirmities (*hōlî*, a word related to *hlh*).' We should note that Gunkel does not attribute the Psalmist's suffering to his or her illness alone as if it were simply produced by a medical condition. Instead, he observes how the suffering arises from the Psalmist's social experience of living with an illness. Regarding Psalm 41, Gunkel writes, 'Ps 41:6–9 portrays how the critically ill person is tormented by the poisonous speech of those who will not believe in his innocence and expect him to die soon. Or we hear how the person who is ill suffered from being held in low esteem, even by his closest friends.'[60] Although Gunkel acknowledges other causes of trouble, he writes that in examples of this genre, 'A person is saved out of great distress—the shipwrecked man who is fortunate enough be brought to land, the prisoner who is liberated, and *especially* the sick person who is restored to health.'[61] Indeed, a disease or illness is the source of distress in Isaiah 38, the one example from Isaiah which Gunkel identifies as reflecting this genre.

We have already observed that Hezekiah's prayer in Isaiah 38 has several connections with Isaiah 53. Yet, unlike the servant in Isaiah 53, Hezekiah recovers in Isaiah 38. Likewise, both Psalms 32 and 41 include a divine deliverance from a disability or illness (32:5–7; 41:2, 12). Furthermore, the apparent similarities between Isaiah 53 and Psalm 30 focus on issues of recovery or deliverance. Certainly, Isaiah

53 promises that the servant will experience some type of honour in vv. 10–12. Yet nothing in our passage suggests that the servant experiences a recovery. The comparison with Psalm 30, however, implies that the servant's deliverance involves the removal of an individual's illness or disease. Psalm 30:2 states, 'O LORD my God, I cried to you for help, and you have healed me.' Nothing in this Psalm addresses social or political oppression. Instead, it recalls divine assistance in the recovery from a near fatal illness or disease of some sort. In 30:3, the Psalmist declares, 'O LORD, you brought up my soul from Sheol, restored me to life from among those gone down to the Pit' (cf. 30:9). Comparisons between our passage and Psalm 30 may create the impression that the servant experienced a healing that Isaiah 53 never states explicitly.

Unlike Isaiah 53, the examples of the individual song of thanksgiving provided above were written in the first person. Since the servant never speaks or narrates his own experience in Isaiah 53, we could question whether this text represents an individual song of thanksgiving. Gunkel, Sigmund Mowinckel, and a number of other scholars, however, suggest that Psalm 107 reflects a thanksgiving liturgy recited on behalf of multiple individuals in the third person.[62] Joachim Begrich, who completed Gunkel's *Introduction to the Psalms* after Gunkel's death, proposed that, like Psalm 107, Isa 53:1–10 also reflects a third person individual psalm of thanksgiving. Begrich saw vv. 2–9 as modelled after the narration of the individual's trouble that typically appear in individual songs of thanksgiving. He interpreted v. 10 as a proclamation of the LORD's deliverance.[63]

To show how v. 10 indicates a divine deliverance, Begrich translated one of the verbs in this verse as '[the LORD] healed him' instead of 'made him diseased'. As we will find in Chapter 3, a Greek translation suggests that the LORD 'cleansed' the servant in this verse. Begrich, however, does not follow this Greek translation. Instead, he derives 'healed' by rearranging the Hebrew consonants and the spacing of the letters from *hhly 'm-tsym* to *hhlym 't-sym*. These moves change the translation from 'make him diseased. When you make' to 'healed the one who made'.[64] A similar form of the word *hhlym* ('to heal him') appears in Hezekiah's prayer for healing (Isa 38:16). Since Isaiah 38 and 53 share other key words and phrases (e.g. 'disease' *hlh* in Isa 38:9; 53:3, 4, 10; 'land of the living' 38:11; 53:8), Begrich's proposal is intriguing. Nevertheless, none of the ancient manuscripts reflects this translation for 53:10. As Brevard Childs correctly observes, 'there is not explicit mention of a healing of the servant up to this point, and the difference between "afflict him with sickness" and "healed him" is hardly inconsequential'.[65] Begrich's translation of v. 10 seems to interpret Isaiah 53 according to the conventions of the individual song of thanksgiving genre and not the text itself.

Despite his translation of v. 10, Begrich does not argue that the verse indicates that the servant recovered from a physical illness or impairment. In fact, he does not view the servant as a figure with disabilities or diseases at any point in the poem. Although he identifies Isaiah 53 as an individual song of thanksgiving, he does not interpret it as commemorating a physical recovery. Instead, he identifies the servant as the supposed author of Isaiah 40–55 (Second Isaiah) and argues that the author used this genre as a poetic way of prophesying about his own death and resurrection.[66] In other words, Begrich thinks the passage predicts the servant's death, but has nothing to do with a recovery from illness as many other individual songs of thanksgiving do. In fact, Begrich's theory implies that the passage has very little to do with a delivery from any of the types of distress that Gunkel proposed. Begrich's theory allows us to divorce the literary form or genre of the text from the typical context in which Gunkel thought it was used in everyday life.

Likewise, Otto Kaiser argues that Isaiah 53 reflects an individual song of thanksgiving. Whereas Begrich interprets the servant as an individual, Kaiser prefers to interpret the servant as a collective reference to Israel's exilic community.[67] Nevertheless, like Begrich, he does not connect it to an experience of illness and impairments. Instead, he views it as a response to a lamentation of the people in exile.[68] According to Kaiser, only 53:1–6 reflect an individual song of thanksgiving. The prophet incorporates vv. 1–6 into a larger 'oracle of salvation' for the exilic community. As in Begrich's interpretation, Kaiser imagines an historical situation for our passage that appears very different than the typical functions of this genre that Gunkel proposes. For both Begrich and Kaiser, a form of poetry often associated with experiences of illness, disease, or other impairments now describes a situation far removed from this context.

It becomes easy to assume a recovery that does not actually appear in the text when we interpret Isaiah 53 according to the conventions of certain poetic genres such as the individual song of thanksgiving. This interpretative strategy may not identify the servant with a presumably able-bodied individual or group. Nevertheless, it may lead to the removal of the servant's disability by interpreting the disability imagery as a stock feature of a genre.

Was the servant an able-bodied prisoner?

Some scholars suggest that the servant's isolation from human society in Isaiah 53 results from imprisonment.[69] For example, Whybray correctly criticizes Begrich and Kaiser for suggesting that Isaiah 53 uses the individual song of thanksgiving in completely idiosyncratic ways. He notes that the Hebrew Bible never uses individual songs of thanksgiving as prophetic references to the author's death and resurrection or as oracles of salvation to comfort the exilic community.[70] By contrast, Whybray proposes a historical context more in keeping with the uses of an individual song of thanksgiving that Gunkel suggests. Whybray hypothesizes that Isaiah 53 was an individual song of thanksgiving composed to commemorate Second Isaiah's release from a Babylonian prison. The song was sung at a religious assembly of the Judean exiles.[71] This hypothesis follows Gunkel's criteria for an individual song of thanksgiving both in its form and its imagined historical context.

As we noted earlier, Gunkel proposes that ancient Israelites could use this genre to celebrate a release from prison. Gunkel uses Psalm 107 as an example: 'Some sat in darkness and in gloom, prisoners in misery and in irons...Then they cried to the LORD in their trouble, and he saved them from their distress; he brought them out of darkness and gloom, and broke their bonds asunder. Let them thank the LORD for his steadfast love, for his wonderful works to humankind' (vv. 10, 13–15). Some forms of the Hebrew words 'restraint' and 'justice' (Isa 53:8) can denote some type of detention and legal proceeding that the servant may have endured. Thus, Whybray follows G. R. Driver as well as a number of other scholars in arguing that 53:8 describes some type of imprisonment.[72]

In this sense, Whybray's identification of Isaiah 53's genre as an individual song of thanksgiving supports the idea that the passage describes an otherwise able-bodied prisoner rather than a figure with disabilities. Furthermore, if Isaiah 53 was composed in the aftermath of the Babylonian destruction of Jerusalem in 587 BCE, then the general historical context may also suggest imprisonment. As we will find in Chapter 4, some scholars connect this passage with the imprisonment and release of King Jehoiachin (2 Kgs 25:27–30). Other post-587 BCE texts from Isaiah that involve a servant figure also mention the release of prisoners (42:9; 61:1). Nonetheless, the historical context of the Babylonian Exile does not mean that the Babylonians imprisoned the majority of the exiles. For example, the Babylonians did not imprison the prophet Ezekiel. While the book of Daniel comes from a later historical period, it does not portray Daniel and other elite Judeans as confined to prison (Daniel 1–6). Jeremiah's letter to the Babylonian exiles of 597 BCE implies that they could acquire property and marry while in Babylon (Jeremiah 29). Thus, we have little reason to assume that the Babylonians would have imprisoned Second Isaiah.

We should also note that while 'without restraint and without justice' in 53:8 means the act was unjustified, these terms could mean many things other than imprisonment. The imagery of oppression within the passage has stronger connections with the social experience of disability. The repeated use of images of disease, illness, impairment and so on throughout Isaiah 53 (the various forms of *ḥlḥ* in vv. 3, 4, 10) as well as references to his 'marred' form and appearance (52:14; 53:2) suggests an overall context of disability much more than imprisonment. Moreover, a recovery from illness represents the most frequent context for extant examples of individual songs of thanksgiving. If we want to connect Isaiah 53 to this genre of poetry, we should remember that issues surrounding illness or disability are the passage's most prominent motif and the genre's most common use, at least based on the biblical examples that Gunkel cites.

We should remain cautious, however, about connecting Isaiah 53 with individual songs of thanksgiving. A focus on the generic affinities between our passage and individual song of thanksgiving distances the description of the servant from the specific experiences of people with disabilities. Unlike Begrich or Whybray, most scholars do not argue that Isaiah 53 provides an actual example of an individual song of thanksgiving because, as Kaiser argues, several of its features do not reflect the genre's typical elements. For example, although Claus Westermann follows Begrich's translation of the verb in v. 10 as 'healed', he only sees the individual song of thanksgiving genre in 'the background' of the passage.[73] Roy F. Melugin agrees with Westermann and writes, 'The structure of the poem is basically the prophet's own creation.'[74] Paul D. Hanson suggests that attention to the form or genre of Isaiah 53 helps us 'establish whatever objective markers [that] can be identified'.[75] Yet he observes only 'affinities' between Isaiah 53 and 'thanksgiving psalms', without making a more specific genre designation. He compares Isaiah 53 to Psalm 30 and 54, although Gunkel did not label the later psalm as an individual song of thanksgiving. While Psalm 54 mentions the Psalmist's 'enemies' (v. 5), it never mentions any disease, illness, or disability of any kind. A comparison to Psalm 54 may obscure the presence of imagery associated with disability in Isaiah 53.

Certainly, like Duhm's identification of the servant as a person with a skin anomaly, Gunkel's attempts to reconstruct the historical situations in which ancient Israelites used the individual song of thanksgiving remain quite speculative. The *Hodayot* found among the Dead Sea Scrolls reflect, or at least imitate, this genre. They suggest, however, a very different historical situation than any of the ones that Gunkel proposes for this genre.[76] Although many scholars argue that the individual song of thanksgiving genre influences Isaiah 53, few of them argue that this passage was composed to give thanks for recovery from an illness or disease. Yet, as we have discovered, these scholars do not reject disability as a possible reason for its composition because of the speculative nature of Gunkel's theory. In fact, several argue that Isaiah 53 was composed to give thanks for a release from imprisonment. This idea, however, is just as speculative as the recovery from illness theory and, according to Gunkel, is a far less frequent reason for reciting an individual song of thanksgiving.

Conclusions

A number of scholars regard the imagery running throughout Isaiah 53 as describing someone with some sort of disability or disease even if they prefer not to diagnose it precisely as a skin anomaly.[77] The imagery that the servant's description uses is usually imagery associated with persons with diseases or disabilities in the Hebrew Bible and other ancient Near Eastern literature. In this chapter, we have emphasized that our inability to diagnose the servant's condition as a skin anomaly should not discourage us from identifying him as a figure with disabilities. The imagery throughout Isaiah 53 depicts the servant as having a chronic but unspecified disability. Yet, in depicting the servant's disability, Isaiah 53 does not focus on a medical description of an anomalous body. The passage provides us with very few, if any, clues that would help us visualize the servant's body, much less diagnose his condition.

Although interpreters often imagine the servant as an otherwise able-bodied person who suffers or even dies, a close examination of our passage provides little support for such interpretations. We suspect that these interpretations of Isaiah 53 are overly influenced by Duhm's other 'servant songs'. Moreover, while God ultimately vindicates the servant, the text does not equate this honour with a removal of his disability. In keeping with texts such as Isaiah 56, our passage depicts a figure with disabilities who is vindicated from social oppression rather than cured of a defective body. However else it may function, Isaiah 53 provides a portrait of disability in the ancient Near East as a social and political experience. If we decide whether Isaiah 53 describes the servant as having a disability based only on our ability to diagnose the servant's condition, we will probably miss how the passage depicts an ancient Israelite experience of disability.

In addition to complicating efforts at a precise medical diagnosis, the lack of specific bodily description in Isaiah 53 prevents us from sentimentalizing the servant's disabled body as an image of individual tragedy. The passage does not contain enough physical description to claim that it arouses pity or pathos for the servant with the specifics of his impaired body. Disability scholarship has frequently examined how characters with disabilities in literature often reinforce the questionable idea that disability imagery naturally evokes individual emotional responses.[78] Yet Isaiah 53 focuses on the servant's social experience rather than his impaired body. Our passage does not approach disability as a tragic embodiment isolated to an individual body in order to produce heartwarming or heartbreaking emotions from its audience. Close attention to the discourse or model that a text uses to approach disability is of paramount importance.

Nothing in Isaiah 53 implies that the servant's disability was a temporary condition or temporary injury. In the following chapters, we discover that commentaries and translations use various exegetical strategies to read a recovery or removal of the servant's disability into the text. Yet the passage's presentation of the servant focuses consistently on his social experience of disability throughout Isaiah 53. This creates a deep irony that runs through the history of scholarship on this passage. Our passage provides a nuanced portrayal of this servant with disabilities. Yet the history of scholarship is largely a record of how we have neglected this portrayal of his disability and invented the able-bodied suffering servant. As we discover in the next two chapters, interpreters have gone to great lengths to show that the suffering servant may be injured, dead, recovered, or imprisoned, but that he is not disabled.

The Servant as Scriptural Sufferer

Christians made use of bits and pieces of psalms or Isaiah 53 until finally a unified interpretation was produced.... What appears to us as coherent interpretation traditions may well be the product of our imaginations. The so-called plots of Psalm 22 or Isaiah 53 may not have been the starting point of Christian interpretation at all but only a later byproduct.

Donald Juel, *Messianic Exegesis: Christological Interpretation of the Old Testament in Early Christianity*

Why, then, does Paul not draw this prophecy into the open and use the servant figure as an explicit basis for his interpretation of Israel, or the church, or of Jesus?... He hints and whispers all around Isaiah 53 but never mentions the prophetic typology that would supremely integrate his interpretation of Christ and Israel. The result is a compelling example of metalepsis: Paul's transumptive silence cries out for the reader to complete the trope

Richard B. Hays, *Echoes of Scripture in the Letters of Paul*

In the previous chapter, we found that various interpreters acknowledge that Isaiah 53 describes the servant as a figure with disabilities. Thus, we should ask why scholars do not typically interpret the servant as having disabilities. In Chapter 4, we will explore this question by reviewing some interpretative strategies that modern scholars use when studying this passage. We will show how these strategies enable scholars to depict the servant as an otherwise able-bodied figure who suffers rather than a figure with disabilities. In this chapter, we trace the roots of this interpretative tendency to early translations and other interpretations of Isaiah 53 from antiquity.

We begin this chapter by examining how ancient Hebrew, Greek, Aramaic, and Latin versions of Isaiah 53 interpret the disability imagery in our passage. We will find a tendency to downplay the servant's disability or to lose it in translation. Second, we examine early typological interpretations that involve Isaiah 53. We will focus on the direct quotations of Isaiah 53 in other biblical texts. Once again, the servant's disability is largely lost in these quotations and their typologies. This chapter shows that while modern scholars may use interpretive methods different from those of their ancient counterparts, modern scholarly depictions of the servant as an able-bodied sufferer reinforce an interpretative tendency that dates back to at least the second century BCE.

Disability imagery lost in translation

We do not have an original manuscript of Isaiah 53. Instead, we have a number of later versions from antiquity in a variety of languages. If we compare these versions, however, we would soon discover that it is very difficult to decide what the original actually said because of the numerous differences between the Hebrew, Greek, and Aramaic versions or even the differences between the Hebrew in the Dead Sea Scrolls versions and in later Masoretic Hebrew manuscripts (sixth to tenth century CE). The NRSV's English translation, which appears with slight modifications in our introduction, does not translate from one ancient manuscript. At some points, it follows a Greek manuscript; at other points, a Hebrew manuscript.[1] We do not have enough space in this book to discuss thoroughly all the NRSV's translation choices. Readers should consult a critical commentary on Isaiah for more detailed discussions of translation issues.[2] For our purposes, our discussion will concentrate on the verses that show a shift from the servant as a figure with disabilities towards an able-bodied servant within different versions of Isaiah 53 from antiquity.

Dead Sea Scrolls (Hebrew). The Great Isaiah Scroll (1QIsa[a]) found among the Dead Sea Scrolls contains one of the oldest extant copies of Isaiah 53. Yet this copy of Isaiah dates to the second century BCE, several centuries after the composition of our passage probably some time in the sixth century BCE. There are several minor differences between 1QIsa^a and other Hebrew versions of Isaiah 53 that need not concern us. Instead, we will concentrate on the two significant variations that have attracted a great deal of scholarly attention. In both cases, it seems unlikely that 1QIsa^a reflects the original Hebrew wording since most other ancient manuscripts do not confirm the wording of 1QIsa^a in these two cases. Both these differences appear in references to the servant's disability in 52:14 and 53:10.

In the Introduction, we translated 52:14 as 'Just as there were many who were astonished at him—so marred was his appearance, unlike human semblance, and his form unlike that of mortals.' This translation suggests that the servant's visible disability, indicated by his 'marred appearance', astonishes others. The word 'marred' translates the Masoretic Hebrew versions that spell the word as *mišḥat*, which comes from the Hebrew root *šḥt*, meaning 'to ruin, destroy, or disfigure'. Yet, since the word *mišḥat* does not appear anywhere else in the Hebrew Bible, scholars debate whether this is the correct spelling of this word. By contrast, 1QIsa^a spells the word as *mšḥy* instead of *mišḥat*.[3] This spelling assumes the word comes from the Hebrew root *mšḥ* meaning 'to anoint'. Thus, if we follow 1QIsa^a, we would translate 52:14 as 'Just as there were many who were astonished at him—so I [God] have anointed his appearance, unlike human semblance, and his form unlike that of mortals.' In 1QIsa^a, the servant's visible disability does not shock those who see him. Instead, his divinely anointed appearance provides the shock.

In the previous chapter, we observed the scholarly tendency to read the other servant songs, especially 50:4–11, into Isaiah 53 when interpreting the servant in our passage. Often, the tendency to use other servant songs to interpret Isaiah 53 helps to explain the description of the servant as referring to something other than disability. Unlike contemporary scholars, the parties that produced 1QIsa^a did not identify Isaiah 53 as belonging to an isolated group of texts called the 'servant songs'. Nonetheless, 1QIsa^a's use of the Hebrew word meaning 'I have anointed' (*mšḥy*) in 52:14 may show the influence of the other servant passages. Rather than a simple spelling correction, Martin Hengel argues that the use of 'anointed' in 52:14 may reflect 'a conscious interpretation' of the servant's mission, possibly influenced by the servant passage in 61:1–4. Hengel cites the reference to a divine anointing in 61:1: 'The spirit of the Lord GOD is upon me, because the LORD has anointed (*mšh*) me.'[4] If Hengel is correct, the tendency to read the other servant passages into Isaiah 53 may have begun as early as the Dead Sea Scrolls in the second century BCE. Yet the description of a future prophetic or priestly figure in 61:1–4 does not include any disability imagery. By claiming that the servant has an anointed appearance instead of a marred appearance in 52:14, the servant in our passage appears more like a presumably able-bodied prophet or priest than a figure with a disability.[5] Similarly, the servant song in 50:4–11 helps modern scholars interpret the servant in Isaiah 53 as fatally injured rather than having a disability.

Other scholars suggest that the use of 'anointed' in 1QIsa[a] shows the influence of biblical texts outside Isaiah. Dominique Barthélemy connects this text to the tradition of anointing a priest in Lev 21:10: 'The priest who is exalted above his fellows, on whose head the anointing (*mšh*) oil has been poured and who has been consecrated to wear the vestments, shall not dishevel his hair, nor tear his vestments.'[6] Interpreting the servant's appearance in Isa 52:14 as anointed instead of marred would avoid a potential conflict with the physical requirements for priests in Leviticus 21–22. Lev 21:10 comes from a set of instructions for priests from Aaron's family. These instructions include an extensive list of physical blemishes that disqualify a priest from certain activities (Lev 21:16–23) as well as restrictions on priests with skin anomalies (Lev 22:4). Leviticus 21–22 seems to influence other discussions of physical requirements in non-biblical texts from the Dead Sea Scrolls.[7] This may increase the likelihood that this material from Leviticus also influences 1QIsa[a], although we cannot know for sure. The use of 'anointed' may mark an interpretative shift away from disability imagery in favour of priestly imagery from Leviticus. The possibility that 1QIsa[a] interprets the servant according to these priestly standards suggests that profiles for the servant that do not typically include disability began to develop early in the history of Isaiah 53's interpretation.[8]

1QIsa[a] not only downplays the disability imagery in 52:14, but in 53:10 as well. In the Introduction, we translated v. 10 as 'The LORD was delighted to crush him, to make him diseased (root: *hlh*).' By contrast, 1QIsaᵃ interprets the word translated as 'diseased' as coming from the Hebrew root *ḥll*, meaning 'to profane' or 'to wound' instead of the root *ḥlh*. If we follow 1QIsaᵃ, we would translate 53:10 as 'The LORD was delighted to crush him and [the LORD] made him profane/wounded him (root: *ḥll*).' Certainly, either to be made profane or to be wounded could imply a disability. According to Lev 21:23, priests with various disabilities could 'profane' sacred spaces. As our translation in the Introduction suggests, 53:5 uses a form of *ḥll* in the context of the servant's disability: 'he was made profane (*ḥll*)'. The use of *ḥll* in v. 5 may have influenced 1QIsaᵃ's use of *ḥll* rather than *ḥlh* in v. 10. Yet this does not mean that 1QIsaᵃ understands *ḥll* in v. 5 in the context of the servant's disability. The NRSV translates *ḥll* in v. 5 as 'he was wounded'. While this wound could imply an acquired disability, this seems unlikely because typically the Hebrew Bible uses forms of *ḥll* to describe human wounds as fatal rather than disabling (Gen 34:27; Josh 13:22; 1 Sam 31:8; 2 Sam 1:19; Isa 34:3; 66:16; Lam 4:9). In these verses, the NRSV usually translates forms of *ḥll* as 'slain' or 'dead'. In other words, 1QIsaᵃ could understand *ḥll* in v. 5 as indicating a fatal injury and use the same root in v. 10 in a similar manner. In this case, the servant appears as an otherwise able-bodied anointed figure who suffers a fatal wound instead of a figure with disabilities.

We find similar types of fatally wounded figures in another Hebrew Bible text from the Second Temple period (515 BCE–70 CE). Although possibly written by a different author than our passage, Isaiah 57:1 describes a figure with language very similar to the description of the servant as 'the righteous one' in 53:11. In Isa 57:1, however, the righteous one dies: 'The righteous one perishes, and no one takes it to heart; the devout are taken away, while no one understands. For the righteous one is taken away from calamity.'[9] Similarly, Zech 12:10 states, 'And I will pour out on the house of David and the inhabitants of Jerusalem a spirit of grace and supplication. They will look on me, the one they have pierced (*dqr* rather than *ḥll*), and they will mourn for him as one mourns for an only child, and grieve bitterly for him as one grieves for a firstborn son.' Although there are significant differences between Isaiah 53 and Isaiah 57 or Zechariah 12, those parties responsible for 1QIsaᵃ may have interpreted the servant in Isaiah 53 with this type of fatally wounded figure in mind.[10] The profile for this type of fatally wounded figure, however, does not usually include disability. Thus, if 1QIsa[a] interprets the servant in Isaiah 53 according to this profile, it moves away from the disability imagery in our passage.

1QIsa[a] does not completely erase the disability imagery associated with the servant in Isaiah 53. As with other ancient manuscripts, 53:3 in 1QIsa[a] describes the servant as 'acquainted with disease (*hlh*)'. Yet forms of *hlh* have a wide semantic range as we discussed in previous chapters. Since this word does not necessarily imply a disability or disease, the servant's description in both 52:14 and 53:10 in 1QIsa[a] could shift the context of *hlh* in 53:3 away from disability and towards a context of more generalized suffering. Given the wide range of possible meanings for *hlh*, this new context for its use in 53:3 allows us to imagine the servant as an able-bodied sufferer.

Non-biblical texts from the Dead Sea Scrolls also use vocabulary found in Isaiah 53 to describe suffering in general rather than an experience of disability. A collection of texts from the Dead Sea Scrolls that scholars call the *Hodayot* or 'Thanksgiving Hymns' (1QH[a]) give thanks for, among other things, divine assistance with various trials and tribulations. Scholars have considered the relationship of 1QH[a] and Isaiah 53. Based on the overlaps in vocabulary and imagery, some argue that the narrator of 1QH[a] is intentionally modelled after the servant in Isaiah 53. Yet other scholars caution against finding a significant connection.[11] Considering that both texts mention 'light' and a positive impact on 'many' (Isa 53:11–12; 1QH[a] XII 27–8)[12] among other possible connections, we agree with Joseph Blenkinsopp that 'there are solid grounds for the conclusion that the profile of the Isaianic Servant formed a significant aspect of the self-image of the author of the hymns'.[13] Yet the servant's profile in Isaiah 53 contributes significantly to the author's self image primarily because he identifies with the servant's suffering rather than his disability.

In 1QH[a] XVI 26–8, the narrator states that his 'residence is with the diseased, my heart is acquainted with plagues, and I am like a forsaken man with plagues... For my plague has increased to bitterness and incurable suffering which does not stop.' This description shares vocabulary with Isaiah 53's description of the servant as 'a man of suffering and acquainted with disease... he has borne our diseases and carried our suffering; yet we accounted him plagued... plagued for the transgression of my people' (53:3, 4, 8). In 1QH^a, however, these lines appear in the context of the narrator's thanksgiving for divine assistance. A few lines later, the narrator uses the words 'suffering' and 'plague' as one example of the hardships that the narrator faces in general. 'As for me, from ruin to annihilation, from suffering to plague, from pangs to labors, my soul reflects on your wonders; you in your kindness, have not rejected me' (1QH^a XVII 6–7). Among these examples, the presumably male narrator lists labour-pangs among his hardships. This birth imagery suggests that the narrator does not describe specific experiences that he has undergone involving labour or illness. Instead, he uses birth and disease imagery to articulate his general experience of suffering (cf. the birth imagery in 1QH^a XI 7–12; Num 11:12). The word translated as 'plague' appears again a few lines later in 1QH^a XVII 10–12. The context of these lines suggest that 'hardship' or 'distress' would be better translations than 'plague' because the context implies a more generalized suffering rather than a plague or illness of some sort: 'I have been pleased in my hardship/plagues, because I hope for your kindness... you have not threatened my life, nor have you removed my health [*shalom*; cf. "made us whole (*shalom*)" in Isa 53:5], nor have you deserted my expectation; rather, in the face of hardship/plague you have upheld my spirit.'

Scholars also connect the so-called 'Self-Glorification Hymn', a hymn reconstructed from fragments of texts found among the Dead Sea Scrolls, to the servant in Isaiah 53.[14] In this hymn, the narrator asks, 'who has been despised like me?... and who carries evil like me?... who bears all sorrows like me? Who carries evil like me?' (4Q471b line 2; 4Q491c line 9). Both Blenkinsopp and Israel Knohl compare these lines with the servant's description in Isa 53:3–4: 'he was despised and we held him of no account. Surely he has borne our diseases and carried our suffering'.[15] According to Blenkinsopp, 'The most significant parallel is the language in which the experience of humiliation and suffering is described. The two compositions share the same verbs: both subjects are despised (verbal stem *bzh*), and in describing their positive acceptance of suffering the paired verbs (*ns'*, *sbl*) occur in both texts.'[16] In other words, the parallels between the two compositions focus on a social experience of suffering. Yet the

Self-Glorification Hymn does not include disability imagery. Instead, it addresses the more generic topics of sorrows and evils.[17] If this hymn invokes the servant's experience in Isaiah 53, it does not invoke a servant with disabilities but a more generic suffering servant.

The profile of the servant in Isaiah 53 that emerges from both the Great Isaiah Scroll and other non-biblical texts from among the Dead Sea Scrolls downplays the disability imagery to the point that it disappears in the Self-Glorification Hymn. Although the interpretative moves are different, we find a similar disappearing act in the early Greek translation of the Hebrew Bible known as the Septuagint (LXX).

Septuagint/LXX (Greek). The LXX's translation of Isaiah 53 does not downplay the disability imagery associated with the servant as 1QIsaᵃ does.[18] Instead, the LXX has the servant's disability removed by translating 53:10 as 'Yet the LORD determined to cleanse him [the servant] of his disease.' This translation suggests a very different meaning than the Hebrew, 'The LORD was delighted to crush him, to make him diseased.' Nonetheless, the LXX may assume that the servant's disease was a skin anomaly before it was cleansed. The LXX uses the same Greek word for 'cleanse' in reference to the 'cleansing' of a skin anomaly when translating Leviticus 13–14 (e.g. 13:6, 13, 23, 28, 34; 14:2, 57). Forms of this word also appear in Greek translations of Lev 22:4, which prohibits priests with skin anomalies from certain rituals until they are 'clean', as well as Num 12:15, which mentions that Miriam was 'cleansed' of her skin anomaly.

Moreover, the LXX uses Greek words meaning 'sickness' (*malakia*) and 'disease' (*plege*; the same Greek word describes skin anomalies in Leviticus 13–14 and Numbers 12) when referring to the servant's condition (Hebrew: *ḥlh*) throughout our passage (53:3, 10). Yet, when translating the same Hebrew word (*ḥlh*) in reference to parties other than the servant in v. 4, the LXX uses a Greek word meaning 'sin' (*amartia*). Since the LXX uses the same word (*amartia*) to translate the Hebrew word for 'iniquity' (*'awon*) in vv. 5 and 6, the LXX seems to interpret *ḥlh* in reference to other parties as a metaphor for their sin (cf. Isa 33:24). By contrast, the LXX interprets *ḥlh* in reference to the servant as a description of a physical anomaly of some sort since it uses Greek words meaning sickness and disease rather than sin to translate *ḥlh* in 53:3, 10.

Furthermore, the later Greek translation by Aquila (second century CE) also depicts the servant as having a disability. Aquila renders the first line of v. 5 as 'he was made profane'. As we discussed earlier, a person with a disability, including a skin anomaly, could profane sacred things. Like the LXX, Aquila translates the Hebrew word for 'diseased' (*ḥlh*) with a Greek word meaning 'illness' (*appostema*), although this is a different word than the LXX uses.

Regarding the two Greek words for 'disease' and 'cleanse' used by the LXX in v. 10, Hengel observes, 'The two words [disease and cleanse] could suggest leprosy, but in fact they are only meant metaphorically.'[19] While Hengel acknowledges that this translation may assume a skin anomaly, he does not provide any reason for why we should take them as metaphors for something other than a physical anomaly or disability in the LXX. Against Hengel's position, we should return to our earlier observation that when the LXX understands disability imagery in Isaiah 53 as a metaphor, it glosses the metaphor (*ḥlh* as 'sin' in v. 4). Rather than taking the servant's condition as a metaphor for sin, the LXX suggests that the servant undergoes a divine removal of a disease when the LORD determines to cleanse him in v. 10. This interpretation of v. 10 fits with a larger tendency in the LXX's version of Isaiah 53. Hebrew versions of Isa 53:8–11 emphasize the servant's suffering as divinely intended. By contrast, as Karen H. Jobes and Moisés Silva observe, the LXX's version of Isaiah 53 contains 'several examples where the translator clearly avoids statements that attribute the servant's suffering to God's actions' (cf. vv. 4, 8 [LXX]).[20]

This attempt to provide an explicit physical healing of the servant in the LXX may reflect an assumption on the translator's part that the servant's glorification in vv. 10–12 would have to include such a healing. This would fit with a theme found in other texts from the Second Temple period. For example, in addition to living in prosperity following his ordeal, Tobit receives a detailed physical restoration from his blindness (Tob 11:10–15). According to the LXX's translation of Job 42:16, Job lived one hundred and seventy years 'after his *plege*'.[21] According to the pseudepigraphic book, *Testament of Job*, special cords given to Job by God restore and even enhance Job's body once he girds his loins (cf. Job 38:3) with them. Once Job puts these cords on, the worms and plagues (cf. Job 7:5) disappear from his body. He becomes as strong as if he had not suffered at all and he forgets the pains of his heart (*T. Job* 47:5–8). The LXX's translation of Isaiah 53:10 may reflect the tendency towards healing that we find in Tobit, the LXX's version of Job, and the *Testament of Job*.

Rather than a deliberate attempt to provide the healing that is absent in the Hebrew texts, the verb 'cleanse' may also have resulted from a simple mistranslation of the Hebrew root *dk'* ('to crush'). The translator(s) of the LXX may not have recognized the root *dk'*. Aramaic was a spoken language in the Second Temple period. Thus, some scholars suggest that translator(s) may have mistaken the Hebrew root *dk'* for the similar Aramaic root *dk'/zkh*, which can mean 'pure' or 'innocent'.[22] This seems unlikely, however, because earlier in the passage the translator(s) seem to have recognized the Hebrew root *dk'* in the phrase 'crushed for our iniquities' (v. 5) because they translate *dk'* with the Greek word meaning 'sick' (*malakia*). The LXX also uses *malakia* to translate the Hebrew word *hlh* in reference to Hezekiah's illness (Isa 38:1, 9; 39:1). Thus, the LXX seems to be playing on the Hebrew and Aramaic meanings of *dk'* to indicate that although the sins of others made the servant sick (v. 5) and diseased (*plege*; vv. 3), God 'cleansed' (Aramaic *dk'*) him of his disease (*plege*) in v. 10. The LXX implies that the servant had a disease or disability of some sort but the LORD chose to heal him. By the end of the passage, the servant emerges as healthy or able-bodied.

Targum (Aramaic). All translation involves some interpretation. Yet the Aramaic Targum of Isaiah 53 (second century CE) differs so extensively from the Hebrew or Greek versions that scholars debate whether it is a translation, paraphrase, commentary, or so on.[23] One significant difference between the Targum and other ancient versions of Isaiah 53 is that the Targum shows no trace of the servant's disability or even generic types of suffering. As Jostein Ådna observes, 'In the Targum, the Suffering Servant has become a triumphant Messiah. The suffering and blows which strike the Servant...are redirected in the Targum to other groups and entities.'[24] We encounter this change in the first verse of our passage, which the Targum renders as 'my servant, the Messiah, shall prosper'; whereas the Hebrew reads as, 'my servant shall prosper' (52:13).[25]

Earlier, we discussed how, according to 1QIsa[a], the servant has an 'anointed' (*mšhy*) appearance rather than a 'marred' (*mišhat*) appearance in 52:14: 'so marred/anointed was his appearance, unlike human semblance, and his form unlike that of mortals'. Unlike 1QIsa[a], the Targum retains the imagery associated with a visible disability in this verse. Yet, it redirects this imagery away from the servant and onto Israel. 'Just as the house of Israel hoped for him [the servant/messiah] many days—their appearances were so dark among the peoples, and their aspect beyond that of the sons of men' (*Tg. Isa.* 52:14). In the Targum, God does not disfigure the servant. Instead, the long wait for the messiah changes the people's appearance.

Our translation of 53:2–4 implies that the servant had a socially undesirable physical appearance: 'He had no form or majesty that we should look at him, nothing in his appearance that we should desire him...a man of suffering and acquainted with disease...he was despised and we held him of no account...we accounted him plagued, struck down by God, and afflicted.' By contrast, the same verses in the Targum present the servant's appearance as extraordinary and worthy of considerable attention. 'His appearance is not a common appearance and his fearfulness is not an ordinary fearfulness and his brilliance will be holy brilliance, that everyone who looks at him will consider him' (*Tg. Isa.* 53:2b). Moreover, according to the Targum, the 'glory of all the kingdoms' rather than the servant will become 'as a man of sorrows [or suffering] and appointed for sicknesses [or diseases]...they are despised and not esteemed.... We were esteemed wounded, smitten before the LORD and afflicted' (*Tg. Isa.* 53:3, 4).

In v. 5 of our translation the LORD makes the servant profane. As discussed in Chapter 2, this could describe a person with a disability or disease. In v. 5 of the Targum, however, the people's sins profane the sanctuary. Furthermore, in the Targum, vv. 7–9 do not depict the servant's experience of social oppression at the hands of others. Instead, these verses claim that the servant will intercede and free the people from exile and Gentile rule. Like the LXX, v. 10 of the Targum uses the verb 'cleanse' (*dk'*) rather than 'crush'. Yet, in the Targum, the servant does not undergo a cleansing of his disease.

Instead, a remnant of the people experiences the cleansing in order to purify them from sin.

Vulgate (Latin). Blenkinsopp makes an important observation regarding the difference between the Targum of Isaiah 53 and Jerome's Latin translation of our passage (early fifth century CE). He writes,

> Jerome was certainly convinced that the Servant passages spoke about Jesus... Unlike the Targumist, however, he was engaged in translating the Hebrew original (the *Hebraica veritus* [or 'Hebrew truth']) as accurately as possible and therefore could not permit himself the freedom to indulge in the kind of paraphrase which is routine in *Targum Jonathan*. This he left to his commentary on the book.[26]

For Jerome, an accurate translation meant that he would use Latin vocabulary for illness, disability, or disease to translate the disability imagery that Isaiah 53 uses to describe the servant's condition. For example, in 53:4, Jerome uses the Latin word *leprosum* for the Hebrew term that we translated as 'plagued'. The Latin word refers to a skin anomaly, although probably not leprosy or Hansen's Disease as we discussed in Chapter 2. In addition, Jerome uses the Latin word *infirmitate* ('illness') for the Hebrew term which we translated as 'diseased' (a form of *ḥlh*).

Jerome's translation of Isaiah 53 presents the servant as a figure with disabilities (cf. *b. Sanh.* 98b) even if Jerome connects the servant with a presumably able-bodied Jesus in other contexts. The servant's disability remains as a prominent trait in Jerome's translation of Isaiah but not in his commentary on Isaiah. Jerome's work provides an example from antiquity of both a recognition that Isaiah 53 depicts a disability and how early interpreters associate the servant with able-bodied figures.

Disability imagery lost in typology

In the non-biblical texts from the Dead Sea Scrolls (1QH[a] and the Self-Glorification Hymn), we found that the narrator presents himself or herself as a type of figure similar to the servant in Isaiah 53. This typological approach, in which two or more figures or characters are interpreted as reflecting a particular character type or profile, represents a common reading strategy for interpreters of Isaiah 53 in antiquity. In order to interpret a figure or character as a type that reflects a certain profile, one must emphasize certain traits and downplay or ignore others. The servant has more traits than simply his disability. Isaiah 53 also presents him as a servant of the LORD who has knowledge and is characterized by righteousness (53:11). Thus, ancient readers did not need to build a typological interpretation around his disability because they had his other traits at their disposal.

In fact, most typologies involving the servant do not include his disability at all. For example, Dan 12:2–3 (second century BCE) reads, 'Many of those who sleep in the dust of the earth shall awake, some to everlasting life, and some to shame and everlasting contempt. Those who are wise shall shine like the brightness of the sky, and those who lead many to righteousness, like the stars forever and ever.' Many scholars claim that this passage reflects an early typological interpretation of the servant based on Isa 52:13, which reads, 'See, my servant shall prosper; he shall be exalted and lifted up, and shall be very high.' Daniel 12:3 creates a typological connection between the 'prospering' (Hebrew root: *skl*) of the servant and those who are 'wise' (Hebrew root: *skl*). The imagery of exaltation, and possibly even resurrection, in both passages furthers this typology. The positive outcome for the 'many' in Dan 12:3–4 reinforces the typology with the servant's experience because references to the 'many' appear throughout Isaiah 53: 'Just as there were many who were astonished at him . . . so he shall startle many nations . . . yet he bore the sin of many' (52:14, 15; 53:12).[27] Thus, Daniel 12 creates a typological connection between the experience of the servant and the experience of the 'wise' in a later period. Yet this connection does not incorporate the servant's disability.

Although Daniel 12 never quotes Isaiah 53 directly, we may still discern an allusion to the servant figure based on the overlaps in the vocabulary, themes, and imagery cited earlier. Like Daniel, many of the typologies involving the servant in Isaiah 53 allude to our passage without quoting it directly. Outside the book of Isaiah, Daniel probably represents the earliest extant allusion to Isaiah 53, but it is not the only one. Scholars have argued that many texts from the New Testament and other Second Temple literature evoke Isaiah 53 (e.g. Aramaic Apocryphon of Levi 4Q540–541; Testament of

Benjamin 3:8; Wisdom 1–6; Mark 10:45; 1 Cor 15:3–5; Rom 4:25; Phil 2:6–9; Heb 9:28).[28]

Some of these typologies, however, come from intertextual connections that scholars make instead of allusions that the texts' authors or editors may have intended.[29] None of them, however, is structured around disability imagery. The New Testament contains eight quotations from Isaiah 53 (Matt 8:17; Mark 15:28; Luke 22:37; John 12:38; Acts 8:32–33; Rom 10:16; 15:21; 1 Pet 2:22–25). We will limit the following discussion to those texts that quote our passage directly due to both space constraints and the fact that a quotation of Isaiah 53 provides a solid criteria for deciding whether a later text alludes to our passage intentionally. These New Testament texts, all in Greek, create typological connections between Isaiah 53 and Jesus or members of the early church.

Jesus as miracle worker and healer (Matt 8:17 and John 12:38). Quotations of Isaiah 53 appear in the context of Jesus' miracles and healings in both Matt 8:17 and John 12:38. Matt 8:16–17 reads, 'That evening they brought to [Jesus] many who were possessed with demons; and he cast out the spirits with a word, and cured all who were sick. This was to fulfill what had been spoken through the prophet Isaiah, "He took our infirmities and bore our diseases."' Matthew's quotation of Isa 53:4 does not come from the LXX's Greek translation. As we noted earlier, the LXX translates the Hebrew word *hlh* ('diseases/ infirmities') as 'sin'. Matt 8:16, however, discusses the healing of sicknesses rather than the forgiveness of sin. Thus, Matthew's Greek rendering of this verse seems to come directly from a Hebrew text rather than the LXX.[30] This translation technique allows Matthew to connect Jesus' healing activities with Isaiah 53. Yet Matthew invokes the servant as one who heals disabilities rather than has disabilities.[31]

Scholars debate whether Matthew quotes Isa 53:4 as an isolated proof text without regard for the quotation's context within Isaiah 53 or if the quotation invites the audience to recall the larger context of Isaiah 53, which would include the servant's suffering as well. Noting the occasional practice in antiquity of quoting scripture without concern for the context of the quotation, Ulrich Luz writes, 'Precisely that part of Isa 53:3–5 is used here that does not speak of the suffering of God's servant. Our quotation is an example of the way early Christian exegesis, like the Jewish exegesis of the time, sometimes quotes individual words of scripture without any regard for their context.'[32] If Luz is correct, at least in the case of Matt 8:17, then the selective quotation of Isa 53:4 ignores aspects of the servant connected to disability that the verses immediately preceding the quoted verse would provide (Isa 53:2–3). This quotation technique helps create a typology in which Jesus and the servant become examples of a healer of disabilities rather than a figure with disabilities.

John connects a different verse from Isaiah 53 to Jesus' healing activities. Yet, like Matthew, John's quotation does not include the verses of Isaiah 53 that contain disability imagery. Instead, John uses the quotation to explain the rejection of Jesus despite his role as a healer.

Although [Jesus] had performed so many signs in their presence, they did not believe in him. This was to fulfill the word spoken by the prophet Isaiah: "Lord, who has believed our message, and to whom has the arm of the Lord been revealed?" And so they could not believe, because Isaiah also said, "He has blinded their eyes and hardened their heart, so that they might not look with their eyes, and understand with their heart and turn—and I would heal them". Isaiah said this because he saw his glory and spoke about him. (John 12:37–41)

Elsewhere, John uses the term 'signs' for Jesus' miracles, often, the healing of the sick (John 4:48; 6:2; 9:16). Thus, the two quotations from Isaiah (Isa 53:1 and 6:10) appear in the context of Jesus' healings or miracles. Nonetheless, these miracles do not convince all of Jesus' audience. John understands this situation as prophesied in Isa 53:1 and quotes the LXX's translation. In Isaiah, the verses immediately surrounding the quotation from Isa 53:1 connect the servant's rejection to his marred and unattractive appearance (Isa 52:14–53:3). Isaiah 53 relates the servant's rejection to his disability. In John, the rejection of Jesus has nothing to do with a disability. In fact, this rejection takes place despite Jesus' healings of disabilities.

John's second quotation from Isaiah further distances Jesus from the disability imagery in Isaiah 53. The disability imagery in John 12:37–41 does not come from the servant's description in Isaiah 53. Instead, it comes from a description of the people who witness the prophecy in Isa 6:10. John quotes this passage to explain why certain people did not believe Jesus (cf. Matt 13:15; Mark 4:12; Luke 8:10).[33] In Isa 6:10, God prevents the people from understanding a prophetic message by blinding their eyes and hardening their hearts. John applies this disability imagery to those who do not believe Jesus rather than to Jesus himself. John associates Jesus with miracles and healings, but associates those who reject Jesus with blindness.

Jesus as innocent figure (Luke 22:37 and Mark 15:28). According to Isa 53:12, the servant 'was numbered with the transgressors'. While certain New Testament passages may allude to other parts of this verse (cf. Matt 20:28; 26:28; Rom 5:15; Phil 2:7–8; Heb 9:28), this phrase is quoted directly in Luke. Jesus instructs his disciples to arm themselves in order to fulfill prophecy. '[Jesus] said to them, "But now, the one who has a purse must take it, and likewise a bag. And the one who has no sword must sell his cloak and buy one. For I tell you, this scripture must be fulfilled in me, 'And he was counted among the lawless'; and indeed what is written about me is being fulfilled"' (Luke 22:36–37). The NRSV translates the same Greek word as both 'transgressors' (Isa 53:12; cf. 53:8) and as 'lawless' (Luke 22:37). In Luke, Jesus draws a connection between himself and an innocent figure associated with wrongdoers. Luke does not use Isaiah 53 to depict Jesus as a figure with disabilities, but as an innocent figure.

Luke 22:35–38 does not comment on Jesus' physical condition. By contrast, Mark 15:25–28 depicts his crucifixion. The NRSV translates vv. 25–27 as 'It was nine o'clock in the morning when they crucified him. The inscription of the charge against him read, "The King of the Jews." And with him they crucified two bandits, one on his right and one on his left.' While the NRSV skips v. 28, it includes the following footnote at the end of v. 27: 'Other ancient authorities add v. 28, *"And the scripture was fulfilled that says, And he was counted among the lawless"'* (italics original). Although v. 28 is most likely a secondary addition since it does not appear in the early Greek manuscripts known as Sinaiticus,[34] if we restore v. 28 to the main body of Mark 15, then, like Luke, Mark uses Isa 53:12 to depict Jesus as an innocent figure associated with wrongdoers.

That Mark quotes Isaiah 53 while narrating Jesus' death could suggest a connection based on physical suffering. Yet, as we discussed in Chapter 2, the servant in Isaiah is not fatally wounded by humans. Rather, Isaiah 53 depicts him as living with an unspecified disability. By contrast, Mark 15 portrays Jesus as an otherwise able-bodied character who suffers and ultimately dies. Moving from able-bodied to dead in a matter of hours does not make Jesus a character with disabilities nor does it parallel the servant's experience as depicted throughout Isaiah 53.[35] Nonetheless, we find Isaiah 53 quoted in other New Testament texts that focus on Jesus as an able-bodied martyr.

Jesus as able-bodied martyr (Acts 8:32–33 and 1 Peter 2:22). In Acts 8, Philip encounters an Ethiopian eunuch reading from the book of Isaiah.

[Philip] heard [an Ethiopian eunuch] reading the prophet Isaiah. He asked, 'Do you understand what you are reading'? He replied, 'How can I, unless someone guides me'? . . . Now the passage of the scripture that he was reading was this: 'Like a sheep he was led to the slaughter, and like a lamb silent before its shearer, so he does not open his mouth. In his humiliation justice was denied him. Who can describe his generation? For his life is taken away from the earth'. The eunuch asked Philip, 'About whom, may I ask you, does the prophet say this, about himself or about someone else'? Then Philip began to speak, and starting with this scripture, he proclaimed to him the good news about Jesus (Acts 8:30–35).

The quotation from Isaiah comes from the LXX's translation of 53:7–8. The LXX differs from our translation of these verses since we followed a Hebrew version for these verses. We translated the last half of v. 8 as 'he was excluded from the land of the living, plagued for the transgression of my people'. As we found in Chapter 2, our translation suggests the servant's isolation, possibly due to some disability ('plagued'). By contrast, Acts' quotation from the LXX implies the servant's death and possible ascension to heaven more clearly than the Hebrew text since the LXX ends with the phrase 'For his life is taken away from the earth'.

Yet, even in the LXX, the portion of v. 8 and v. 9 that immediately follows the quotation in Acts does not suggest that the servant died or ascended to heaven. Acts 8 does not include the last line of 53:8 or the first half of v. 9, which the LXX translates as 'Due to the transgressions [cf. Isa 53:12 LXX] of my people, he was led to death, but I [God] turned over the wicked instead of his grave and the rich instead of his death' (author's translation). In the LXX, the larger context of vv. 8–9 suggests that the servant's life was threatened but that God delivered him. As we discussed earlier, the next verse (v. 10) depicts the servant's 'cleansing' with Greek terms used for the cleansing of skin anomalies elsewhere in the LXX. Moreover, the LXX may interpret the servant's condition as a skin anomaly based on its translation of vv. 3 and 4. By quoting v. 7 and only the first part of v.8 rather than vv. 3–4 or vv. 8–10, Acts ignores the disability and healing imagery in the LXX's translation of Isaiah 53. The isolated quotation from v. 7 and only the first part of v. 8 allows the servant to appear as an otherwise able-bodied figure who loses his life.

The discussion of whom the prophecy refers to does not consider a figure with disabilities. Instead, the candidates include Isaiah and Jesus. The eunuch's mention of Isaiah may reflect a tradition, that may date to the first century CE if not earlier, that Isaiah was martyred by Manasseh and ascended to heaven (cf. *Lives of the Prophets* 1; *Martyrdom of Isaiah* 5; Justin, *Dialogues with Trypho* 120.5; Tertullian, *De patientia* 14; Josephus, *Jewish Antiquites* 10.38; *Yebamot* 49b; Heb 11:37).[36] Philip's connection between the experience of suffering and death in the quotation from Isa 53:7–8 and the 'good news about Jesus' recalls events that include Jesus' death (cf. Luke 24:19–27). Yet the traditions about either Isaiah or Jesus' death present them as otherwise able-bodied people who suffer and die from humanly inflicted torture. Even if Acts hints at a connection between the eunuch and the servant's respective social experiences of disability,[37] the selective quotation of Isa 53:7–8 shifts Philip and the eunuch's discussion onto able-bodied martyrs rather than persons with disabilities.

In 1 Peter 2, we also find a reference to the servant's suffering as that of an able-bodied martyr rather than part of a social experience of disability. In this passage, the author of 1 Peter advises slaves to accept the authority of their masters, even if their masters abuse them. The passage holds up Jesus as an example for how to handle suffering. In the process, the author connects Jesus with an innocent sufferer by quoting from Isa 53:9:

If you endure when you are beaten for doing wrong, what credit is that? But if you endure when you do right and suffer for it, you have God's approval. For to this you have been called, because Christ also suffered for you, leaving you an example, so that you should follow in his steps. 'He committed no sin, and no deceit was found in his mouth'. When he was abused, he did not return abuse; when he suffered, he did not threaten; but he entrusted himself to the one who judges justly. He himself bore our sins in his body on the cross, so that, free from sins, we might live for righteousness; by his wounds you have been healed. For you were going astray like sheep, but now you have returned to the shepherd and guardian of your souls (1 Pet 2:20–25).

1 Pet 2:18–25 shows some awareness of the context of its quotation from Isaiah 53. Although it only quotes Isa 53:9 directly, it alludes to Isaiah 53 elsewhere with near quotations from the LXX such as 'bore our sins' (cf. 53:4), 'by his wounds you have been healed' (cf. 53:5) and 'you were going astray like sheep' (cf. 53:6). Attention to the larger context of Isaiah 53 requires greater focus on the servant's physical condition than we found in the Gospels' isolated quotations from Isaiah 53.

Yet, unlike Isaiah 53, 1 Peter does not connect this physical condition with disability. Instead, it understands Isaiah 53 as a prophecy about Jesus' suffering and death. According to 1 Pet 1:11, the Spirit of Christ through the prophets 'testified in advance to the sufferings destined for Christ and the subsequent glory' (cf. 1 Pet 3:18). If, for 1 Peter, these testimonies include Isaiah 53, then Isaiah 53 becomes a prophecy about a future martyr and not a depiction of a social experience of disability. In this prophecy, the suffering involves fatal wounds through crucifixion rather than a social byproduct of living with disabilities. This use of Isaiah 53 should not surprise us since 1 Peter largely focuses on persecution and suffering.

The experience of disability becomes experiences of enslavement or martyrdom. 1 Peter also uses references to the servant's suffering as an example for how others should handle hardships. As we found in 1QH[a], however, these hardships are the generalized suffering of presumably able-bodied persons rather than persons with disabilities. For example, 1 Pet 2:20 connects the servant's suffering with the beatings endured by slaves rather than anything to do with disability. Both in terms of the suffering of Jesus and the slaves whom 1 Peter 2 addresses, the servant's experience in Isaiah 53 describes the suffering and social oppression of the presumably able-bodied. The servant's disability is lost in this appropriation of his experience.

Outside of the New Testament, we also find the use of the servant's suffering to encourage others to imitate Jesus in 1 Clement. Like 1 Peter, 1 Clement comes from the late first century CE and shows awareness of the larger context of Isaiah 53. In fact, it cites all of Isa 53:1–12, mainly from the LXX.[38] First Clement calls the Corinthian church to keep the peace by living in humility.[39] Nevertheless, although 1 Clem 16:3–14 cites a large portion of our passage, the focus shifts from an experience of disability to an experience of humility. 1 Clement connects the servant with a presumably able-bodied Jesus as humble figures who should be imitated by the members of the Corinthian church.

Reactions to the servant (Rom 10:16 and 15:21). Paul quotes Isaiah 53 twice in Romans. As Richard Hays observes in the epigram for this chapter, he does not invoke the servant directly in either case. Instead, Paul quotes the verses that focus on reactions to the servant's experience or mission. In Rom 10:16, Paul explains the widespread rejection of the gospel message (or 'good news') as the fulfilment of prophecy. Like John 12:38, Paul quotes the LXX's translation of Isa 53:1. Paul writes, 'But not all have obeyed the good news [or "gospel"]'; for Isaiah says, 'Lord, who has believed our message?' (Rom 10:16). In the verses that immediately precede Isa 53:1, the disbelief over the servant comes from the fact that God exalts him (52:13) despite his marred appearance (52:14). In fact, the LXX emphasizes this point when it translates the first line in 52:15 as 'he shall startle many nations' instead of 'he shall sprinkle many nations' as some Hebrew versions do. In this context, 53:1 helps to depict the servant's disability as not just a physical description but a social experience. By contrast, the context in which Paul quotes Isa 53:1 has nothing to do with a report involving an experience of disability. Rather, Paul uses Isa 53:1 as a prophetic explanation for a very different experience, namely, the rejection of his gospel message. This social experience differs considerably from the one described in Isaiah 53.

Paul quotes the LXX's translation of Isaiah 53 again in Rom 15:21. He uses 52:15 to explain why he is spreading the gospel among the Gentiles (cf. Rom 15:16). Paul writes, 'Thus I make it my ambition to proclaim the good news [or "gospel"], not where Christ has already been named, so that I do not build on someone else's foundation, but as it is written, "Those who have never been told of him shall see, and those who have never heard of him shall understand"' (Rom 15:20–1). Paul does not quote the first half of Isa 52:15, which reads, 'so he shall startle many nations'. Yet this unquoted phrase may explain why he associates the last half of Isa 52:15 with his mission to the Gentiles. The LXX uses the same Greek word for 'nations' in Isa 52:15 as the NRSV translates as 'Gentiles' throughout Rom 15:15–21.[40] While this connection may show some awareness of the larger context for the quotation, it does not include the disability imagery in the surrounding verses. The nations (or 'Gentiles') are startled by the servant's marred appearance in Isaiah 53. Yet, for Paul, what the nations will learn has nothing to do with the nuanced portrayal of living with a disability that Isaiah 53 commemorates.

Conclusion: the invention of the able-bodied suffering servant

The servant in Isaiah 53 has a number of traits and experiences other than disability. Thus, while disability imagery saturates this passage, later biblical texts tend to draw on these other traits. Other Hebrew Bible texts may connect the servant to the experience of righteous martyrs (Isa 57:1; Dan 12:1–3). Likewise, some recent scholarship also interprets Isaiah 53 in relation to violence experienced by contemporary oppressed communities. Jorge Pixley interprets the servant's suffering as violence inflicted upon exiles that resist the Babylonian empire. He connects the political violence in Isaiah 53 to the political violence in Nicaragua.[41] Similarly, François Kabasele Lumbala and Cyris Heesuk Moon connect the servant's suffering to violence experienced by communities in Africa and Asia respectively.[42] Nevertheless, the specific examples of violence focus on violence inflicted on the able-bodied in these comparisons of Isaiah 53 to contemporary communities.

In fact, only one reference to people with disabilities appears in these essays. Lumbala recounts the story of a mother who goes to prison to serve her oldest daughter's sentence. During her incarceration, she worries that she cannot care for two of her other children described as 'epileptic' and 'mentally retarded' respectively.[43] Lumbala does not compare the servant to the children with disabilities, but rather their elderly, but otherwise able-bodied, mother. As with their ancient typological counterparts, the servant's disability disappears in these contemporary comparisons.

Yet, within ancient typological interpretations, the servant was not only positioned as an example of an able-bodied sufferer. Certain New Testament texts quote isolated verses from Isaiah 53 as examples of various other typological figures such as a healer, an innocent one, or a martyr. Along with early translations of Isaiah 53, these typologies show how quickly interpretations can move away from our passage's focus on the servant's experience of disability. At the same time, the ancient translations and quotations of our passage do not suggest that there was a unified interpretation of the servant as an able-bodied sufferer that began with Isaiah 53 itself. Instead, Isaiah 53 describes the servant as a figure with disabilities while other biblical texts incorporate the servant into a variety of typologies that have little to do with disability.

Nor does this mean that interpretations involving the servant began with a unified understanding of the servant as the typical able-bodied sufferer. That would not account for the diversity among early typological uses of the servant. In other words, the idea of the able-bodied suffering servant does not naturally arise from Isaiah 53's depiction of the servant. Rather, this idea emerges slowly from a long process of interpretation in which the servant becomes increasingly used as an example in typologies of able-bodied suffering.

Eventually, the servant becomes more than an example of a suffering type. Instead, he becomes identified as a suffering *character* independent of not only his disability but also his typological framework. Once the servant is not understood as representing a typological figure nor as having a disability, interpreters are free to identify him as biblical characters traditionally understood as suffering but able-bodied. In short, this interpretative process invented the suffering servant of Isaiah 53 as we will discover in our next chapter.

Several of the biblical texts that we discussed in this chapter quote verses from Isaiah 53 but never address the passage as a whole (Isa 52:13–53:12). This practice changed by the end of the first century CE when 1 Clem 16:3–14 quotes all Isa 53:1–12. As interpreters focused more on Isaiah 53 as a whole, the servant became more worthy of study in his own right. Over time, the primary focus for interpretation of the servant began to shift from the type of figure that he represents to the historical person or community that he represents. In our next chapter, we find that scholars identified the servant with individuals or communities rarely associated with disability. Nevertheless, translations and typological interpretations from antiquity had already begun to sever the link between the servant and disability long before historical identification of the servant became the dominant scholarly approach to Isaiah 53.

The Servant as Historical or Collective Sufferer

[W]e have to contend with an entire catalogue of historical individuals who have figured in the discussions of the Servant.... Undeniably the list resembles the contents of a successful big-game hunt on the exegetical savannah.... Duhm's theory about the 'Servant Songs' has crippled the study of Isaiah 40–55.

Tryggve N. D. Mettinger, *A Farewell to the Servant Songs: A Critical Examination of an Exegetical Axiom*

[T]he expressions used [to describe the servant] go far beyond biography, indeed they go far beyond the description of anyone who might have existed in the past or the present.

Gerhard von Rad, *Old Testament Theology*, vol. 2: *The Theology of Israel's Prophetic Traditions*

Over the last few centuries, biblical scholarship has focused on the origins of the Bible. Often, modern scholars examine to whom or what a particular biblical passage referred before it became part of the Bible as we know it. When studying Isaiah 53, they have become increasingly interested in discovering the original identity of the servant in contrast to the typological reading strategies discussed in the previous chapter. Attempts to discover the servant's historical identity have blunted our ability to recognize Isaiah 53's association of disability imagery with the servant. Scholars have made numerous attempts to identify the servant with either an individual or a community. Traditionally, they have debated whether to identify the servant as an individual person or collective Israel. We will not attempt to settle this debate in this chapter. Instead, this chapter will examine why a serious debate has not developed around the question of whether to identify the servant as a figure with disabilities or as an able-bodied figure. We will explore the process through which 'servant as able-bodied sufferer' became the largely uncontested default interpretation during the search for the servant's identity.

We begin this chapter by showing that, like Duhm, a minority of interpreters throughout history have focused on the disability imagery in order to identify the servant with a person with disabilities. Second, we discover that more recent scholars have downplayed disability as a prominent clue to the servant's historical identity. Instead, they locate his identity among characters traditionally understood as able-bodied or as healed by God. Third, we turn to scholars who identify the servant with the personification of a collective group rather than one particular individual. For such scholars, the servant's experience becomes Israel's collective experience of exile. Often, the collective identification of the servant results in an interpretation of the servant's disability as describing the experience of exile rather than disability.

Identifying the servant through disability

In the middle of the twentieth century Christopher R. North surveyed the various proposals for the servant's identity. North found that scholars had identified the servant with no less than fifteen individuals.[1] In 2007, Kristin Joachimsen's list of scholarly identifications included over twenty individuals. Joachimsen writes,

> In Duhmian exegesis, no-one has adopted Duhm's identification, that is, an unknown contemporary of the prophet Second Isaiah suffering leprosy.... Among the identifications of the servant as an individual, are: the prophet Isaiah, 'Second Isaiah', an anonymous contemporary of the prophet 'Second Isaiah', King David, King Uzziah, King Hezekiah, King Josiah, King Jehoiachin, the Persian kings Cyrus or Darius, Zerubbabel or his son Meshullam, Shesbazzar, the prophets Ezekiel, Jeremiah, or Moses, Job, an unknown teacher of the Law, Eleazar (a martyr in the time of the Maccabees), the high-priest Onias, a eunuch, a vaguely defined mythical figure, Christ or a forerunner of Christ, and an eschatological or Messianic figure.[2]

While we do not have enough space to review all these identifications in detail, we should note that very few of the individuals from this list are traditionally interpreted or remembered as having disabilities. Instead, interpreters typically search for the servant's identity among the able-bodied.

As Joachimsen's list indicates, historical analysis of the servant's identity has largely abandoned Duhm's identification of the servant as an individual with disabilities. Yet Duhm was certainly not the only scholar or the first scholar to suggest that the servant had a disability of some sort. Long before Duhm, early Jewish and Christian interpretations identified the servant as having a skin anomaly or some other disability.[3]

While some seem more convincing than others, the examples that we will review in this section show an ongoing recognition of disability as a viable identification marker of the servant throughout the history of biblical interpretation. Since this option has never disappeared completely, scholars could choose to identify the servant as a figure with disabilities at any point in the history of interpretation. This choice, however, represents a minority position among interpreters.

In his translation of Isa 53:4 in the early fifth century CE, Jerome uses the Latin word *leprosum* in reference to the servant's condition. John F. A. Sawyer suggests that this translation influenced Matthais Grünewald's famous sixteenth century CE painting of Jesus' crucifixion on the Isenheim Altar at St Anthony's monastery. In the painting, lesions cover Jesus' body. As part of their treatment, patients at the monastery with blood and skin diseases were brought before the altar.[4]

In the Talmud, the rabbis refer to the messiah's name as 'the leprous one' based on Isa 53:10 (*Sanhedrin* 98b).[5] Regardless of whether the rabbis thought the messiah would actually have a skin anomaly, at minimum, they imply that Isaiah 53 describes the servant as having one (cf. *Sanhedrin* 98a). Drawing on this tradition, the medieval Jewish apocalypse, *Sefer Zerubbabel* uses language found in Isa 53:3–5 to describe a heavenly being as 'a man, despised and wounded, lowly and in pain'.[6] Although they identify the servant with Israel collectively, both Rashi and Ibn Ezra (twelfth century CE) acknowledge that 53:3–4 compares the servant to a person with a skin anomaly. Ibn Ezra observes similar vocabulary in Isa 53:4 and the discussion of skin anomalies in Lev 13:5. The sixteenth-century CE rabbinic scholar Maharal (Judah Loew ben Bezalel), however, argues that *Sanhedrin* 98b does not mean that the messiah will have a skin anomaly. Rather, his decaying body provides a fitting metaphor for someone so spiritual that this person is the antithesis of the physical. Maharal's position provides an early example of how disability imagery becomes a literary trope that describes an able-bodied figure rather than a figure with a disability.

Eliezer ben Elijah Ashkenazi, also a sixteenth-century rabbi, identified the servant with Job, whom the satan struck with a skin anomaly (Job 2:7). Building on a Talmudic tradition that Job was a symbolic figure (*Bava Batra* 15a), Ashkenazi argues that both Job and the servant in Isaiah 53 serve as parables for the experience of Israel collectively. While Ashkenazi does not make this identification based solely on disability imagery, this imagery plays a role. He includes several parallels between Isaiah 53 and Job that describe the respective subjects' physical condition and the reaction to it by others (e.g. Isa 52:14/Job 2:12; 21:5; Isa 53:3/Job 2:13; 31:34; Isa 53:5/Job 6:9; Isa 53:6/Job 7:20).[7]

Like Duhm, some of his predecessors in the eighteenth century also focused on the disability imagery in order to identify the servant with a person with disabilities. In 1795, Johann Christian Wilhelm Augusti proposed that King Uzziah was the servant because 2 Chr 26:22 states that 'the rest of the acts of Uzziah, from first to last, the prophet Isaiah son of Amoz wrote'. In 2 Chr 26:19–21, Uzziah acquires a skin anomaly as a punishment for a religious infraction. Augusti reasoned that Isaiah 53 provides a more positive explanation for his skin anomaly as an alternative to the one given in Chronicles. In 1783, Karl Friedrich Bahrdt identified the servant as Hezekiah because of the king's illness (Isaiah 38; 2 Kgs 20:1–11), which he diagnosed as cancer. In 1795, J. Konynenburg interpreted Isaiah 53 as referring to Hezekiah because of repeated vocabulary involving illness and recovery.[8]

The nineteenth-century CE rabbinic scholar Ya'qob Yoseph Mord'-khai Hayyim Passani also interpreted the disability imagery in relation to Hezekiah. In fact, he connected the servant's suffering to a social experience. He writes, 'when [the Judeans] saw [Hezekiah]

afflicted with severe illness, their hatred carried itself still further...
judging maliciously that his sufferings were because he had despised
their own wicked faith'.[9] Nevertheless, as with Ashkenazi's interpretation of the servant as Job, the disability imagery occurs more as one
incidental parallel among many other parallels than a central character trait for Ya'qob Yoseph Mord'khai Hayyim Passani and other
scholars who connect the servant with Hezekiah.[10] As we will discover later in this chapter, scholars have connected individuals who
have a recorded disease, such as Hezekiah, to the servant because of
some trait other than just a disease.

Following Duhm's proposal in 1892, a number of scholars continued
to use disability imagery to help them identify the servant, although
they did not always diagnose the disability as a skin anomaly. While
Karl Budde strongly opposed Duhm's theory of the 'servant songs', he
does state that in Isa 53:3–4, the servant 'is afflicted with a loathsome
disease, which is beyond all doubt leprosy'.[11] Nevertheless, he interprets this condition as only one of many types of suffering used to
describe the servant. In 1900, Richard Kraetzschmar found similarities between the servant and Ezekiel based on Ezek 4:4–8, in which
Ezekiel experiences a divinely caused temporary paralysis.[12] Both the
servant in Isa 53:12 and Ezekiel in Ezek 4:5 must 'bear' (*ns'*) the sin or
iniquity of others. While Walther Zimmerli does not identify the
servant as Ezekiel, he argues that both Ezek 4:4–8 and Isaiah 53 serve
as examples of a tradition about a suffering messenger.[13] In 1916,
Lauri Itkonen identified the servant in Isaiah 53 as Uzziah because of
the king's skin anomaly.[14] In 1954, John Skinner followed Duhm in
identifying the servant as an anonymous individual with a skin
anomaly.[15] Likewise, in 1993, John F. A. Sawyer interpreted the
servant as having a skin anomaly.[16] As the epigraph for Chapter
2 indicates, in Michael L. Barré's 1999 presidential address to the
Catholic Biblical Association of America, he argues that Isaiah 53
uses language for skin anomalies in the servant's description.[17]

In 1922, Ernst Sellin drew several parallels between the servant and
Moses. Relying on a vague reference in Exod 15:26 (cf. Deut 7:15;
28:60), Sellin claimed that Moses experienced Egyptian diseases. For
Sellin, the disability imagery in Isa 53:2–5 reflects this tradition about
Moses.[18] More recently, Klaus Baltzer identified the servant as
Moses. He cites numerous parallels between the servant and Moses,

including the following: 'The Servant is familiar with sickness.... According to Exod 4:6–8, Moses' hand becomes leprous and is healed.'[19] There are traditions that identify Moses with an Egyptian priest who has a chronic skin anomaly (cf. the third-century BCE Egyptian historian Manetho cited in Josephus, *Against Apion*, 1.250) and a number of Egyptian works that associate Moses and the Jews with the purging of 'lepers' from Egypt (e.g. Lysimachos, Chaeremon, Pompeius Trogus, Tacitus).[20] Yet, in Exod 4:6–8, God heals Moses' skin anomaly immediately. Thus, if we compare the servant's disability to Moses' skin anomaly, we imply that the servant recovered quickly from a temporary impairment.

By contrast, Beverly J. Stratton identifies the servant as an exiled Israelite eunuch, which qualifies as a chronic disability, in the Babylonian court. She observes that the servant is 'marred' (Isa 52:14) and 'crushed' (Isa 53:5, 10) and that these Hebrew words describe genital damage in Lev 22:24–5: 'Any animal that has its testicles bruised or crushed or torn or cut, you shall not offer to the LORD; such you shall not do within your land, nor shall you accept any such animals from a foreigner to offer as food to your God; since they are marred, with a blemish in them, they shall not be accepted in your behalf.'[21] Additionally, Stratton noted that in Isa 56:3, a eunuch describes himself as a 'withered tree'. While the vocabulary is different from 53:2, she sees a similarity in imagery when the servant is compared to 'a root out of dry ground'.[22] Moreover, the isolation of the servant in Isaiah 53 would appear consistent with the ostensible experience of eunuchs in ancient Israel (cf. Deut 23:1 and our discussion in Chapter 2). Although possibly written by a different author, Stratton observes that Isa 39:7 portrays the Judean exiles as 'eunuchs' when the prophet says to Hezekiah that 'Some of your own sons who are born to you shall be taken away; they shall be eunuchs in the palace of the king of Babylon.'[23]

The various scholars discussed in this section, however, provide an exception which proves the rule that interpreters prefer to identify the servant with individuals traditionally understood as able-bodied. Able-bodied identifications of the servant represent an interpretative choice so overwhelmingly popular and strongly reinforced over time that it seems like an obvious or natural starting point by default rather than a choice made by many contemporary scholars. Nevertheless, such identifications are a historical development that we may trace to at least the Jewish–Christian dialogues beginning in the second century CE.

The servant as messiah

As we discovered in the previous section, attempts to identify the servant with a historical figure or circumstance predate modern historical analysis of the Bible. Early Christians did not connect the servant to Jesus only because both were examples of a particular typology. Instead, in early dialogues with (sometimes fictitious) Jews, they argued that the servant in Isaiah 53 was a prophecy about Jesus as an individual. Read as prophecy, the servant became identified with Jesus.

In the second century CE, Justin Martyr interprets Isaiah 53 as a prophecy about Jesus (*1 Apology* 50–1).[24] In his *Dialogue with Trypho*, Justin quotes Isa 52:10–54:6 (*Dialogue* 13:2–9) and applies this passage to Jesus' suffering during his passion. His Jewish interlocutor Trypho contends that the messiah would appear in glory unlike Jesus who suffered crucifixion. Even if one grants that the messiah must suffer, Trypho reasons, this does not prove that the messiah must die by crucifixion, since this form of death indicates a divine curse according to Deut 21:23 (*Dialogue* 32:1; 89:1). He objects to Justin's claim that Isa 53:3–4, 7–8, 12 prove that the prophecy refers to Jesus and no one else (*Dialogue* 89:3). For Trypho, the comparison of the messiah to 'a lamb that is led to the slaughter' (Isa 53:7) does not mean that the messiah must be crucified (*Dialogue* 90:1).

Justin responds to Trypho with a number of typological connections between Hebrew Bible passages and the cross. These typologies culminate with a claim that Jesus was the Passover lamb based on a comparison between the lamb in Isa 53:7, understood by Justin as a prophecy of Jesus, and the lamb in Exodus 12 (cf. John 1:29).[25] Yet, according to Exod 12:5, the Passover lamb must 'be without blemish'. This implies that Justin interprets Isa 53:7 as a reference to Jesus as an unblemished lamb rather than a servant with a disability of any sort.

In the third century CE, Origen objects to his Jewish interlocutor Celsus' claim that the servant's suffering refers to the Jews' collective experience of exile. Following the Septuagint (LXX), Origen notes that 53:8 differentiates between the servant and the people when it states, 'Due to the transgressions of my people, he was led to death' (*Contra Celsum* 1:55).[26] Celsus also claims that if Jesus was divine, his body would have differed from other human bodies. Yet, according to Isa 53:2, Jesus, 'had no form or majesty'. Origin responds with an allegory to show that those who do not see Jesus in a more divine form but only with 'no form or majesty' have not advanced beyond what Paul refers to as 'the foolishness of our proclamation' (1 Cor 1:21).[27] In this sense, the disability imagery in Isaiah 53 does not actually describe Jesus as having disabilities. Instead, the imagery is merely an allegory for those who do not have the ability to see that Jesus had a more divine form.

We also find a response to potential Jewish objections to a crucified messiah in the Syriac *Demonstrations of Aphrahat* (fourth century CE). Citing Dan 9:26–7, Aphrahat argues that the messiah will be killed. He supports this argument by claiming that Isaiah referred to the messiah's suffering in Isa 52:13–15; 53:2, 5.[28] Aphrahat connects this suffering to Jesus' death by crucifixion. He does not consider the possibility that these verses describe a chronic condition instead of the death of a presumably able-bodied Jesus. In fact, he rejects the idea that the servant could refer to David, whom God calls 'my servant' in Isa 37:35, because David was not killed but died at an old age (*Demonstrations* 17:10).

In the centuries following these so-called dialogues with Jews, the overwhelming consensus within Christian interpretation understood Isaiah 53 as a prophecy about Jesus. The consensus held through at least the Reformation.[29] In fact, Sawyer observes that by the twelfth century CE, Christian interpreters understood Isaiah as more of a 'Prophet of the Passion' than a 'Prophet of the Annunciation' (cf. Isa 7:14; 11:1–2).[30] Indeed, connections between Isaiah 53 and Jesus' passion appear in the writings of Theodoret of Cyrus (fifth century CE), Thomas Aquinas (thirteenth century CE), Martin Luther (sixteenth century CE) and John Calvin (sixteenth century CE), among others.[31] Artwork and literature of this period emphasized Jesus' agony with frequent references to Isaiah 53.[32] For example, Chaucer quotes Isa 53:5 in the *Parson's Tale* as a reminder of human responsibility for Jesus' pain.[33] Nevertheless, with few exceptions such as the aforementioned

Isenheim Altar, identifications of Jesus with the servant depicted an otherwise able-bodied person who suffers and dies.

Certainly, the identification of the servant with Jesus encountered strong objection. When Ashkenazi identified the servant with Job, he wrote, 'Now it should be clear to you that Isaiah uttered this whole passage in relation to Job.... And I have explained it at such length "because I was vexed by the wantonness" [Ps 73:3] with which [the Christians] have sought to interpret it in accordance with their faith.'[34] Moreover, Jesus is not the only messianic figure with which the servant was identified. As we found in Chapter 3, the Targum of Isaiah 53 portrays the servant as a messiah with no indications of either suffering or disability. Over against Christian interpretations, later rabbinic scholars such as Isaac Abarbanel (fifteenth century CE) or Moshe Alshech (sixteenth century CE) affirmed the Targumic identification of the servant with the messiah. Yet, while a few possible references to a messiah with disabilities exist (*Sanhedrin* 98b; *Sefer Zerubbabel*), most identifications of the servant as a messiah figure other than Jesus depict a presumably able-bodied messiah who may or may not suffer.[35]

Interest in the servant's historical identity predates modern attempts at historical analysis of the Bible. While we cannot account for this interest solely as a result of early Jewish–Christian dialogues, these dialogues helped to shift the focus of the servant's interpretation away from typological approaches and towards historical identification. Although identification with a historical person may help bring the servant to life, this shift only further distances the servant from his disability.

The servant as king

Isaiah 53 not only describes the servant with disability imagery. It also uses imagery associated with royalty elsewhere in the Hebrew Bible. This does not mean that disability and kingship are mutually exclusive identities. Kings with disabilities exist within the Hebrew Bible and other ancient Near Eastern literature.[36] Yet, although royal imagery may not appear as prominently as disability imagery in Isaiah 53, scholars have nevertheless searched for the servant's identity among able-bodied kings more often than kings with disabilities.

As we noted earlier, scholarly associations between the servant and Uzziah or Hezekiah based on disability imagery provide exceptions that prove the rule. Moreover, Hezekiah has a temporary condition which God heals. By contrast, we discovered in Chapter 2 that Isa 53:10–12 indicates that the servant experiences divine exaltation, but not a change in his physical condition. Thus, although a healing of the servant does not appear anywhere in Isaiah 53, we may create the impression that God heals him if we identify the servant as Hezekiah, who was diseased (*ḥlh*) but ultimately recovered (Isa 39:1).

More often, disability imagery in Isaiah 53 provides an incidental parallel for scholars who connect the servant with biblical kings. For example, prior to identifying the servant as Moses, Sellin identified the servant as Jehoiachin, the last Judean monarch whom the Babylonians imprisoned for thirty-seven years (2 Kgs 24:10–16; 25:27–30).[37] Almost a century later, Michael D. Goulder returned to Sellin's hypothesis by finding several points of contact between the servant and Jehoiachin. The disability imagery refers to Jehoiachin because, according to Goulder, thirty-seven years in a damp, dark, Babylonian prison would disfigure the king and cause severe health problems.[38] Yet Jehoiachin's disability is entirely the creation of scholars who supply a back story for his experience in prison. The Bible never suggests that Jehoiachin has a disability nor gives any details about his time in prison that would suggest an acquired disability. In other words, we probably understand the servant as able-bodied if we identify him as Jehoiachin.

Other royal candidates for the servant's identity are also traditionally remembered as able-bodied (e.g. Cyrus).[39] Scholars identify some kings or political leaders as the servant largely because of traditions about their murders or deaths (e.g. Zerubbabel or Meshulam).[40] Abarbanel provides a detailed interpretation of Isaiah 53 in connection with Josiah's death in a battle with Pharaoh Neco of Egypt (2 Kgs 23:29–30; 2 Chr 35:20–5). He attributes the servant's marred and stricken appearance to Josiah's fatal battle wounds. For Abarbanel, Isaiah 53 depicts Josiah as a valiant warrior who dies a tragic death. He recognizes the phrase 'a man of suffering' in 53:4 as indicating a chronic disability, but interprets it as a description of Neco's mobility impairment rather than Josiah's condition.

Since the Hebrew spelling of the name 'Neco' is similar to a Hebrew word meaning 'lame', various traditions held that the Pharaoh acquired a mobility impairment. According to these traditions, one of the lions on Solomon's throne injured Neco when he tried to sit on the throne (cf. *Qohelet Rabbah* 9:2; *Leviticus Rabbah* 20:1; the Targum's translation of 'Neco' as 'lame' in 2 Kgs 23:29).[41] Abrabanel seems to invoke these traditions when he explains that 'After describing the perfections of Josiah, the prophet then depicts the insignificance of the man who caused his ruin, Phar'oh Necho. In view of his bodily defects he says, He was despised and forlorn of men: for Necho was not a valiant man . . . but lame in his feet from gout . . . so here he terms him "a man of pains".'[42] For Abrabanel, the disability imagery describes Neco rather than the servant in Isaiah 53. The servant is Josiah, a valiant and presumably able-bodied warrior who suffers fatal injuries.

The servant as prophet

As with the royal imagery, scholars frequently rely on the prophetic imagery to identify the servant. Wolfgang M. W. Roth argues that the anonymous servant presents the prophetic office in its ideal form. Noting that the title 'servant' often designates a prophet in the Hebrew Bible, Roth concludes that the servant represents '*the* prophet of Yahweh . . . known by his function: to stand between man and God in service and in suffering'.[43] Unlike Duhm, however, scholars rarely interpret the servant as a prophet with disabilities. As we observed earlier, disability represents only one of many parallels that some scholars use to identify Moses as the servant. Thus, they do not interpret Moses as primarily a prophet with disabilities.

In this section, we do not mean to suggest that Isaiah 53 does not portray the servant in a prophetic role. We do not have to choose between identifying the servant as a prophet or a figure with disabilities. These identities are not mutually exclusive. The comparisons of the servant with Moses and Ezekiel mentioned earlier suggest that we could describe the servant as a prophet with disabilities. Instead, our point is that we should not turn the disability imagery into prophetic imagery.

Moses. Since at least the time of the Talmud, scholars have associated the servant with Moses without focusing on disability. In *Sotah* 14a, the rabbis quote Isa 53:12 as a reference to Moses' role as an intercessory prophet who offered his life on behalf of the people during the Golden Calf incident (Exod 32:32). Later rabbinic interpreters such as Abarbanel and Solomon b. Moses ha-Levi (sixteenth century CE) affirm this connection between Isa 53:12 and Moses.[44] Yet Isa 53:12 contains none of the disability imagery present elsewhere in our passage. Despite Moses' disability in Exod 4:6–12 and 6:12, 30, the use of Isa 53:12 to connect Moses with the servant focuses on his intercessory role rather than his disability.[45]

Among modern scholars, Sellin, Baltzer, and Chavasse champion the identification of the servant as Moses. Yet, as we discussed earlier, Moses' disability serves as one incidental parallel among many for Sellin and Baltzer. Their primary point of comparison is the deaths of Moses and the servant. Sellin argues that passages such as Isaiah 53 and other biblical passages (Hos 5:1; 9:7–14; 12:14; 13:1; Zech 11:4–17) reflect a tradition that the people murdered Moses, rather than Zimri, during the Baal Poer incident at Shittim (Numbers 25).[46] For Baltzer, Isaiah 53 is 'an interpretation of Deuteronomy 34, with Moses' rise, death and burial. The Servant's grave "among criminals and beside a rich man" can be understood as a contemporary interpretation, referring to the death of Moses in Moab, on Mount Nebo, opposite Baal-poer, before the entry into the promised land'.[47] Chavasse connects the reference to the servant's grave being with the wicked in Isa 53:9 to repeated references to Moses' death outside of Israel and on behalf of others (Deut 1:37; 3:23–6; 4:21–2). He also connects Moses' unparalleled humility (Num 12:3) with the servant's meekness (Isa 53:7).[48]

Other scholars prefer to identify the servant as an unnamed prophet in the tradition of Moses (cf. Deut 18:15–19). While Gerhard von Rad acknowledges in passing that 'the idea that [the servant] was a leper is old',[49] he argues that the hyperbolic language could not describe an actual individual because of its 'flowery' and 'extreme' style.[50] This leads him to the conclusion that the servant represents a future prophet in the tradition of Moses. He writes, 'The songs have as their theme proclamation and suffering—the basic prophetic functions at the time ... by the seventh century [BCE] the idea of the prophetic role had changed, and the prophet was portrayed as a suffering mediator.'[51] More recently, both Gordon P. Hugenberger and Christopher R. Seitz refer to the servant as a 'second Moses' figure. Yet Seitz interprets the disability imagery in relation to the servant's Moses-like intercessory activity in 53:12 (cf. Deut 9:25–29).[52] Hugenberger connects Isa 53:3–8 to the repeated rejections of Moses by the people in Exodus and Numbers.[53]

Jeremiah. For some scholars, Jeremiah has a great deal in common with the servant.[54] In fact, Duhm originally thought the four 'servant songs' described Jeremiah before he decided that the servant was an unnamed teacher of the law who had a skin anomaly.[55] While the Bible never indicates that Jeremiah has a disability, it does record a great deal of his suffering. Jeremiah uses very similar imagery to what we find in Isa 53:7–8 when he complains, 'But I was like a gentle lamb led to the slaughter. And I did not know it was against me that they devised schemes, saying, "Let us destroy the tree with its fruit, let us cut him off from the land of the living, so that his name will no longer be remembered!"'(Jer 11:9).

Scholars have compared the servant to Jeremiah since at least Saadia Gaon in the tenth century CE.[56] In addition to the similar imagery in Jer 11:9 and Isa 53:7–8, Saadia Gaon also understands the description of the servant as a 'young plant' (53:2) as a reference to Jeremiah's youth (Jer 1:6). He takes the phrase 'he bore the sin of many' in 53:12 as a reference to Jeremiah's intercession before God on behalf of the people (Jer 18:20). The servant's 'portion' in 53:12 refers to the provisions with which the captain of the guard provides Jeremiah (Jer 40:5). Although Abarbanel criticized Saadia Gaon's identification, other early rabbinic scholars, such as Ibn Ezra, affirmed it.[57] Saadia Gaon's references to Jeremiah, however, come from the parts of Isaiah 53 that do not include disability imagery. Thus, our focus may shift towards an able-bodied sufferer like Jeremiah if we follow Saadia Gaon.

By at least the time of the Reformation, some Christian interpretations begin to identify the servant with persons other than Jesus. Jeremiah provided an attractive alternative. In 1644, Hugo Grotius proposed that, although several references to a servant in the preceding chapters referred to Isaiah, the servant in Isaiah 53 referred to

Jeremiah as a prefiguring of Jesus. As modern biblical scholarship began to emerge over the next few centuries, Anthony Collins (1727) and Christian Karl Josais Freiherr von Bunsen (1857) followed Grotius' proposal.[58]

More recently, Brevard Childs acknowledges that, 'Verse 3b speaks even of [the servant] being afflicted with sickness or disease. However, almost immediately one senses that the chief interest of the narrative is not biographical; rather, the concrete features that encompass the ensuing description focus largely on the response of others to him.'[59] Correctly, Childs observes that Isaiah 53 focuses primarily on the servant's social experience. Nonetheless, he does not comment on the servant's social experience to further explore the servant's physical condition or disability. Rather, Childs criticizes Duhm's attempt to diagnose the servant's condition as a skin anomaly by stating that 'it is a mistake to specify the sickness too precisely'.[60] Yet Childs is not criticizing a medical model approach to Isaiah 53. Instead, this lack of precision allows him to apply this imagery to experiences other than sickness and disease, such as the difficulties faced by innocent sufferers or those holding the prophetic office. Although Childs acknowledges that the verbs in 53:10 mean 'to make sick', he understands this imagery as an idiom for innocent suffering (cf. Pss 22:6–7; 88:8) rather than a description of disability. He writes that Isaiah 53 'begins to resonate with the typical idiom of the innocent suffering one of the Psalter... [forming] a continuing lament of the suffering innocent of the Psalter (Pss. 35:13; 41:4; 77:16)... Much like the idiom of the Psalter, physical and spiritual suffering are combined without carefully defined boundaries and so probe its multifaceted aspects.'[61]

While he does not identify the servant as Jeremiah, Childs finds parallels to the servant's suffering in the book of Jeremiah (Jer 15:17; 20:7, 10). The texts from Jeremiah that Childs cites, however, do not contain any disability imagery. Instead, Jeremiah describes his social experience as a prophet rather than as a person with disabilities. For example, in 20:7, Jeremiah describes his social experience as follows: 'O LORD, you have enticed me, and I was enticed; you have overpowered me, and you have prevailed. I have become a laughingstock all day long; everyone mocks me.'[62] Using such comparisons, Childs concludes, 'Much like Jeremiah, the description of prophetic suffering depicts a calling, even an office, into which the servant of God has been summoned. However, the confession that then follows in chapter 53 begins to probe a new dimension of obedient suffering, unknown to Jeremiah or the other prophets.'[63] Yet Childs never implies that this 'new dimension' of suffering somehow relates to the servant's experience of disability, be it a skin anomaly or some other unspecified 'sickness or disease'. Intentionally or not, this could lead us to overlook a figure with disabilities as a subject of Isaiah 53. The experiences of such a figure may get lost in the shuffle.

Second Isaiah. As we discussed in the Introduction, most scholars maintain that Isaiah 40–55 comes from a period after the Babylonian destruction of Jerusalem in 587 BCE. While we can connect the content of these chapters to the historical circumstances of the Babylonian exile or its aftermath, we have no personal details or biographic information about whoever produced them. Scholars personify the source(s) of these chapters as an anonymous prophet that they call 'Second Isaiah' (although some argue that Isaiah 53 comes from 'Third Isaiah' or some other figure(s) within the Isaianic tradition). This process of personification involves speculation about the back story of Second Isaiah even though we have no specific information about his or her life.[64] Some scholars even use the conjectured personification of Second Isaiah to fill in the missing back story of the servant's experience. Identifying the servant with a personification allows scholars to propose that the details of Isaiah 53 refer to a range of imagined events within an unknown life. Yet, few, if any, scholars personify Second Isaiah as a person with disabilities.

In 1921, Sigmund Mowinckel popularized the identification of the servant as Second Isaiah. His proposal received immediate acclaim from other prominent biblical scholars such as Otto Eissfeldt, Hermann Gunkel, and Hans Schmidt.[65] According to Mowinckel, the fact that we do not know anything about Second Isaiah is an exaggerated problem. He focused on a number of passages from Isaiah 40–55 to flesh out Second Isaiah's back story. Thus, for Mowinckel, the servant in our passage is an otherwise able-bodied prophet based mostly on passages outside of Isaiah 53.[66] Throughout the twentieth century, Second Isaiah remained one of the most popular individual candidates for the servant's identification. As we discussed in Chapter 2, Begrich argues that Second Isaiah prophesies his or her own death in our passage and Roger N. Whybray and G. R. Driver suggest that the Babylonians imprisoned Second Isaiah based on the imagery in 53:8 (cf. Isa 42:9; 61:1). Yet the idea of the servant's imprisonment is a complete conjecture that goes far beyond what our passage says.

More recently, Joseph Blenkinsopp argues that Isaiah 53 is a eulogy for Second Isaiah that originated among Second Isaiah's disciples before the chapter was inserted into Isaiah 40–55. Blenkinsopp observes that, with the exception of 54:17, in Isaiah 49–55, the term 'servant' refers to an individual prophetic figure (Second Isaiah). According to Blenkinsopp, we encounter the activities of this prophet's disciples in the repeated references to a disenfranchised prophetic group called the 'servants' in Isaiah 56–66 (Isa 56:6; 63:17; 65:9, 13–15; 66:14).[67] While Blenkinsopp's theory seems slightly less speculative than Whybray or Driver's theory, none of these identifications of the servant as Second Isaiah include disability as part of the imaginative back stories for this hypothetical figure.

Often, interpreting Isaiah 53 as primarily describing the prophetic experience has reconfigured the servant as a presumably able-bodied prophetic sufferer. In such readings, parallels with other prophetic literature suggest that our passage uses disability imagery to communicate the difficulties of the prophetic experience rather than an experience of disability. This interpretative strategy risks the erasure of the servant's disability from the passage.

The search for the servant's identity has produced more individual candidates than we have room to discuss in this book. Yet scholars often overlook his status as a figure with disabilities even though they acknowledge that the imagery in Isaiah 53 depicts the servant as having an often unspecified disability. Certainly, some of the individuals identified as the servant have disabilities or diseases. For example, God causes Ezekiel's temporary paralysis and loss of speech (Ezek 3:22–27; 4:4–8), but heals him in Ezek 24:27. Likewise, Hezekiah recovers from his illness. Unlike the servant, these individuals have temporary disabilities. Such identifications allow us to imagine the servant without a disability in the end.

Furthermore, those candidates with temporary disabilities or diseases represent a minority of the individuals that scholars have identified as the servant. The majority of the candidates do not require any type of healing because they do not have a recorded disability. More often than not, scholars have identified the servant with a traditionally able-bodied individual. Disability does not factor heavily into these identifications. The servant needs no healing because the various proposals for the historical identity of the servant have removed the servant's disability altogether by associating him with various able-bodied individuals.

The servant as a collective reference

The search for the servant's identity among historical individuals reached its peak in the late nineteenth and early twentieth centuries. Nevertheless, even in this period, some scholars raised strong objections to this approach. In 1899, Budde wrote a lengthy article with detailed criticisms of Duhm and the various attempts to identify the servant with an individual.[68] He preferred to identify the servant with the personification of a collective group.[69]

Budde was not the first scholar to offer a collective identification. As we discussed above, as early as the third century CE, Origen mentioned the identification of the servant as a collective reference to Israel as the position of his Jewish interlocutor Celsus. By the twelfth century CE, this identification of the servant was commonplace among Jewish interpreters such as Rashi, Ibn Erza, David Kimhi (Radak), and others. For example, Radak wrote that Isaiah 53 'refers to the captivity of Israel, who are here called "my servant" as in xli 8'.[70] Radak identifies the servant as Israel based on Isa 41:8, which reads, 'But you, Israel, my servant, Jacob, whom I have chosen.' Likewise, several other passages in Second Isaiah refer to a singular servant as Israel /Jacob (cf. 43:10; 44:1–2, 21; 45:4; 49:3). Thus, there is precedent for identifying the servant in Isaiah 53 as Israel.

A number of medieval Jewish interpreters commend this collective interpretation to counter the Christian associations of the servant with Jesus. Yet we cannot attribute the collective interpretation of the servant to an anti-Christian polemic alone. As we discussed in the previous chapter, Dan 12:3 typologically connects a Jewish group referred to as the 'wise' (a plural form of *skl*) with the servant because Isa 52:13 describes the servant as 'prosperous' (a singular form of *skl*).

Thus, the collective interpretation of the servant may predate Christianity by well over a century.

Furthermore, some scholars have used *skl* to argue that Isaiah 53 itself identifies the servant as Israel long before later interpreters identified the servant with various individuals. Harry Orlinsky observes that the form of *skl* in 52:13 is *yaskil*. He argues that the phrase 'my servant shall prosper (*yaskil*)' sounds like 'my servant Israel (Hebrew: *yisrael*)'. For Orlinsky, 52:13 creates an intentional pun with the word 'Israel' as a clue to the audience that the servant in Isaiah 53 is a collective reference to Israel.[71] This suggestion attempts to address the problem that, unlike Isa 41:8 or 49:3, Isaiah 53 does not clearly identify the servant as Israel but repeatedly refers to him with singular rather than plural or collective words.

Disability imagery as exilic imagery. As Jill Middlemas emphasizes, the identification of the servant with Israel focuses on the suffering of Israel in exile.[72] This identification understands the disability imagery in our passage as describing the experience of siege or exile rather than the experience of disability. Fredrik Hägglund observes that various forms of Hebrew words in Isa 53:3–4 that we translated as 'suffering' and 'diseased' appear in other prophetic passages that describe Jerusalem or Judah in the context of exile. In Jer 10:19, the inhabitants of Judah collectively lament their exilic experience with vocabulary very similar to that used in our passage: 'Woe is me because of my hurt! My wound (*nkh*) has become diseased (*hlh*). But I said, "Truly this is my disease (*hlh*), and I must bear (*ns'*) it."' In Isa 53:4, we read, 'Surely he has borne (*ns'*) our diseases (*hlh*) and carried our suffering; yet we accounted him plagued, struck down (*nkh*) by God, and afflicted. But he was made profane for our transgressions, crushed for our iniquities; upon him was the punishment that made us whole, and by his bruises (*brh*) we are healed' (cf. Jer 51:8; Lam 1:12, 18). Like Jer 10:19, Isa 1:4–6 personifies the 'sinful nation' of Judah (v. 4) with imagery similar to Isa 53:4–5. It reads, 'Why should you be struck (*nkh*) anymore? Why do you persist in rebellion? The whole head is diseased (*hlh*), and the whole heart faint. From the sole of the foot even to the head, there is no soundness in it, but sores and bruises (*brh*) and fresh wounds (*nkh*); they have not been drained, or bound up, or softened with oil' (Isa 1:5–6).[73]

Furthermore, both Isa 53:4 and 8 use the Hebrew word 'plagued' (*ngʿ*) to describe the servant's condition. We observed in Chapter 2 that this word often describes skin anomalies in Leviticus 13–14. Yet, when depicting the destruction of Israel, Amos 9:5 uses the word 'plagued' in reference to the land of Israel rather than a figure with a skin anomaly: 'The Lord, GOD of hosts, the one who plagues (*ngʿ*) the earth and it melts.'[74] The use of disability imagery to identify the servant as exiled Israel, however, creates further distance between the disability imagery in Isaiah 53 and the social experience of disability. Few, if any, scholars claim that the servant's disability functions as a description of the exiles' actual physical condition.

Tryggve N. D. Mettinger explains the disability imagery in Isaiah 53 as a reference to Israel's reduced population during exile. He translates the second verb in Isa 53:3 (*ḥdl*) as 'lacking' as in 'he was despised and lacking humans'. Connecting this verse to Isa 41:14 and 54:1, Mettinger argues that Isaiah 53 'speaks of an Israel which has been reduced to a small and insignificant group'.[75] Mettinger also cites Gerleman's observation (which we discussed in Chapter 2) that the phrase 'land of the living' in 53:8 may refer to the land of Israel rather than a state of life as opposed to death. Thus, according to Mettinger, the phrase 'excluded from the land of the living' refers to the Judeans collective experience of exile from the land of Israel.[76]

Mettinger's interpretation does not adequately account for the repeated descriptions of the servant as 'diseased' (vv. 3, 4, 10) or 'plagued' (vv. 4, 8) throughout our passage. Instead of analysing these specific images, Mettinger compares our passage with Isa 50:4–11 and 51:4–8 in order to arrive at what he calls 'a meaningful interpretation of the expressions of [the servant's] suffering'.[77] Yet the comparison with these other passages allows Mettinger to generalize the nature of the servant's suffering in Isaiah 53 because these other passages from Isaiah do not contain disability imagery. As we discussed in Chapter 2, scholars have understood the servant as a (sometimes fatally) injured able-bodied figure by reading Isa 50:4–11 into Isaiah 53. Isaiah 51:4–8 addresses Israel collectively and shares specific imagery with 50:4–11 (compare the phrase 'wear out like a garment' in 50:9 and 51:6). Yet the imagery of suffering in 51:4–8 is too general to compare with the disability imagery of Isaiah 53.[78]

In contrast to Mettinger, we argued in Chapter 2 that both 53:3 and 8 use this imagery to describe disability as a social experience in the ancient Near East. We translated the verb *ḥdl* in 53:3 as 'withdrew' rather than 'lacking'. Thus, we prefer the translation 'he was despised and withdrew from humanity' to 'he was despised and lacking humans'. Correctly, Barré observes, 'the Servant is depicted as a person tending to withdraw from others, perhaps in a way similar to lepers who kept their distance from others in the community'.[79] As we discussed in Chapter 2, this phrase fits well with our passage's description of disability as a social experience. Earlier in this chapter, we observed that both Rashi and Ibn Ezra acknowledge that 53:3-4 compare the servant to a person with a skin anomaly even though both Rashi and Ibn Ezra identify the servant with Israel collectively. Regarding the servant's exclusion from 'the land of the living' in 53:8, we agree with Mettinger that the phrase can refer to the land of Israel or possibly human society more generally. Yet, as with 53:3, this phrase describes a figure with disabilities' social isolation from the larger population more clearly than a collective experience of exile from the land of Israel. The rest of 53:8 supports our interpretation when it describes the servant as 'plagued': 'he was excluded from the land of the living, plagued for the transgression of my people'. In the larger context of v.8, the phrase 'excluded from the land of the living' helps to describe the servant's social experience of disability.

Both Hägglund and Mettinger, among others, support their identification of the servant as exiled Israel by comparing Isaiah 53 with Ezekiel 37 because of similar vocabulary.[80] Ezekiel 37 includes a vision of a valley full of dry bones. After Ezekiel prophesies to the dry bones, they come to life (Ezek 37:4-10). Then, God tells Ezekiel, 'these bones are the whole house of Israel. They say, "Our bones are dried up, and our hope is lost; we are excluded." Therefore prophesy, and say to them [Israel], "Thus says the Lord GOD: I am going to open your graves, and bring you up from your graves, O my people; and I will bring you back to the land of Israel"' (Ezek 37:11-12). The bones (Israel) claim that they are 'excluded'. The same Hebrew term appears in Isaiah 53:8, which states that the servant 'was excluded from the land of the living'. Also, both passages refer to the 'grave' (Ezek 37:12; Isa 53:9). A key difference, however, is that Israel is already in its grave in Ezekiel 37, whereas Isa 53:9 only states that others prepared a grave for the servant, as we discussed in Chapter 2. Yet, more important for our purposes is the fact that Ezekiel 37 includes a physical restoration of the dry bones to an able-bodied state. Comparing this recovery of the dry bones to the servant's experience may allow us to assume that God also heals the servant and that the servant becomes able-bodied by the end of Isaiah 53.

Yet the comparison between Isaiah 53 and Ezekiel 37 obscures the typical way that most prophetic texts composed after the Babylonian destruction of Jerusalem use disability imagery in reference to Israel's experience of restoration from exile. Usually, they do not include a healing. Healing was not a standard element in the literary trope that uses disability imagery to depict the exilic experience. For example, Mic 4:6–7 states, 'In that day, says the LORD, I will assemble the lame and gather those who have been driven away, and those whom I have afflicted. I will make the lame a remnant, those driven away a strong nation. The LORD will rule over them in Mount Zion from that day and forever.' Jeremiah 31:8 declares, 'See, I am going to bring them from the land of the north, and gather them from the farthest parts of the earth, among them the blind and the lame, those with child and those in labour, together; a great company, they shall return here' (cf. Zeph 3:19).[81] This reinforces our claim in Chapter 2 that the servant does not recover from his disability in Isaiah 53.

Nevertheless, these passages use imagery of disability to describe the suffering and hardships of the presumably able-bodied in exile. Such passages provide precedent for interpreting the servant's disability in Isaiah 53 as describing the experience of exile rather than disability. As with Isaiah 53, most of the passages that use disability imagery to express the experience of exile do not focus on or even include a removal of the disability. Isaiah 35:5–6 provides an exception that proves the rule when it describes the return of the exiles to Zion in the following terms: 'Then the eyes of the blind shall be opened, and the ears of the deaf unstopped; then the lame shall leap like a deer, and the tongue of the speechless sing for joy.' More frequently, biblical passages that use disability to describe the exilic experience do not need to include healings because they divorce the disability imagery from the lived experience of persons with disabilities. Regarding such passages, Rebecca Raphael observes,

The key passages in Hebrew prophecy that are known for speaking of healing for disabled persons are not about disabled persons, and usually do not speak of healing. Indeed, a lack of reference to mended bodies indicates that the disability terms are doing something other than referring to actual disabled persons. The most obvious cases of non-healing are in Jeremiah, Micah and Zephaniah . . . Ingathering is not healing, nor is healing used as a metaphor for ingathering.[82]

This phenomenon may very well represent the highpoint of biblical literature's use of disability imagery as a literary trope that articulates the suffering of otherwise able-bodied people. Healing is unnecessary when the communities described in the passage are presumably able-bodied to begin with.

The servant and personified Zion.   Since at least the twelfth century CE, scholars favouring the collective interpretation have also appealed to the passages that immediately surround Isaiah 53 to resolve the problem that the servant is referred to in the singular throughout our passage. Ibn Erza observes that Isaiah 54 personifies the conquered city of Zion as an individual woman. Furthermore, immediately preceding our passage, Isa 52:1–12 personifies Zion as a captured woman to whom God promises liberation: 'Shake yourself from the dust, rise up, O captive Jerusalem; loose the bonds from your neck, O captive daughter Zion' (52:2). Both Isaiah 52 and 54 depict the personified city in a state of captivity or exile. Zion personifies the Judean people's experience of exile in the passages immediately surrounding Isaiah 53. Thus, even if Isaiah 53 depicts the servant as an individual, the context of the passage suggests that he represents a personification of Israel in exile just as 'Uncle Sam' personifies the United States government collectively.[83]

The changes in gender in Isaiah 52–4 from a female Zion to a male servant back to a female Zion do not present a problem for this interpretation. We find a similar gender switch in the book of Lamentations. Lamentations 3 personifies exiled Israel as a man in pain (Lam 3:1–4, 30; cf. Isa 50:6). Yet, Lamentations 1–2 and 4 surrounds this male personification with personifications of exiled Israel as 'daughter Zion' (Lam 1:6, 17; 2:1, 4, 6, 8, 10, 13, 18; 4:2, 22). Moreover, Leland Edward Wilshire observes that Isa 51:16 uses the Hebrew masculine singular pronoun for 'you' when God personifies Zion: 'I have put my words in your mouth . . . saying to Zion, "You [masculine singular pronoun] are my people."'[84] Seitz notes that Isa 49:14–15 compares God to a mother and Zion to a male child when it states, 'But Zion said, "The LORD has forsaken me, my Lord has forgotten me." Can a woman forget her nursing child, or show no compassion for the son of her womb? Even these may forget, yet I will not forget you.'[85]

Both Wilshire and Seitz develop the identification of the servant as the city of Zion. After citing the similarities between the personification of the servant and of Zion in Second Isaiah, Wilshire observes parallels between Isaiah 53 and other Mesopotamian poems that describe fallen cities. For example, Isa 53:7 compares the servant to 'a lamb that is led to the slaughter'. Regarding the fallen Sumerian city of Ur, the 'Lament over the Destruction of Ur' (second millennium BCE) declares, 'O my city, like an innocent ewe thy lamb has been torn away from thee; O Ur, like an innocent goat thy kid has perished' (*ANET*, 456).[86] Wilshire interprets the servant's 'marred' and 'despised' state as references to Zion's destruction and humiliation rather than as images of disability.[87] As the final servant song, Isaiah 53 promises the restoration of Zion after a period of exile and humiliation.[88]

Seitz draws parallels between the suffering of the servant and the suffering of Zion (e.g. Isa 49:13; 51:21; 54:11). He argues that, in contrast to Ezekiel or Lamentations, Second Isaiah does not focus on the sinfulness of Zion itself. Picking up on the specific images of disability in our passage, Seitz writes 'an interpretation of the servant in 52:13–53:12 as Zion . . . is in continuity with the depiction of Zion-King in Isa 38. Hezekiah is sick and at the point of death. The emphasis is not on his sinfulness (38:17), but on his state of illness (28:9–20) and his prior faithfulness. The psalm narrates the movement from sickness, to near death, to new life, to awaiting full health. Has the final servant poem been composed for Zion on analogy with the psalm of Hezekiah?'[89] In answer to Seitz's question, we would caution against pressing this analogy very far. Certainly, as we discussed in Chapter 2, Isaiah 38 shares imagery of disability with Isaiah 53. The difference is that Hezekiah's has a temporary illness whereas the servant has a chronic disability. As we noted earlier, the comparison with Hezekiah's illness allows us to imagine a divine healing of the servant that does not appear in Isaiah 53.

Similarly, comparisons with Zion may also imply a healing of the servant. In Isaiah 53–4, the servant and Zion share imagery involving disability. Both Isa 49:21 and 54:1 refer to a personified Zion as infertile. As we discussed in Chapter 1, the Hebrew Bible and other ancient Near Eastern texts portray infertility as a disability and associate it with several other physical and cognitive disabilities. Yet, Isa 54:1 explicitly promises that the infertile Zion will have many children. 'Sing, O barren one who did not bear; burst into song and shout, you who have not been in labor! For the children of the desolate woman will be more than the children of her that is married, says the LORD.' Unlike the servant, the personified Zion experiences a removal of her disability. If we interpret both the servant and Zion as personifying the same thing, we find yet another way to imply that God healed the servant's disability.

Conclusions

In our last two chapters, we have traced the transformation of the servant from a figure with disabilities in a poem to a typological figure to a historically identifiable and usually able-bodied person or group. The disappearance of the servant's disability does not occur in the text but in the process of interpretation. The servant's transformation into an able-bodied sufferer results from a long series of interpretative choices by scholars. Biblical scholarship has a venerable tradition of divorcing the imagery of disability in Isaiah 53 from the experience of disability. The search for the servant's identity is no exception. Throughout this search, many interpreters use the disability imagery to focus on the suffering of almost any person or group except those with disabilities. The servant with disabilities fades from our memory while the suffering servant emerges.

| Conclusion

The Servant as Able-Bodied
Passer

[People with disabilities passing as able-bodied] recognize that in most
societies there exists no common experience or understanding of
disability on which to base their identity. For where a common acceptance of disability exists, passing is unnecessary.

Tobin Siebers, *Disability Theory*

The analogy with the Servant is clear, but like all analogies, it walks
with a limp.

Joseph Blenkinsopp, *Isaiah 40–55: A New Translation
with Introduction and Commentary*

In his programmatic work *I, He, We, and They*, David J. A. Clines
declares, 'Isaiah 53 is a casualty of historical-critical scholarship.'[1]
Rather than approaching the poem as a source of historical information, he calls for us to approach the poem as a 'language-event'. For
Clines, the language of the poem 'creates a world...It sets forth a
vision of the world which is radically different from our prior expectations; it is a new "world" in that its scale of values differs from
the conventional.'[2] We can appreciate Clines' shift from a scholarly
focus on *whom* Isaiah 53 describes to *how* it describes, and thereby
how it creates new worlds. Nevertheless, even allowing for the text to
create multiple meanings, worlds, and even characters, it amazes us
how often this passage has created a world and a character without
disabilities within the history of its interpretation. As we have discovered throughout this book, the 'scale of values' of the brave new

worlds that Isaiah 53 creates for most scholars does not include disability.

Brave new worlds without disabilities

Unfortunately, the history of the servant's interpretation remains largely an exercise in creating new worlds and characters without disabilities. The widespread dismissal of Duhm's skin anomaly diagnosis contributed to the widespread dismissal of the servant's disability. Yet we should not mistake misguided attempts to understand a literary representation of disability through a medical model for the absence of disability in the passage. As we discussed in Chapter 1, interpreting disability involves much more than a medical diagnosis. In Chapter 2, we discovered that these new worlds without disability do not reflect Isaiah 53's depiction of the servant's experience. Isaiah 53 describes the servant with imagery usually associated with disability as a social experience in the Hebrew Bible and other ancient Near Eastern literature. As we traced the interpretative history of the servant in Chapters 3 and 4, we found that the servant with disabilities in the poem helped create typological connections for early interpreters and create identifications with presumably able-bodied individuals or communal experiences of exile rather than disability for later interpreters. The identification of the servant with historical individuals or communities not only created new worlds for interpreters but a new character in the servant as an able-bodied sufferer.

We may wonder why scholars tend to create worlds and characters without disabilities when interpreting Isaiah 53. Contrary to a popular assumption, these worlds do not represent a natural or default starting point for reading our passage. Such worlds are in fact the products of repeated interpretive choices or preferences. Yet we should not speculate about the reasons why scholars repeatedly make these choices or preferences, which seem to reflect and reinforce what Robert McRuer refers to as 'compulsory able-bodiedness'.[3] Certainly, we would caution against reading a conscious ablist or eugenics conspiracy theory behind these preferences. Nevertheless, while we cannot know why scholars tend to neglect the servant's disability, we do know that this neglect contributes to the creation of worlds and characters without disability.

By contrast, this book has chosen the reasonable starting point that disability imagery describes a figure with disabilities in Isaiah 53. Yet we have not claimed that our reading of the servant is the only legitimate way to interpret the servant. As we discussed in Chapter 1, most of the biblical language for disability is broad enough semantically to describe conditions or circumstances other than experiences of disability. We could interpret the disability imagery as an idiomatic description of experiences of prophetic or exilic suffering. Yet, while our reading of the servant as a poetic figure with disabilities is not the only way we could interpret him, it remains as viable an option as any. Since Isaiah 53 uses disability imagery, the burden of proof falls on those who would claim that such imagery does not describe a disability. We have not found any convincing reason why we should not choose to start from the position that disability imagery describes experiences of disability. Throughout this book, however, we have found a number of unconvincing reasons used to justify other presumably able-bodied starting points.

Democratizing the servant or appropriating disability?

As we discussed in the Introduction, much of Isaiah 1–33 comes from a period before the destruction of Jerusalem and the end of the Davidic monarchy in 587 BCE. Isaiah 40–55 comes from some time after these horrific events. In other words, our passage reflects a very different world from that of First Isaiah. We could argue that this historical context of Isaiah 40–55 encourages the creation of newly imagined worlds. Nevertheless, the later chapters of Isaiah create a literary world from several of the motifs that appear repeatedly throughout First Isaiah, including 'Zion' (e.g. 1:8; 12:6; 14:32) and 'servant' (20:3; 22:20; cf. 37:35).[4] Some scholars have suggested that, in the wake of the destruction of both the Davidic monarchy and Jerusalem, Second Isaiah reapplies these motifs to the Judean people more generally rather than limiting them to a specific royal line or city. For example, in Isa 55:3, God applies 'an everlasting covenant, my steadfast, sure love for David' to all Israel (cf. 2 Sam 7:15–16). Likewise, Isa 51:16 refers to all Israel as 'Zion' (cf. Zech 2:7).[5]

In a way, this broader reapplication of these motifs ensures the survival of the divine promises associated with such motifs in a historical situation very different from the one preceding the destruction of the Davidic line and Jerusalem. Often, scholars refer to this phenomenon as the 'democratization' of the Davidic promise (or 'Zion theology'[6]) to Judean parties beyond the royal family. This so-called democratization of motifs found elsewhere in the Isaianic tradition allows our passage to create 'a vision of the world which is radically different from our prior expectations', to borrow Clines' words quoted earlier.

Regarding the servant figure in Isaiah 53, Mettinger argues that a similar process occurs in our passage. Mettinger writes, 'This was the development during the Exile by means of which the Davidic theology became "nationalized". Ideas which were previously attached to the king were now transferred to the people...In Isaiah 40–55 this tendency is most clearly observable in 55:3–5.'[7] As with other motifs associated with the Davidic monarchy, Mettinger claims that the servant figure becomes a collective reference for the exilic community in Second Isaiah. As with many other creative reapplications of the servant discussed throughout this book, the servant's democratization helps to ensure his continued survival within our scholarly and popular imaginations.

Nevertheless, there is an important difference between the democratization of Zion or kingship and that of the servant figure in Isaiah 40–55. We may acknowledge the expansion of kingship or Zion motifs to new and broader circles without denying that the terms 'David' or 'Zion' also describe a specific person and geographic location respectively. Regarding the servant with disabilities, however, scholars tend to read Isaiah 53 as an expansion of a servant motif that does not also describe a figure with disabilities. The imagery of disability in Isaiah 53 is not democratized. Rather, it is appropriated. In fact, the appropriation of the servant has left little room for people with disabilities to claim the servant as one of their own.

The servant's afterlife: creative reapplying or passing?

We do not raise the issue of the appropriation of Isaiah 53's disability imagery in order to make an exclusive claim of ownership over this passage for one group or another. As Benjamin Sommer correctly remarks, 'In this chapter, Deutero-Isaiah's allusive art reaches a high point.'[8] In other words, Isaiah 53 fleshes out the servant through a wide variety of imagery, including but not limited to royal, national, prophetic, and disability imagery.

Unfortunately, interpretative interest in the servant would probably have faded long ago if the disability imagery were not reapplied to persons or situations other than those of disability. People rarely bother with stories of persons with disabilities if they do not somehow inform the experience of the able-bodied, be it for their medical, entertainment, or even theological value. In many ways, the servant's ability to 'pass' as an otherwise able-bodied prophet, king, or exiled persona has ensured his literary survival among the dominant figures within the history of biblical interpretation. We suspect that if he had not passed as able-bodied he would not have had much of an interpretative afterlife at all. Rather, he would remain buried deep within a prophetic corpus whose imagery often overshadows its humanity.

In this sense, the servant's interpretative afterlife most closely approximates an unfortunately frequent experience of persons with disabilities. Passing as able-bodied represents the dominant strategy for ensuring the servant's survival in literature beyond Isaiah 53. Likewise, passing as able-bodied represents a dominant strategy for acceptance, if not survival, for many persons with disabilities in real-life situations. Earlier, we quoted Clines' claim that Isaiah 53 presents 'a new "world" in that its scale of values differs from the conventional'. Yet the scale of values reflected in the new worlds created throughout the history of the servant's interpretation still require the servant to pass as able-bodied. The values of these new worlds seem to reflect the all too conventional values of an able-bodied world.

While we may appreciate the creative reapplication of the servant's experience to wider circles throughout the history of interpretation, it remains important to contextualize this process within the cultural history of disability. Traditionally, as with other minority groups, this history has had an uneasy relationship with how dominant groups have exploited persons with disabilities as sources of medical, moral, scientific, and even theological enquiry. This does not mean that Isaiah 53 cannot inform interpretations, theological or otherwise, that do not focus on the servant as a figure with disabilities. Rather, it means that we should recognize how and state why we choose to interpret the servant as either able-bodied or as having a disability just as scholars routinely state why they interpret the servant as an individual or a collective reference.

Even if we do not focus on the servant as a figure with disabilities, we do not have to repeat the tendency to make him pass as able-bodied. We can make a different interpretative choice. Some scholars writing from a self-identified Christian standpoint have creatively reapplied the servant's experience to that of the Church while recognizing that Isaiah 53 does not describe the servant as a Christian or the Church collectively.[9] Such scholars can reapply the servant's experience to that of Jesus or the Church without trying to make the servant pass as Jesus or a Christian. Those that interpret the servant outside the context of disability should make a similar distinction between creatively reapplying the servant's experience of disability and imagining him as an able-bodied passer.

In the epigraph, we quoted Tobin Siebers' statement that 'where a common acceptance of disability exists, passing is unnecessary'. Unfortunately, that the history of the servant's interpretation reviewed in this book has produced worlds upon worlds that are free of disabilities reminds us how necessary passing, in a multiplicity of forms, still is within biblical scholarship. Studying Isaiah 53 in the context of disability studies does more than ask who the servant is for each one of us. It asks us to state clearly how we have imagined and organized the biblical world and whom we have allowed to occupy it.

| *Notes*

INTRODUCTION

1. For the sake of convenience, throughout this book, we use 'Isaiah 53' as a less cumbersome title for Isa 52:13–53:12.

2. On vicarious suffering in Isaiah 53, see, with citations, Daniel P. Bailey, 'Concepts of *Stellvertretung* in the Interpretation of Isaiah 53', in William H. Bellinger and William R. Farmer (eds), *Jesus and the Suffering Servant: Isaiah 53 and Christian Origins* (Harrisburg: Trinity, 1998), 223–50; Bernd Janowski, *Stellvertretung: alttestamentliche Studien zu einem theologischen Grundbegriff* (Stuttgart: Verlag Katholisches Bibelwerk, 1997); *idem*, 'He Bore Our Sins: Isaiah 53 and the Drama of Taking Another's Place', in Bernd Janowski and Peter Stuhlmacher (eds), *The Suffering Servant: Isaiah 53 In Jewish And Christian Sources*, trans. Daniel P. Bailey (Grand Rapids: William B. Eerdmans, 2004), 48–74; Hermann Spieckermann, 'The Conception and Prehistory of the Idea of Vicarious Suffering in the Old Testament', in Janowski and Stuhlmacher (eds), *The Suffering Servant*, 1–47.

3. For a helpful discussion of this topic, see Martha Stoddard Holmes, *Fictions of Affliction: Physical Disability in Victorian Culture* (Ann Arbor: University of Michigan Press, 2004).

4. On this issue within the cultural history of disability, see Sharon L. Snyder and David T. Mitchell, *Cultural Locations of Disability* (Chicago: University of Chicago Press, 2006); *idem*, *Narrative Prosthesis: Disability and the Dependencies of Discourse* (Ann Arbor: University of Michigan Press, 2000); Shelley Tremain (ed.), *Foucault and the Government of Disability* (Ann Arbor: University of Michigan Press, 2005).

5. See Colin G. Cruse, 'The Servant Songs: Interpretative Trends since C. K. North', *Studia Biblica et Theologica* 8 (1978): 3–27; Samuel R. Driver and Adolf Neubauer, *The Fifty-Third Chapter of Isaiah according to the Jewish Interpreters* (Oxford and London: James Parker and Company, 1877); Herbert Haag, *Der Gottesknecht bei Deuterojesaja* (Darmstadt: Wissenschaftliche, 1985), 34–195; Wolfgang Hüllstrung and Gerlinde Feine, updated by Daniel P. Bailey, 'A Classified Bibliography on Isaiah 53', in Janowski and Stuhlmacher (eds), *The Suffering Servant*, 462–92; Christopher R. North, *The Suffering Servant in Deutero-Isaiah: A Historical and Critical Study*, 2nd edn (London: Oxford University Press,

1956); Harold Henry Rowley, 'The Servant of the Lord', in Harold Henry Rowley, *The Servant of the Lord and Other Essays* (London: Lutterworth, 1952), 1–57; John D. W. Watts, *Isaiah 34–66*, rev. edn, WBC 25 (Nashville: Nelson Reference & Electronic, 2005), 791. For further references to surveys of the history of Isaiah 53's interpretation, see Kristin Joachimsen, 'Steck's Five Stories of the Servant in Isaiah lii 13–liii 12, and Beyond', *VT* 57 (2007): 209 n. 2 and 3; 217 n. 33.

6. The NRSV and our translation follow the Greek version known as the Septuagint in translating 52:15 as 'so he shall startle many nations'. Yet other translations follow Hebrew and other Greek manuscripts by Aquila and Theodorion in translating this verse as 'so shall he sprinkle many nations' (KJV). Our translation fits the context of the passage well as we discover in Chapter 2.

7. The NRSV translates this phrase as 'He was despised and rejected by others.' While the first Hebrew verb is a passive form ('was despised'), the second verb is active ('rejected'). Thus, we prefer to translate the phrase as 'He was despised and withdrew from humanity.' See, with citations, Michael L. Barré, S.S., 'Textual and Rhetorical-critical Observations on the Last Servant Song (Isaiah 52:13–53:12)', *CBQ* 62 (2000): 13 n. 62. The emphasis on the servant's separation from society fits the context of the passage well as we discover in Chapter 2.

8. The NRSV translates this phrase as 'as one from whom others hide their faces'. Yet, our translation 'like someone who hides his face from us' is also grammatically possible and fits the context of the passage well as we discover in Chapter 2. See D. Winton Thomas, 'A Consideration of Isaiah liii in the Light of Recent Textual and Philological Study', *Ephemerides Theologicae Lovanienses* 44 (1968): 83.

9. The NRSV translates this phrase as 'yet we accounted him stricken'. We translate the Hebrew *ng'* as 'plagued' instead of 'stricken' in both its verb and noun forms (vv. 4 and 8 respectively) in order to reflect its use as a term for disability or disease. For example, *ng'* in both its noun and verb forms appears 61 times in Leviticus 13–14, mostly as a reference to a skin anomaly. We will discuss this translation in Chapter 2.

10. The NRSV translates the Hebrew *mhll* as 'he was wounded' (*meholal*). Our translation follows the early Greek text by Aquila, who translates *mhll* as 'made profane' (*mehullal* as in Ezek 36:23; cf. Ezek 24:21). An Aramaic translation also translates the Hebrew word as 'profaned' rather than 'wounded'. We will discuss this translation in Chapter 2 (cf. 53:10).

11. The NRSV translates the first part of v. 8 as 'by a perversion of justice'. Our translation understands the two Hebrew prepositions (*min*) that appear respectively before the nouns 'restraint' and 'justice' as negating

these nouns. Similarly, the passage uses a pair of the preposition *min* in a similar way when it negates the nouns 'human semblance' and 'mortals' in 52:14 ('unlike [*min*] human semblance, and his form unlike [*min*] that of mortals'). This repeated use of the preposition *min* to negate nouns also appears in Isa 54:9, which the NRSV translates as, 'I will not (*min*) be angry with you and will not (*min*) rebuke you'. Elsewhere, a verbal form of the word for 'restrain' appears in contexts in which a plague is stopped (Num 17:13, 15; 25:8; 2 Sam 24:25). The idea in 53:8 is that those who took the servant away showed no restraint or justice in their actions. See G. Brooke Lester, 'Daniel Evokes Isaiah: The Rule of the Nations in Apocalyptic Allusion-Narrative' (Ph.D. diss., Princeton Theological Seminary, 2007), 235 n. 54. On this use of the preposition *min*, see Bruce K. Waltke and Michael O'Connor, *An Introduction to Biblical Hebrew Syntax* (Winona Lake: Eisenbrauns, 1990), 214.

12. The NRSV translates the root *dwr* as 'generation' rather than 'dwelling'. Although 'generation' is the most common meaning of this root, a similar form of this root means 'dwelling' during Hezekiah's prayer for recovery from an illness (Isa 38:12) . Furthermore, cognates of *dwr* in other Near Eastern languages mean 'to dwell'. See Barré, 'Textual and Rhetorical-critical Observations on the Last Servant Song (Isaiah 52:13–53:12)', 17, with citations.

13. Unlike the NRSV, we have translated the various forms of *ḥlh* as 'diseased' or 'diseases' consistently (vv. 3, 4, 10). In v. 10, a text from the Dead Sea Scrolls (1QIsa^a) has a slightly different word that reflects the Hebrew root *ḥll* and means, 'profaned him' (cf. v. 5) instead of 'make him diseased'. The Septuagint translates this verse as 'the LORD desired to cleanse him of his disease'. We discuss how 1QIsa^a and the Septuagint render v. 10 further in Chapter 3.

14. David J. A. Clines, *I, He, We, and They: A Literary Approach to Isaiah 53*, JSOTSup 1 (Sheffield: JSOT, 1976), 33.

15. For example, see Ernst Haag, 'Die Botschaft vom Gottesknecht. Ein Weg zur Überwindung der Gewalt', in Norbert Lohfink (ed.), *Gewalt und Gewaltlosigkeit im Alten Testament* (Freiburg: Herder, 1983), 166–72; Reinhard Gregor Kratz, *Kyros im Deuterojesaja-Buch: Redaktions-geschichtliche Untersuchungen zu Entstehung und Theologie von Jes 40–55*, FAT 1 (Tübingen: Mohr-Siebeck, 1991), 217. Odil Hannes Steck argues for five layers of redaction, beginning in 530 and continuing until 270 BCE. Odil Hannes Steck, *Gottesknecht und Zion: Gesammelte Aufsätze zu Deu-terojesaja*, FAT 4 (Tübingen: Mohr-Siebeck, 1992), 149–72. For a helpful discussion of Steck's redactional proposal, see Kristin Joachimsen,

'Steck's Five Stories of the Servant in Isaiah lii 13-liii 12, and Beyond', 208–28.

16. I would like to thank Patrick D. Miller for bringing this point to my attention in a personal communication.

17. For discussions of these issues, see Brevard S. Childs, *Introduction to the Old Testament as Scripture* (Philadelphia: Fortress, 1979), 311–23, with citations; John J. Collins, *Introduction to the Hebrew Bible* (Minneapolis: Fortress, 2004), 379–400; Marvin Sweeney, 'The Book of Isaiah in Recent Research', *Currents in Research: Biblical Studies* 1 (1993): 141–62; Marvin E. Tate, 'The Book of Isaiah in Recent Study', in James W. Watts and Paul R. House (eds), *Forming Prophetic Literature: Essays on Isaiah and the Twelve in Honor of John D. W. Watts*, JSOTSup 235 (Sheffield: Sheffield Academic Press, 1996), 22–56.

18. As early as 1933, Karl Elliger argued that Isaiah 53 comes from Third Isaiah rather than Second Isaiah. See Karl Elliger, *Deuterojesaja in seinem verhältnis zu Tritojeseja* (Stuttgart: W. Kohlhammer verlag, 1933). For a critique of Elliger, see North, *The Suffering Servant in Deutero-Isaiah*, 161–77. More recently, see Fredrick Hägglund, *Isaiah 53 in the Light of Homecoming after Exile*, FAT 31 (Tübingen: Mohr-Siebeck, 2008), 137–9, with citations. Recently, some scholars have argued against the idea of a 'Third Isaiah'. Benjamin D. Sommer attributes Isaiah 35, 40–66, including Isaiah 53, to Second Isaiah (*A Prophet Reads Scripture: Allusion in Isaiah 40–66* [Stanford: Stanford University Press, 1998], 187–95); cf. Shalom M. Paul, *Isaiah 40–66: Introduction and Commentary*, 2 vols, Mikra Leyisrael (Jerusalem: Magnes, 2008 [Hebrew]).

19. On this possibility, see the discussions and citations in Zoltán Kustár, *'Durch seine Wunden sind wir geheilt': eine Untersuchung zur Metaphorik von Israels Krankheit und Heilung im Jesajabuch*, BWANT 154 (Stuttgart: Kohlhammer, 2002), 160–204; Jill Middlemas, 'Did Second Isaiah Write Lamentations III?', *VT* 56 (2006): 506–25; Sommer, *A Prophet Reads Scripture*, 64–6, 93–6; Patricia Tull Willey, *Remember the Former Things: The Recollection of Previous Texts in Second Isaiah*, SBLDS 161 (Atlanta: Society of Biblical Literature, 1997), 214–21.

20. For example, see the extensive list of parallels in Ivan Engell, 'The 'Ebed Yahweh Songs and the Suffering Messiah in Deutero-Isaiah', *BJRL* 31 (1948): 54–93; cf. Helmer Ringgren, *The Messiah in the Old Testament*, Studies in Biblical Theology 18 (London: SCM Press, 1956), 50–3. For critiques of these parallels, see Harry M. Orlinsky, 'The So-Called "Servant of the Lord" and "Suffering Servant" in Second Isaiah', in *Studies on the Second Part of the Book of Isaiah*, VTSup 14 (Leiden: E. J. Brill, 1967), 65–6, with citations; Joseph Scharbert, 'Stellvertretendes

Sühneleiden in den Ebed-Jahwe-Liedern und in altorienta-lischen Ri-tualtexten', *BZ* 2 (1958): 190–213.

21. For example, Roger N. Whybray argues that whereas 52:13–53:12 as a whole does not conform to any known genre of poetry found in the Hebrew Bible, 53:1–12 follows the pattern of the 'individual song of thanksgiving' genre (see our discussion in Chapter 2). Therefore, ac-cording to Whybray, 52:13–15 and 53:1–12 represent different sources. See Roger N. Whybray, *Thanksgiving for a Liberated Prophet: An Interpreta-tion of Isaiah Chapter 53*, JSOTSup 4 (Sheffield: JSOT, 1978), 109–15; 163 n. 1. Prior to Whybray, several scholars near the turn of the last century argued that either Isa 52:13–15 or 52:13–53:1 come from a different source than Isa 53:1–12 or 2–12. For example, see the discussion of Schian and Bertholet in North, *The Suffering Servant in Deutero-Isaiah*, 48–9. Yet there is no definitive textual evidence to support these proposals.

22. See Claus Westermann, *Isaiah 40–66: A Commentary*, OTL, trans. David M. G. Stalker (Philadelphia: Westminster, 1969), 255–8; cf. Brevard S. Childs, *Isaiah: A Commentary*, OTL (Louisville: Westminster John Knox, 2001), 411.

23. Jeremy Schipper, *Disability Studies and the Hebrew Bible: Figuring Me-phibosheth in the David Story*, LHBOTS 441 (New York: T & T Clark, 2006), 27–8.

24. Welcomed exceptions include the discussions and citations in Brenda Brueggemann, 'On (Almost) Passing', in *The Disability Studies Reader*, 3rd edn, ed. Lennard J. Davis (New York: Routledge, 2010), 209–19; Rosemarie Garland-Thomson, *Staring: How We Look* (New York: Oxford University Press, 2009), esp. 18–20, 42; Ellen Samuels, 'My Body, My Closet: Invisible Disability and the Limits of Coming-Out Discourse', *Gay Lesbian Quarterly* 9 (2003): 233–55; Tobin Siebers, *Dis-ability Theory* (Ann Arbor: University of Michigan Press, 2008), 96–119.

25. See Saul M. Olyan, *Disability in the Hebrew Bible: Interpreting Mental and Physical Differences* (New York: Cambridge University Press, 2008); *idem*, 'The Ascription of Physical Disability as a Stigmatizing Strategy in Biblical Iconic Polemics', *JHS* 9, article 14 (2009): 1–15, available online: www.arts.ualberta.ca/JHS/Articles/article_116.pdf (accessed 11 February 2011); Rebecca Raphael, *Biblical Corpora: Representations of Disability in Hebrew Biblical Literature*, LHBOTS 445 (New York: T & T Clark, 2008). For a helpful study of disability in the Qumran Scrolls, see Johanna Dorman, *The Blemished Body: Deformity and Dis-ability in the Qumran Scrolls* (Groningen: Rijksuniversiteit, 2007).

26. See Lennard J. Davis, *Bending Over Backwards: Disability, Dismodernism and Other Difficult Positions* (New York: New York University Press,

2002), 79–101; Snyder and Mitchell, *Cultural Locations of Disability*; *idem, Narrative Prosthesis*. Regarding the role of disability as an aesthetic object in modern art and visual culture, see Tobin Siebers, *Disability Aesthetics* (Ann Arbor: University of Michigan Press, 2010).

CHAPTER 1

1. See Saul M. Olyan, *Disability in the Hebrew Bible: Interpreting Mental and Physical Differences* (New York: Cambridge University Press, 2008); Rebecca Raphael, *Biblical Corpora: Representations of Disability in Hebrew Biblical Literature*, LHBOTS 445 (New York: T & T Clark, 2008); Jeremy Schipper, *Disability Studies and the Hebrew Bible: Figuring Mephibosheth in the David Story*, LHBOTS 441 (New York: T & T Clark, 2006); Hector Avalos, Sarah Melcher, and Jeremy Schipper (eds), *This Abled Body: Rethinking Disability and Biblical Studies*, Semeia Studies 55 (Atlanta: Society of Biblical Literature, 2007).

2. For a detailed discussion of those physical disabilities that do or do not qualify as a *mum* in the Hebrew Bible, see Olyan, *Disability in the Hebrew Bible*, 26–61.

3. Raphael, *Biblical Corpora*, 14–15.

4. For a detailed treatment of this issue, see Schipper, *Disability Studies and the Hebrew Bible*, 64–73. We appreciate Olyan's suggestion that we should label this conceptual category as 'somatic dysfunction' rather than 'disability' as we did in *Disability Studies and the Hebrew Bible*. See Olyan, *Disability in the Hebrew Bible*, 147–8, n. 5. In the present book, we use the term 'disability' according to the cultural model definition provided later in this chapter.

5. On disability and queer studies, including the pathologization of these identities, see the discussions and citations in Eli Clare, *Exile and Pride: Disability, Queerness, and Liberation* (Cambridge: South End, 1999); Robert McRuer, *Crip Theory: Cultural Signs of Queerness and Disability* (New York: New York University Press, 2006).

6. On the relationship between disability and illness, see Susan Wendell, *The Rejected Body: Feminist Philosophical Reflections on Disability* (New York: Routledge, 1996), 19–22.

7. See Nils Heessel, *Babylonisch-assyriche Diagnostik*, AOAT 43 (Münster: Ugarit-Verlag, 2000); René Labat, *Traité akkadien de diagnostics et prognostics médicaux*, 2 vols (Paris: Académie internationale d'histoire des sciences, 1951); Franz Köcher, *Die babylonisch-assyrische Medizin in Texten und Untersuchungen*, 6 vols (Berlin: Walter de Gruyter, 1963–80). For recent attempts at medical diagnoses of Mesopotamian illnesses, diseases, and

disabilities, see JoAnn Scurlock and Burton R. Anderson, *Diagnoses of Assyrian and Babylonian Medicine: Ancient Sources, Translations, and Modern Medical Analyses* (Urbana: University of Illinois Press, 2005).

8. See Colin Barnes, Len Barton, and Michael Oliver (eds), *Disability Studies Today* (Cambridge: Polity, 2002).

9. Lennard J. Davis, *Enforcing Normalcy: Disability, Deafness, and the Body* (New York: Verso, 1995), 130.

10. Lennard J. Davis, *Bending Over Backwards: Disability, Dismodernism and Other Difficult Positions* (New York: New York University Press, 2002), 23.

11. Jenny Morris, *Pride Against Prejudice: Transforming Attitudes to Disability* (London: The Women's Press, 1991) 10.

12. In a private communication, Josh Lukin, my colleague in Temple University's English department and affiliated faculty member of Temple's Institute on Disabilities, noted the importance of distinguishing between an inability and a prohibition when discussing differences between experiences of disability and that of race, sexuality, and so on.

13. Davis, *Bending Over Backwards*, 23.

14. On the 'cultural model' see the discussions and citations in Sharon L. Snyder and David T. Mitchell, *Cultural Locations of Disability* (Chicago: University of Chicago Press, 2006), 5–11; Schipper, *Disability Studies and the Hebrew Bible*, 18–21; Raphael, *Biblical Corpora*, 8–11.

15. Rebecca Raphael, 'Things Too Wonderful: A Disabled Reading of Job', *PRSt* 31 (2004): 400.

16. For a further discussion of this tendency, see Jeremy Schipper, 'Embodying Deuteronomistic Theology in 1 Kings 15:22–24', in Tamar Kamionkowski and Wonil Kim (eds), *Bodies, Embodiment and Theology of the Hebrew Bible*, LHBOTS 465 (New York: T & T Clark, 2010), 77–89; idem, 'Deuteronomy 24:5 and King Asa's Foot Disease in 1 Kings 15:23b', *JBL* 129 (2009): 643–8.

17. For example, see Gen 27:1; 32:26, 32; 48:10; Exod 4:6, 10–11; Lev 13–14; Num 12:10–12; Deut 31:2; Judg 16:21; 1 Sam 3:2; 4:18; 11:2; 2 Sam 4:4; 5:6–8; 6:23; 9:3, 13; 19:27; 2 Kgs 7:10–11; 14:4; 5:1, 12; 9:30–37; 15:5; 25:7; Pss 6:2; 22:14–15, 17; 31:10; 102:52; Job 2:7; 7:5; 19:20; 30:30; 2 Chr 26:16–23. On this point, see Schipper, 'Embodying Deuteronomistic Theology in 1 Kings 15:22–24'.

18. McRuer, *Crip Theory*, 1.

19. On this point in relation to infertility in the Hebrew Bible, see Joel S. Baden, 'The Nature of Barrenness in the Hebrew Bible', in Candida

Moss and Jeremy Schipper (eds), *Disability Studies and Biblical Literature* (New York: Palgrave Macmillan, forthcoming).

20. Martha C. Nussbaum, *Frontiers of Justice: Disability, Nationality, Species Membership* (Cambridge, MA: Harvard University Press, 2006), 101. For Nussbaum, a society's notion of disability is contingent upon the demands of the society on its citizens' bodies.

21. See Rosemarie Garland Thomson, *Extraordinary Bodies: Figuring Physical Disability in American Culture and Literature* (New York: Columbia University Press, 1997), 141, n. 14.

22. Tobin Siebers, *Disability Theory* (Ann Arbor: University of Michigan Press, 2008), 71.

23. Thomson, *Extraordinary Bodies*, 13–14.

24. This does not mean that ancient Near Eastern societies considered infertility as an exclusively female disability. Deuteronomy 7:14 mentions male infertility alongside female infertility (cf. Gen 20:17). Additionally, for a large number of Mesopotamian male fertility incantations see Robert D. Biggs, *Šà.zi.ga, Ancient Mesopotamian Potency Incantations* (Locust Valley, NY: J. J. Augustin, 1967).

25. See the discussions and citations in Neal H. Walls, 'The Origins of the Disabled Body: Disability in Ancient Mesopotamia', in Avalos, Melcher, and Schipper (eds), *This Abled Body*, 16–19; Jeremy Schipper, 'Disabling Israelite Leadership: 2 Samuel 6:23 and Other Images of Disability in the Deuteronomistic History', in Avalos, Melcher, and Schipper, *This Abled Body*, 109–12.

26. For a thoughtful treatment of female infertility in the Hebrew Bible as a social experience with cultic restrictions, see Susan Ackerman, 'The Blind, the Lame, and the Barran shall not Come into the House', in Moss and Schipper, *Disability Studies and Biblical Literature* (forthcoming).

27. According to *Sefer ha-Yashar*, a collection of midrashim from the Middle Ages, Lamech also lost his sight due to advanced age (cf. Gen 4:18–24).

28. Although Rebekah and Jacob take advantage of Isaac's visual impairment, Isaac maintains his status as patriarch within the family structure. For a detailed discussion, see Kerry Wynn, 'The Normate Hermeneutic and Interpretations of Disability in Yahwistic Narratives', in Avalos, Melcher, and Schipper, *This Abled Body*, 93–6.

29. On this issue, see R. K. Harrison, 'Blindness', *IDB* 1:448–9. Rosemary Ellison suggests that Vitamin A deficiencies due to diets heavy in barley may have resulted in eye problems among some Mesopotamian workers. See Rosemary Ellison, 'Some Thoughts on the Diet of Mesopotamia from c. 3000–600 B.C.E.', *Iraq* 45 (1983): 146–50; *idem*, 'Diet in

Mesopotamia: The Evidence of the Barley Ration Texts (c. 3000 to 1400 B.C.E.)', *Iraq* 43 (1981): 35–45. On euphemisms for blindness in Akkadian with some discussion of biblical material, see David Marcus, 'Some Antiphrastic Euphemisms for a Blind Person in Akkadian and Other Semitic Languages', *JAOS* 100 (1980): 307–10.

30. On the rhetorical significance of Moses' eyesight in relation to other leaders throughout the Deuteronomistic History, see Schipper, 'Disabling Israelite Leadership', 105.

31. Americans with Disabilities Act of 1990, S. 933, section 3, paragraph 2. http://caselaw.lp.findlaw.com/casecode/uscodes/42/chapters/126/toc.html (accessed 4 February 2011).

32. This is not to say that disability imagery did not intersect with legal discourses in ancient Near Eastern literature. On this issue, see F. Rachel Magdalene, 'The ANE Legal Origins of Impairment as Theological Disability and the Book of Job', *PRSt* 34 (2007): 23–60; *idem, On the Scales of Righteousness: Neo-Babylonian Trial Law and the Book of Job*, BJS 48 (Atlanta: Society of Biblical Literature, 2007).

33. Miriam Lichtheim, *Ancient Egyptian Literature*, 3 vols (Berkley: University of California Press, 1973), vol. 2, 160.

34. See Frances Reynolds (ed.), *The Babylonian Correspondence of Esarhaddon and Letters to Assurbanipal and Sin-Šarru-Iškun from Northern and Central Babylonia*, SAA 18 (Helsinki: Helsinki University Press, 2003), 95–97.

35. See the references in n. 7.

36. For a detailed study of this character, see Schipper, *Disability Studies and the Hebrew Bible*.

37. Autopsies of Egyptian mummies reveal that a number of rulers acquired impairments through injuries and various bodily traumas during their lifetimes. If this was common among the ruling class, it seems reasonable to induce that significant non-fatal injuries frequently resulted in acquired impairments among the wider population. See Walter M. Whitehouse, 'Radiologic Findings in the Royal Mummies', in James Harris and Edward Wente (eds), *An X-Ray Atlas of the Royal Mummies* (Chicago: University of Chicago Press, 1980), 286–327; cf. Calvin Wells, *Bones, Bodies, and Disease: Evidence of Disease and Abnormality in Early Man* (New York: Frederick A. Praeger, 1964). For a variety of reasons, scholars have not devoted much study to ancient Israelite human remains. For an accessible discussion of diseases and disability in relation to ancient Israelite dietary practices based on paleopathology, see Nathan MacDonald, *What Did the Ancient Israelites Eat?: Diet in Biblical Times* (Grand Rapids: Eerdmans, 2008), 80–87, with citations; cf.

Hector Avalos, *Illness and Health Care in the Ancient Near East: The Role of the Temple in Greece, Mesopotamia, and Israel*, HSM 54 (Atlanta: Scholars, 1995), 120–24 with citations.

38. Rashi infers Jacob's healing from Gen 33:18a, which reads, 'Jacob came safely [or 'in wholeness' *shalem*] to the city of Shechem.' Yet, in this verse, *shalem* most likely alludes to Jacob's request of the LORD that he may return to his father's house 'in peace' (*beshalom*) in Gen 28:21.

39. For a critique of scholarly opinions on this issue, see Wynn, 'The Normate Hermeneutic and Interpretations of Disability in Yahwistic Narratives', 99.

40. For more detailed discussions of *ḥlḥ* including related terms and ancient Near Eastern cognates, see Schipper, *Disability Studies and the Hebrew Bible*, 80–84, with citations.

41. Roger N. Whybray, *Thanksgiving for a Liberated Prophet: An Interpretation of Isaiah Chapter 53*, JOTSup 4 (Sheffield: JSOT, 1978), 148, n. 116.

42. For a review of the interpretive history, see Jeffery Tigay, '"Heavy of Mouth" and "Heavy of Tongue": On Moses' Speech Difficulty', *BASOR* 231 (1978): 57–67; cf. Nyasha Junior and Jeremy Schipper, 'Mosaic Disability and Identity in Exodus 4:10; 6:12, 30', *BibInt* 16 (2008): 428–41.

43. Tigay, '"Heavy of Mouth" and "Heavy of Tongue"', 59, 62.

44. Raphael, *Biblical Corpora*, 119.

45. John N. Oswalt, *The Book of Isaiah: Chapters 40–66*, NICOT (Grand Rapids: William B. Eerdmans, 1998), 383–4.

46. For example, see the quotations of James Muilenburg, David F. Payne, George Wöosung Wade, and Claus Westermann cited in Clines, *I, He, We, and They: A Literary Approach to Isaiah 53*, JSOTSup 1 (Sheffield: JSOT, 1976), 27.

47. We could argue that we know Song of Songs 4 describes the woman as beautiful because v. 1 begins the passage by stating, 'How beautiful you are, my love, how very beautiful!' We could also argue, however, that we know Isaiah 53 describes the servant as having a disability because v. 3 states that he was 'acquainted with diseases'.

48. 'The Poem of the Righteous Sufferer' uses rare and technical language for disease or disability to describe the righteous sufferer. Several of the terms appear elsewhere in Mesopotamian medical, ritual, or omen texts. Furthermore, the Mesopotamian commentary on the poem translates a number of these terms with other Akkadian words for illness, disease, or disability. See Amar Annus and Alan Lenzi, *Ludlul Bēl Nēmeqi*, State Archives of Assyria Cuneiform Texts 8 (Helsinki: The Neo-Assyrian Text Corpus Project, 2010), xxvii. Moreover, the initial portions of the poem praise the god Marduk as a healer. See D. J.

Wiseman, 'A New Text of the Babylonian Poem of the Righteous Sufferer', *Anatolian Studies* 30 (1980): 101–07.

49. William L. Holladay, *Isaiah: Scroll of a Prophetic Heritage* (Grand Rapids: William B. Eerdmans, 1978), 152 (emphasis added).

CHAPTER 2

1. On this topic, see Andrew Davies, 'Oratorio as Exegesis: The Use of the Book of Isaiah in Handel's *Messiah*', *BibInt* 15 (2007): 464–84.

2. Bernhard Duhm, *Die Theologie der Propheten als Grundlage für die innere Entwicklungsgeschichte der israelitischen Religion* (Bonn: Marcus, 1875); cf. *idem, Das Buch Jesaia uJbersetzt und erklärt* (Göttingen: Vandenhoeck & Ruprecht, 1922).

3. Duhm, *Das Buch Jesaia*, 396–401. See also Odil Hannes Steck, *Gottesknecht und Zion: Gesammelte Aufsätze zu Deuterojesaja*, FAT 4 (Tübingen: Mohr-Siebeck, 1992), 22; Claus Westermann, *Isaiah 40–66: A Commentary*, OTL, trans. David M. G. Stalker (Philadelphia: Westminster, 1969), 92.

4. On this issue, see the discussion and bibliography in Hector Avalos, *Illness and Health Care in the Ancient Near East: The Role of the Temple in Greece, Mesopotamia, and Israel*, HSM 54 (Atlanta: Scholars, 1995), 311–16; Richard N. Jones and David P. Wright, 'Leprosy', *ABD* 4.277–82.

5. Duhm, *Das Buch Jesaia*, 368.

6. See, among others, Johannes Lindblom, *The Servant Songs in Deutero-Isaiah: A New Attempt to Solve an Old Problem* (Lund: CWK Gleerup, 1951); James Muilenburg, 'Isaiah, Chapters 40–66', in G. A. Buttrick (ed.), *The Interpreter's Bible* (New York and Nashville: Abingdon, 1956), 406–08; Hugh G. M. Williamson, *Variations on a Theme: King, Messiah and Servant in the Book of Isaiah* (Carlisle: Paternoster, 1998), 131. For challenges to Duhm's 'servant songs' theory as well as a review of scholarship that questions the theory, see Hans M. Barstad, 'The Future of the "Servant Songs": Some Reflections on the Relationship of Biblical Scholarship to its own Tradition', in Samuel E. Balentine and John Barton (eds), *Language, Theology, and the Bible: Essays in Honour of James Barr* (Oxford: Claredon, 1994), 261–70; Tryggve N. D. Mettinger, *A Farewell to the Servant Songs: A Critical Examination of an Exegetical Axiom*, trans. Frederick H. Cryer (Lund: CWK Gleerup, 1983).

7. For example, see the discussion of Schian and Bertholet in Christopher R. North, *The Suffering Servant in Deutero-Isaiah: A Historical and Critical Study*, 2nd edn (London: Oxford University Press, 1956), 48–9.

8. Karl Budde, 'The So-Called "Ebed-Yahweh Songs," and the Meaning of the Term "Servant of Yahweh" in Isaiah, Chaps. 40–55', *AJT* 3 (1899): 503.

9. See Rebecca Raphael, 'Things Too Wonderful: A Disabled Reading of Job', *PRSt* 31 (2004): 400. This does not necessarily mean that theological and diagnostic frameworks represented mutually exclusive options in the ancient Near East. Mesopotamian cultures could attribute the source of an illness to a deity while still studying the illness through empirical observations and inductive experiments. See JoAnn Scurlock, *Magico-Medical Means of Treating Ghost-Induced Illnesses in Ancient Mesopotamia*, Ancient Magic and Divination 3 (Leiden: Brill, 2006), 77–81.

10. Avalos, *Illness and Health Care in the Ancient Near East*, 332.

11. Michael L. Barré, S.S., 'Textual and Rhetorical-critical Observations on the Last Servant Song (Isaiah 52:13–53:12)', *CBQ* 62 (2000): 13 n. 66.

12. J. J. M. Roberts, 'Hand of Yahweh', *VT* 21 (1971): 244–51; cf. René Labat, *Traité akkadien de diagnostics et prognostics médicaux*, 2 vols (Paris: Académie internationale d'histoire des sciences, 1951).

13. See the discussion in Avalos, *Illness and Health Care in the Ancient Near East*, 178–9.

14. Joseph Blenkinsopp, *Isaiah 40–55: A New Translation with Introduction and Commentary*, AB 19A (New York: Doubleday, 2000), 352.

15. For example, see William L. Holladay, *Isaiah: Scroll of a Prophetic Heritage* (Grand Rapids: William B. Eerdmans, 1978), 152.

16. John F. A. Sawyer, *Prophecy and the Biblical Prophets* (Oxford: Oxford University Press, 1993), 93.

17. Barré, 'Textual and Rhetorical-critical Observations on the Last Servant Song', 19 n. 94, with citations; cf. J. V. Kinnier Wilson, 'Leprosy in Ancient Mesopotamia', *RA* 60 (1966): 47–58.

18. On this omen and prayer, see, with citations, Avalos, *Illness and Health Care in the Ancient Near East*, 180–1.

19. For a more detailed treatment of skin anomalies in the Pentateuch, see Joel S. Baden and Candida R. Moss, 'The Origin and Interpretation of sara 'at in Leviticus 13-14', *JBL* (forthcoming).

20. For other possible connections between Isaiah 53 and Number 10–12, see Klaus Baltzer, *Deutero-Isaiah: A Commentary on Isaiah 40–55*, Hermeneia, trans. Margaret Kohl (Minneapolis: Fortress, 2001), 408–9. We should note, however, that unlike Miriam in Numbers 12, our passage does not include the servant as a member of the guilty party in Isaiah 53. Elsewhere, an individual's skin anomaly represents a household punishment (2 Sam 3:29).

21. See Louis Ginzberg, *The Legends of the Jews*, 7 vols, trans. Henrietta Szold and Paul Radin (Baltimore: The Johns Hopkins University Press, 1998), vol. 4, 272; vol. 6, 366 n. 72.

22. Jon D. Levenson, *Resurrection and the Restoration of Israel: The Ultimate Victory of the God of Life* (New Haven: Yale University Press, 2006), 174; cf. 38–9.

23. For detailed discussions of purity and impurity, see Jonathan Klawans, *Impurity and Sin in Ancient Judaism* (New York: Oxford University Press, 2000), 21–42; David P. Wright, 'The Spectrum of Priestly Impurity', in Gary A. Anderson and Saul M. Olyan (eds), *Priesthood and Cult in Ancient Israel*, JSOTSup 125 (Sheffield: JSOT Press, 1991); *idem*, 'Unclean and Clean (OT)', *ABD* 6: 729–41.

24. Jacob Milgrom, *Leviticus 1–16: A New Translation with Introduction and Commentary*, AB 3 (New York: Doubleday, 1991), 818.

25. David J. A. Clines, *I, He, We, and They: A Literary Approach to Isaiah 53*, JSOTSup 1 (Sheffield: JSOT, 1976), 27.

26. See Jeremy Schipper, *Disability Studies and the Hebrew Bible: Figuring Mephibosheth in the David Story* (New York: T & T Clark, 2006), 76.

27. Josef Scharbert, 'Stellvertretendes Sühneleiden in den Ebed-Jahwe-Lieden und in altorientalischen Ritualtexten', *BZ* 2 (1958): 190–213.

28. John H. Walton, 'The Imagery of the Substitute King Ritual in Isaiah's Fourth Servant Song', *JBL* 122 (2003): 737–9.

29. The best evidence for a humanly inflicted injury or fatality comes from the reference to 'bruises' (*brh*) in 53:5. This word describes humanly inflicted injuries in Gen 4:23 and Exod 21:25. Yet, this word also appears in Isa 1:6 in the context of a divinely inflicted 'striking' (*nkh*) and a 'sickness' (*ḥōli*) that seems consistent with the descriptions of divinely caused diseases mentioned earlier. It also appears in Ps 38:5 (Hebrew v. 6) in the context of a prayer for recovery from an illness. The context and genre of Isa 53:5 appear closer to Isaiah 1 and Psalm 38 than to Gen 4:23 or Exod 21:25.

30. Westermann, *Isaiah 40–66*, 258.

31. Barré, 'Textual and Rhetorical-critical Observations on the Last Servant Song', 25, 24.

32. Roger N. Whybray, *Thanksgiving for a Liberated Prophet: An Interpretation of Isaiah Chapter 53*, JSOTSup 4 (Sheffield: JSOT, 1978), 135.

33. Whybray, *Thanksgiving for a Liberated Prophet*, 96. On this particular interpretation, Whybray follows D. Winton Thomas, 'A Consideration of Some Unusual Ways of Expressing the Superlative in Hebrew', *VT* 18 (1953): 209–44.

34. John Goldingay and David Payne, *A Critical and Exegetical Commentary on Isaiah 40–55*, 2 vols, ICC (New York: T & T Clark International,

2006), vol. 2, 302. For a similar argument, see Westermann, *Isaiah 40–66*, 264.

35. See our discussion of this use of metaphor in Chapter 1.
36. We will discuss the Septuagint's translation of Isaiah 53 in greater detail in Chapter 3.
37. Gillis Gerleman, *Studien zur alttestamentlichen Theologie* (Heidelberg: Schneider, 1980), 41–2.
38. Whybray, *Thanksgiving for a Liberated Prophet*, 101.
39. Jan Alberto Soggin, 'Tod und Auferstehung des leidendes Gottes-Knechtes: Jesaja 53, 8–10', *ZAW* 85 (1975): 346–55.
40. See, among others, Clines, *I, He, We, and They*, 28; Harry M. Orlinksky, 'The So-Called "Servant of the Lord" and "Suffering Servant" in Second Isaiah', in Harry M. Orlinksky, *Studies on the Second Part of the Book of Isaiah*, VTSup 14 (Leiden: E. J. Brill, 1967), 62; Whybray, *Thanksgiving for a Liberated Prophet*, 103–4.
41. See Levenson, *Resurrection and the Restoration of Israel*, 76–8.
42. For example, see Mettinger, *A Farewell to the Servant Songs*, 41. For a review and critique of scholars who hold this position, see Bernd Janowski, 'He Bore Our Sins: Isaiah 53 and the Drama of Taking Another's Place', in Bernd Janowski and Peter Stuhlmacher (eds), *The Suffering Servant: Isaiah 53 in Jewish And Christian Sources*, trans. Daniel P. Bailey (Grand Rapids: William B. Eerdmans, 2004), 67–70.
43. See the discussion and overview of scholarly opinions in Goldingay and Payne, *A Critical and Exegetical Commentary on Isaiah 40–55*, vol. 2, 294–5.
44. In 1 Sam 9:24, the cook (or 'butcher/slaughterer' [a noun form of *tbh*]) gives Saul the thigh portion of the meat. According to Num 18:18, the right thigh of a sacrificed animal was reserved for priests. Nonetheless, although 1 Sam 9:24 may invoke a ritual sacrifice involving priests, it does not reflect any of the sacrifices discussed in the ritual texts of the Pentateuch.
45. Isaiah 34:6 may contain the one exception that proves the rule since the word 'slaughter' parallels the phrase 'sacrifice (*zbh*) to the LORD', which suggests a ritual sacrifice (Exod 13:15; 1 Sam 15:15; 1 Kgs 8:63; Jon 1:16). Ritual texts throughout the Pentateuch use the word 'sacrifice (*zbh*)' repeatedly in the context of ritual sacrifices for various offerings, especially peace offerings, performed by priests (Exod 29:28; Lev 3:1; 4:10; 22:21; Num 7:17; 10:10; Deut 27:7).
46. See, Fredrick Hägglund, *Isaiah 53 in the Light of Homecoming after Exile*, FAT 31 (Tübingen: Mohr-Siebeck, 2008), 67–73, 98–9, with citations; Bernd Janowski, 'He Bore Our Sins', 65–70.

47. Janowski, 'He Bore Our Sins', 68–9.
48. The similarities between Isaiah 53 and 1 Samuel 6 do not determine whether the use of *ʾšm* in 53:10 reflects the use of this word in 1 Samuel 6 rather than Leviticus. As we noted earlier, the word translated as 'plagued' in Isa 53:4 and 8 in both its noun and verb forms appears sixty-one times in Leviticus 13–14. As in Isa 53:5, the word 'heal' (*rpʾ*) occurs repeatedly during discussions of the healing of ritual impurities (Lev 13:18, 37; 14:3, 48) and the *ʾšm* required for their accompanying purification (Lev 14:12–31).
49. We will further discuss how some translations and interpretations find references to a healing of the servant in Chapter 3.
50. See Saul M. Olyan, *Disability and the Hebrew Bible: Interpreting Mental and Physical Differences* (New York: Cambridge University Press, 2008), 10–12, 28–9, 84–5.
51. Olyan, *Disability and the Hebrew Bible*, 85.
52. This promise also appears in a Greek text from a much later period. Wisdom 3:14 declares, 'Blessed also is the eunuch whose hands have done no lawless deed, and who has not devised wicked things against the Lord; for special favor will be shown him for his faithfulness, and a place of great delight in the temple of the Lord.'
53. Hägglund, *Isaiah 53 in the Light of Homecoming after Exile*, 100–1.
54. See Jeremy Schipper, 'Healing and Silence in the Epilogue of Job', *Word and World* 30 (2010): 16–22.
55. See the comment in Olyan, *Disability and the Hebrew Bible*, 9–10, 134 n. 28.
56. For a survey of scholarly proposals regarding the genre of Isaiah 53, see Jan Leunis Koole, *Isaiah, Part III*, Historical Commentary on the Old Testament (Kampen: Kok Pharos, 1997), 260–2.
57. See Hermann Gunkel, *Introduction to the Psalms: The Genres of the Religious Lyric of Israel*, completed by Joachim Begrich, trans. James D. Nogalski (Macon: Mercer University Press, 1998), 199–221.
58. Gunkel, *Introduction to the Psalms*, 199 n. 2.
59. Gunkel, *Introduction to the Psalms*, 202.
60. Gunkel, *Introduction to the Psalms*, 203.
61. Hermann Gunkel, *The Psalms: A Form-Critical Introduction*, trans. Thomas M. Horner (Philadelphia: Fortress, 1967), 17 (italics added).
62. See the references provided in Whybray, *Thanksgiving for a Liberated Prophet*, 169 n. 106.
63. Joachim Begrich, *Studien zu Deuterojesaja* (München: C. Kaiser, 1963), 62–5.
64. Begrich, *Studien zu Deuterojesaja*, 64.

65. Brevard S. Childs, *Isaiah: A Commentary*, OTL (Louisville: Westminster John Knox, 2001), 417.

66. Begrich, *Studien zu Deuterojesaja* , 145–51.

67. Otto Kaiser, *Der königliche Knecht; eine traditionsgeschichtlich-exegetische Studie über die Ebed-Jahwe-Lieder bei Deuterojesaja* (Göttingen: Vandenhoeck & Ruprecht, 1959), 88.

68. Recently, several scholars have studied how Second Isaiah, including Isaiah 53, responds to the material in the book of Lamentations. See Tod Linafelt, *Surviving Lamentations: Catastrophe, Lament, and Protest in the Afterlife of a Biblical Book* (Chicago: University of Chicago Press, 2000), 62–79, with citations; Jill Middlemas, 'Did Second Isaiah Write Lamentations III'?, *VT* 56 (2006): 506–25; Benjamin Sommer, *A Prophet Reads Scripture: Allusion in Isaiah 40–66* (Stanford: Stanford University Press, 1998), 127–30; Patricia Tull Willey, *Remember the Former Things: The Recollection of Previous Texts in Second Isaiah*, SBLDS 161 (Atlanta: Society of Biblical Literature, 1997), 209–28.

69. G. R. Driver, 'Isaiah 52:13–53:12: The Servant of the Lord', in Matthew Black and Georg Fohrer (eds), *In memoriam Paul Kahle*, BZAW 103 (Berlin: A. Töpelmann, 1968), 95; Whybray, *Thanksgiving for a Liberated Prophet*, 134–9.

70. Whybray, *Thanksgiving for a Liberated Prophet*, 10–12.

71. Whybray, *Thanksgiving for a Liberated Prophet*, 134–9.

72. For example, see the scholars cited by Barré, 'Textual and Rhetorical-critical Observations on the Last Servant Song', 17 n. 82.

73. See Westermann, *Isaiah 40–66*, 254, 257.

74. Roy F. Melugin, *The Formation of Isaiah 40–55*, BZAW 141 (Berlin: Walter de Gruyter, 1976), 74.

75. Paul D. Hanson, *Isaiah 40–66*, Interpretation (Louisville: John Knox, 1995), 153–4.

76. See our discussion of the *Hodayot* in relation to Isaiah 53 in Chapter 3. In fairness to Gunkel, the Dead Sea Scrolls were discovered years after his death. Furthermore, we may explain how the use of the *Hodayot* in the Qumran community differs from Gunkel's proposal by noting that the *Hodayot* imitate the genre seen in the biblical texts rather than reflect an example of this genre from ancient Israel.

77. For example, see Muilenburg, 'Isaiah, Chapters 40–66', 622; Westermann, *Isaiah 40–66*, 262.

78. For a helpful discussion of this topic with a focus on Victorian literature, see Martha Stoddard Holmes, *Fictions of Affliction: Physical Disability in Victorian Culture* (Ann Arbor: University of Michigan Press, 2004).

CHAPTER 3

1. For example, while the Hebrew in the Masoretic version of v. 11 reads 'he will see', the NRSV follows the Greek manuscripts and the Hebrew manuscripts from the Dead Sea Scrolls that both read 'he will see light'.
2. For example, see Michael L. Barré, S.S., 'Textual and Rhetorical-critical Observations on the Last Servant Song (Isaiah 52:13–53:12)', *CBQ* 62 (2000): 1–27. For a detailed discussion and bibliography, see also John Goldingay and David Payne, *A Critical and Exegetical Commentary on Isaiah 40–55*, 2 vols, ICC (New York: T & T Clark International, 2006), vol. 2, 288–336.
3. For the Hebrew text of 1QIsa^a as well as a bibliography of scholarship on 1QIsa^a, see Donald W. Parry and Elisha Qimron (eds), *The Great Isaiah Scroll (1QIsa^a): A New Edition*, Studies on the Texts of the Desert of Judah 32 (Leiden: Brill, 1999).
4. Martin Hengel with Daniel P. Bailey, 'The Effective History of Isaiah 53 in the Pre-Christian Period', in Bernd Janowski and Peter Stuhlmacher (eds), *The Suffering Servant: Isaiah 53 in Jewish and Christian Sources*, trans. Daniel P. Bailey (Grand Rapids: Eerdmans, 2004), 105.
5. In addition to a priestly or prophetic figure, Hengel also observes that Ps 45:7 uses very similar vocabulary and syntax to that of Isa 52:14 when the Psalm describes a king: 'Therefore God, your God, has anointed you with the oil of gladness unlike your companions'. See Hengel, 'The Effective History of Isaiah 53 in the Pre-Christian Period', 104–5. Unlike Isa 52:14, this Psalm describes the king's appearance as exceedingly handsome. Ps 45:2 states, 'You are the most handsome of mortals (Hebrew: *mbny 'dm*).' Ps 45:2 and Isa 52:14 are the only verses in the Hebrew Bible that compare a person's appearance to the rest of humanity with the Hebrew phrase *mbny 'dm*. Yet, Psalm 45 describes a king as having a handsome rather than marred appearance. If the use of 'anointed' in 1QIsa^a connects the servant with a royal figure like the one in Psalm 45, it further distances the imagery in Isa 52:14 from a description of disability.
6. Dominique Barthélemy, *Critique textuelle de l'Ancien Testament*, 4 vols (Göttingen: Vandenhoeck & Ruprecht, 1982–2005), vol. 2, 387–90. For critiques of Barthélemy's argument, see Joseph Blenkinsopp, *Opening the Sealed Book: Interpretations of the Book of Isaiah in Late Antiquity* (Grand Rapids: William B. Eerdmans, 2006), 268.
7. For a more detailed discussion of the influence of Leviticus 21 on non-biblical texts from the Dead Sea Scrolls, see Johanna Dorman, *The*

Blemished Body: Deformity and Disability in the Qumran Scrolls (Groningen: Rijksuniversiteit, 2007), 15–47, 243–5; cf. Saul M. Olyan, *Disability in the Hebrew Bible: Interpreting Mental and Physical Differences* (New York: Cambridge University Press, 2008), 101–18.

8. Hengel observes that a priestly anointing would help make sense of the Hebrew rendering of the first line of 52:15 as 'so shall he sprinkle many nations' (cf. the Greek translations by Aquila and Theodorion), rather than 'he will startle many nations' as we discussed in Chapter 2. See Hengel, 'The Effective History of Isaiah 53 in the Pre-Christian Period', 104.

9. For connections between Isa 53:11 and 57:1–2, see Blenkinsopp, *Opening the Sealed Book*, 258–9.

10. We do not mean to suggest that Zechariah 12 alludes to Isaiah 53 specifically as some scholars have. For example, see Hengel, 'The Effective History of Isaiah 53 in the Pre-Christian Period', 85–90. The vocabulary does not overlap much and the violent imagery remains too vague to support a clear connection between the two texts. Instead, we are suggesting that 1QIsa^a may interpret the servant according to a general profile for a fatally wounded figure reflected in texts and traditions available by the Second Temple period.

11. For a review of scholarly opinions of this issue, see Blenkinsopp, *Opening the Sealed Book*, 271 n. 46; John J. Collins, 'Teacher and Servant', *RHPR* 80 (2000): 37–50.

12. The referencing system and translations, with some modifications, for the non-biblical texts from the Dead Sea Scrolls come from Florentino García Martínez and Eibert J. C. Tigchelaar (eds), *The Dead Sea Scrolls: Study Edition*, 2 vols (Leiden: Brill, 1997–8).

13. Blenkinsopp, *Opening the Sealed Book*, 271. Collins cites allusions to Jer 20:9 in 1QH^a XVI 30 to argue that the narrator does not identify himself as the servant in Isaiah any more than he identifies himself as the prophet Jeremiah. Rather, both of these prophetic figures inform the narrator's self presentation. See Collins, 'Teacher and Servant', 47.

14. For a detailed discussion of this hymn, see Esther Eshel, '4Q471b: A Self-Glorification Hymn', *RevQ* 17 (1996): 175–203.

15. Blenkinsopp, *Opening the Sealed Book*, 279; Israel Knohl, *The Messiah before Jesus: The Suffering Servant of the Dead Sea Scrolls*, trans David Maisel (Berkeley: University of California Press, 2000), 15–18; cf. 44–5; *idem*, 'The Suffering Servant: from Isaiah to the Dead Sea Scrolls', in Deborah A. Green and Laura S. Lieber (eds), *Scriptural Exegesis: The Shapes of Culture and the Religious Imagination: Essays in Honour of Michael Fishbane* (Oxford: Oxford University Press, 2009), 89–104.

16. Blenkinsopp, *Opening the Sealed Book*, 279.
17. Knohl argues that the line 'who bears all sorrows like me?' is a claim that the narrator has 'the capacity to bear physical suffering' (*The Messiah before Jesus*, 17–18; cf. *idem*, 'The Suffering Servant', 97). Yet the Hebrew word translated as 'sorrows', which Knohl translates as 'afflictions', has too wide a semantic range to argue that it refers specifically to a physical condition.
18. For a detailed discussion of the LXX's rendering of Isaiah 53, see Karen H. Jobes and Moisés Silva, *Invitation to the Septuagint* (Grand Rapids: Baker Academic, 2000), 215–27, with citations.
19. Hengel, 'The Effective History of Isaiah 53 in the Pre-Christian Period', 125.
20. Jobes and Moisés Silva, *Invitation to the Septuagint*, 221; cf. their discussion of vv. 8, 10 on pp. 224, 226; cf. David A. Sapp, 'The LXX. 1QIsa, and MT Versions of Isaiah 53 and the Christian Doctrine of Atonement', in William H. Bellinger and William R. Farmer (eds), *Jesus and the Suffering Servant: Isaiah 53 and Christian Origins* (Harrisburg: Trinity, 1998), 180–2.
21. This phrase, which does not appear in the Hebrew versions of Job, may suggest an attempt to make a physical restoration more explicit than in the Hebrew versions. The LXX uses the same term (*plege*) to translate the Hebrew word for 'suffering' in Job 2:13, although we could translate the Greek word *plege* as 'affliction' or 'ordeal' as well as 'plague' or 'wound'.
22. For example, see Jobes and Moisés Silva, *Invitation to the Septuagint*, 226; Ronald L. Troxel, *LXX-Isaiah as Translation and Interpretation: The Strategies of the Translator of the Septuagint of Isaiah*, JSJSup 124 (Leiden: Brill, 2008), 206; cf. Karl Friedrich Euler, who suggests that the Septuagint translates the verb as if it was a form of the Hebrew root *zkh* meaning 'clean' (*Die verkündigung vom leidenden Gottesknecht aud Jes 53 in der griechischen Bibel* [Berlin: W. Kohlhammer, 1934], 79).
23. For a review of scholarly opinions, see Jostein Ådna, 'The Servant of Isaiah 53 as Triumphant and Interceding Messiah: The Reception of Isaiah 52:13–53:12 in the Targum of Isaiah with Special Attention to the Concept of Messiah', in Janowski and Stuhlmacher (eds), *The Suffering Servant*, 190–4.
24. Ådna, 'The Servant of Isaiah 53 as Triumphant and Interceding Messiah', 190–1; cf. Bruce D. Chilton, *The Isaiah Targum: Introduction, Translation, Apparatus and Notes*, ArBib 11 (Wilmington: Michael Glazier, 1987), 105.

25. All translations of the Targum of Isaiah come from Chilton, *The Isaiah Targum*, 103–5 (italics removed).
26. Blenkinsopp, *Opening the Sealed Book*, 267.
27. See Harold L. Ginsberg, 'The Oldest Interpretation of the Suffering Servant', *VT* 3 (1953): 400–4.
28. See the discussion of several of these passages in Walther Zimmerli and Joachim Jeremias, *The Servant of God*, SBT 20, trans. Harold Knight (London: SCM Press, 1957), 50–60, 79–104; Hans Walter Wolff, *Jesaja 53 im Urchristentum*, with an introduction by Peter Stuhlmacher (Giessen: Brunnen Verlag, 1984). Wolff argues that the early church understood Jesus' death as fulfilling Isaiah 53 (pp. 86–103). By contrast, Morna D. Hooker argues that Isaiah 53 does not play a significant role in how the gospels understood the meaning of Jesus' death. See Morna D. Hooker, *Jesus and the Servant: The Influence of the Servant Concept of Deutero-Isaiah in the New Testament* (London: SPCK, 1959); idem, 'Did the Use of Isaiah 53 to Interpret His Mission Begin with Jesus?', in Bellinger and Farmer (eds), *Jesus and the Suffering Servant*, 88–103; idem, 'Response to Mikeal Parsons', in Bellinger and Farmer (eds), *Jesus and the Suffering Servant*, 120–4.
29. Some scholars distinguish between 'allusion' and 'intertextuality'. Allusion refers to an intentional reference to an earlier text, person, or event by the author(s) or editor(s) of a later text. Intertextuality refers to a connection between two or more texts, persons, or events that an interpreter makes regardless of authorial or editorial intention. For more detailed discussions, see G. Brooke Lester, 'Daniel Evokes Isaiah: The Rule of the Nations in Apocalyptic Allusion-Narrative' (Ph.D. diss., Princeton Theological Seminary, 2007), 5–27; Benjamin Sommer, *A Prophet Reads Scripture: Allusion in Isaiah 40–66* (Stanford: Stanford University Press, 1998), 6–31. For example, following the model of the Protestant reformer John Calvin, John D. W. Watts cites numerous New Testament passages that may connect with Isaiah 53 even though many of these texts do not allude to our passage as clearly as others. See John D. W. Watts, *Isaiah 34–66*, rev. edn, WBC 25 (Nashville: Nelson Reference & Electronic, 2005), 792–4. Other scholars make connections between the servant in Isaiah 53 and other biblical characters but state clearly that the biblical authors or editors may not have intended such connections. For example, see David M. Gunn, 'Samson of Sorrows: An Isaianic Gloss on Judges 13–16', in Danna Nolan Fewell (ed.), *Reading between Texts: Intertextuality and the Hebrew Bible* (Louisville: Westminster/John Knox, 1992), 225–53.

30. For a detailed discussion of this issue, see Maarten J. J. Menten, 'The Source of the Quotation of Isaiah 53:4 in Matthew 8:17', *NovT* 39 (1997): 313–27, with citations.

31. Menten observes, 'while the servant of Isaiah 53 is himself plagued by illness, the Matthean Jesus is not, but he removes the diseases others are suffering from'. He goes on to critique unconvincing attempts by scholars to resolve this difference between Matthew and Isaiah. See Menten, 'The Source of the Quotation of Isaiah 53:4 in Matthew 8:17', 324.

32. Ulrich Luz, *Matthew 8–20: A Commentary*, 3 vols, Hermeneia, trans. James E. Crouch (Minneapolis: Fortress Press, 2001), vol. 2, 14.

33. Although John attributes this quotation to the prophet Isaiah, it is unclear whether the quotation comes from the book of Isaiah or another early Christian source since variations of this quotation also appear in Matthew, Mark, and Luke.

34. Mark 15:28 seems to have been added to Mark under the influence of Luke 22:37. Mark 15:28 follows the Greek wording of Luke 22:37's citation of Isa 53:12 rather than the LXX's translation of Isa 53:12. The absence of 15:28 in Sinaiticus and its agreement with Luke over the LXX suggests that it is a secondary addition to Mark. For further discussion of the manuscript evidence for Mark 15:28, see Adela Yarbro Collins, *Mark: A Commentary*, Hermeneia (Minneapolis: Fortress, 2007), 730, n. c.

35. The New Testament describes Jesus' post resurrection body as physically scarred. Citing Luke 24:36–9 (cf. John 20:19–28), Nancy L. Eiesland writes, 'In changing the symbol of Christ, from that of suffering servant, model of virtuous suffering, or conquering lord, toward a formulation of Jesus Christ as disabled God, I draw implications for the ritual and doctrine of the Eucharist based on this new symbol. . . . In presenting his impaired hands and feet to his startled friends, the resurrected Jesus is revealed as the disabled God.' See Nancy L. Eiesland, *The Disabled God: Toward a Liberatory Theology of Disability* (Nashville: Abingdon, 1994), 94, 100. Eiesland focuses on Jesus' body as a sacramental symbol. Correctly, she does not claim that, through his crucifixion wounds, he acquires a disability in terms of a social experience.

36. For a discussion of several of these texts, see Blenkinsopp, *Opening the Sealed Book*, 46–55, with citations.

37. Mikeal C. Parsons argues that the eunuch may have identified with the servant in Isa 53:7–8 because they shared similar social experiences of oppression related to their physical impairments. Both characters would have been considered polluted. See Mikael C. Parsons, 'Isaiah 53 in Acts 8: A Reply to Morna Hooker', in Bellinger and Farmer (eds), *Jesus and the Suffering Servant*, 111–15; *idem, Body and Character in Luke and Acts:*

The Subversion of Physiognomy in Early Christianity (Grand Rapids: Baker Academic, 2006), 138–40.

38. For a detailed treatment of 1 Clem 16:3–14 in relationship to the LXX's translation of Isa 53:1–12, see Daniel P. Bailey, 'Appendix: Isaiah 53 in Codex A Text of 1 Clement 16:3–14', in Janowski and Stuhlmacher (eds), *The Suffering Servant*, 321–3.

39. Wolff argues that 1 Clement does not quote the servant's exaltation in Isa 52:13–15 in order to keep the focus on humility (Wolff, *Jesaja 53 im Urchristentum*, 108).

40. J. Ross Wagner, *Heralds of the Good News: Isaiah and Paul in Concert*, NovTSup 101 (Leiden: Brill, 2002), 333–4. Wagner's book provides detailed studies of the quotations of Isaiah 53 in Romans.

41. Jorge Pixley, 'Isaiah 52:13–53:12: A Latin American Perspective', in John R. Levison and Priscilla Pope-Levison (eds), *Return to Babel: Global Perspectives on the Bible* (Louisville: Westminster John Knox, 1999), 93–100.

42. François Kabasele Lumbala, 'Isaiah 52:13–53:12: An African Perspective', in *Return to Babel*, 101–6; Cyris Heesuk Moon, 'Isaiah 52:13–53:12: An Asian Perspective', in Levinson and Pope-Levison, *Return to Babel*, 107–13.

43. Lumbala, 'Isaiah 52:13–53:12: An African Perspective', 101.

CHAPTER 4

1. Christopher R. North, *The Suffering Servant in Deutero-Isaiah: A Historical and Critical Study*, 2nd edn (London: Oxford University Press, 1956).

2. Kristin Joachimsen, 'Steck's Five Stories of the Servant in Isaiah lii 13-liii 12, and Beyond', *VT* 57 (2007): 220.

3. See Walther Zimmerli and Joachim Jeremias, *The Servant of God*, SBT 20, trans. Harold Knight (London: SCM Press, 1957), 62–4, with citations.

4. John F. A. Sawyer, *The Fifth Gospel: Isaiah in the History of Christianity* (Cambridge: Cambridge University Press, 1996), 91.

5. We also find the Talmudic image of a 'leper messiah' in popular music, although without any obvious reference to Isaiah 53 or a figure with disabilities. In David Bowie's classic song, 'Ziggy Stardust' the 'leper messiah' reference describes the hollowness of celebrity rock stardom rather than a person with disability (David Bowie. 'Ziggy Stardust', The Rise and Fall of Ziggy Stardust and the Spiders from Mars, RCA Records, 1972). The band Metallica's song titled 'Leper Messiah'

describes a corrupt but presumably able-bodied televangelist (Metallica, 'Leper Messiah', Master of Puppets, Elektra Records, 1986).

6. Martha Himmelfarb, 'Sefer Zerubbabel', in David Stern and Mark J. Mirsky (eds), *Rabbinic Fantasies: Imaginative Narratives from Classical Hebrew Literature* (New Haven: Yale University Press, 1990), 72. Himmelfarb provides an introduction and translation of Sefer Zerubbabel.

7. For a detailed discussion of Ashkenazi as well as modern scholars who connect the servant with Job, see Alan Cooper, 'The Suffering Servant and Job: A View from the Sixteenth Century', in Clairia Mathews McGillis and Patricia K. Tull (eds), *'As Those Who are Taught': The Reception of Isaiah from the LXX to the SBL*, SBLSymS 27 (Atlanta: Society of Biblical Literature, 2006), 189–200.

8. On Bahrdt's, Konyenburg's, and Augusti's interpretations, see North, *The Suffering Servant in Deutero-Isaiah*, 39–41.

9. Samuel R. Driver and Adolf Neubauer, *The Fifty-Third Chapter of Isaiah according to the Jewish Interpreters* (Oxford and London: James Parker and Company, 1877), 409.

10. For example, in addition to Ya'qob Yoseph Mord'khai Hayyim Passani, see also the interpretation of the servant in relation to Hezekiah by Sa'adyah Ibn Danân (fifteenth century CE) in Driver and Neubauer, *The Fifty-Third Chapter of Isaiah*, 202–16.

11. Karl Budde, 'The So-Called "Ebed-Yahweh Songs", and the Meaning of the Term "Servant of Yahweh" in Isaiah, Chaps. 40–55', *AJT* 3 (1899): 503.

12. See Richard Kraetzschmar, *Das Buch Ezechiel übersetzt und erklärt* (Göttingen: Vandenhoeck & Ruprecht, 1900), 46.

13. Walther Zimmerli, 'Zur Vorgeschichte von Jes 53', in *Studien zur alttestamentlichen Theologie und Prophetie* (München: Kaiser, 1974), 213–21; cf. Fredrick Hägglund, *Isaiah 53 in the Light of Homecoming after Exile*, FAT 31 (Tübingen: Mohr-Siebeck, 2008), 89–90; Henning Graf Reventlow, 'Basic Issues in the Interpretation of Isaiah 53', in William H. Bellinger and William R. Farmer (eds), *Jesus and the Suffering Servant: Isaiah 53 and Christian Origins* (Harrisburg: Trinity, 1998), 36–7.

14. Lauri Itkonen, *Deuterojesaja (Jes. 40–55) metrisch untersucht* (Helsinki: Finnischen Literatur-Gesellschaft, 1916), 81–2.

15. John Skinner, *The Book of the Prophet Isaiah: Chapters XL–LXVI*, CBC (Cambridge: Cambridge University Press, 1954), 139–41.

16. John F. A. Sawyer, *Prophecy and the Biblical Prophets* (Oxford: Oxford University Press, 1993), 92–5.

17. Michael L. Barré, S.S., 'Textual and Rhetorical-critical Observations on the Last Servant Song (Isaiah 52:13–53:12)', *CBQ* 62 (2000): 19.

18. Ernst Sellin, *Mose und seine Bedeutung für die israelitisch-jüdische Religionsgeschichte* (Leipzig: Deichert, 1922), 134–5.

19. Klaus Baltzer, *Deutero-Isaiah: A Commentary on Isaiah 40–55*, Hermeneia, trans. Margaret Kohl (Minneapolis: Fortress, 2001), 407.

20. On these sources, see Jan Assmann, *Moses the Egyptian: The Memory of Egypt in Western Monotheism* (Cambridge, MA: Harvard University Press, 1997), 29–44, with citations.

21. Beverly J. Stratton, 'Engaging Metaphors: Suffering with Zion and the Servant in Isaiah 52–53', in Stephen E. Fowl (ed.), *The Theological Interpretation of Scripture: Classic and Contemporary Readings* (Cambridge: Blackwell, 1997), 228–9.

22. Stratton, 'Engaging Metaphors', 228.

23. Stratton, 'Engaging Metaphors', 228. Nevertheless, Isa 53:10 presents problems for identifying the servant as a eunuch since it states 'he shall see his offspring'. The reference to the servant's children seems odd unless we imagine him having children before becoming a eunuch. Such speculation, however, creates a back story for the servant that goes far beyond what Isaiah 53 states.

24. For detailed discussions of Justin's use of Isaiah 53, see D. Jeffrey Bingham, 'Justin and Isaiah 53', *VC* 53 (2000): 248–61. Daniel P. Bailey, '"Our Suffering and Crucified Messiah" (Dial. III.2): Justin Martyr's Allusions to Isaiah 53 in His Dialogue with Trypho with Special Reference to the New Edition of M. Marcovich', in Bernd Janowski and Peter Stuhlmacher (eds), *The Suffering Servant: Isaiah 53 in Jewish And Christian Sources*, trans. Daniel P. Bailey (Grand Rapids: William B. Eerdmans, 2004), 324–417. The following discussion of Justin, Origen, and Aphrahat relies heavily on Christoph Markschies, 'Jesus Christ as a Man before God: Two Interpretative Models for Isaiah 53 in the Patristic Literature and Their Development', in Janowski and Stuhlmacher (eds), *The Suffering Servant*, 225–323.

25. See Markschies, 'Jesus Christ as a Man before God', 265–6.

26. Modern biblical scholars use this type of argument to support the identification of the servant as an individual rather than a collective reference. For example, see the discussion of Isa 40:2b; 43:23b; 53:9b in Hans Walter Wolff, 'Wer ist der Gottesknecht in Jesaja 53?' *EvT* 22 (1962): 340–1.

27. See Markschies, 'Jesus Christ as a Man before God', 288–9.

28. See Markschies, 'Jesus Christ as a Man before God', 269–70.

29. For a concise review of this period, see North, *The Suffering Servant in Deutero-Isaiah*, 26–7.

30. Sawyer, *The Fifth Gospel*, 83.

31. For a helpful overview of these and other Christian interpreters' use of Isaiah, including chapter 53, see Brevard S. Childs, *The Struggle to Understand Isaiah as Christian Scripture* (Grand Rapids: William B. Eerdmans, 2004); Mark W. Elliot (ed.), *Isaiah 40–66*, ACCS 11 (Downers Grove: InterVarsity, 2007), 154–73; Robert Louis Wilken (ed.), *Isaiah: Interpreted by Early Christian and Medieval Commentators*, The Church's Bible (Grand Rapids: William B. Eerdmans, 2007), 416–30.

32. See James H. Marrow, *Passion Iconography in Northern European Art of the Late Middle Ages and Early Renaissance: A Study of the Transformation of Sacred Metaphor into Descriptive Narrative* (Kortrijk: Van Ghemmert, 1979), 54–7; cf. Martin O'Kane, 'Picturing "The Man of Sorrows": The Passion-Filled Afterlives of a Biblical Icon', *RelArts* 9 (2005): 62–100.

33. Sawyer, *The Fifth Gospel*, 83. Sawyer provides an overview of artistic uses of Isaiah 53 from the twelfth century onward (pp. 83–99).

34. Cooper, 'The Suffering Servant and Job', 198.

35. For several of these Jewish messianic interpretations, see Driver and Neubauer, *The Fifty-Third Chapter of Isaiah*. For a more concise summary, see North, *The Suffering Servant in Deutero-Isaiah*, 11–17.

36. For a detailed discussion, see Jeremy Schipper, *Disability Studies and the Hebrew Bible: Figuring Mephibosheth in the David Story* LHBOTS 441 (New York: T & T Clark, 2006), 79–87.

37. Ernst Sellin, *Studien zur Entstehungsgeschichte der jüdischen Gemeinde nach dem babylonischen Exil. I. Der Knecht Gottes bei Deuterojesaja* (Leipzig: Deichert, 1901).

38. Michael D. Goulder, 'Behold my servant Jehoiachin', *VT* 52 (2002): 178–9, 181.

39. For example, see Johannes Lindblom, *The Servant Songs in Deutero-Isaiah: A New Attempt to Solve an Old Problem* (Lund: CWK Gleerup, 1951), 75–93; cf. Antti Laato, *The Servant of YHWH and Cyrus: A Reinterpretation of the Exilic Messianic Programme of Isaiah 40–55*, ConBOT 35 (Stockholm: Almqvist & Wiksell, 1992). For earlier scholars who identify the servant as Cyrus, see North, *The Suffering Servant in Deutero-Isaiah*, 57.

40. See North, *The Suffering Servant in Deutero-Isaiah*, 42, 49–50, 89–90. More recently, see John D. W. Watts, *Isaiah 34–66*, rev. edn, WBC 25 (Nashville: Nelson Reference & Electronic, 2005), 757–61 with citations.

41. See Louis Ginzberg, *The Legends of the Jews*, 7 vols, trans. Henrietta Szold and Paul Radin, (Baltimore: The Johns Hopkins University Press,

1998), vol. 4, 160; vol. 6, 297 n. 71; cf. Lynn Holden, *Forms of Deformity*, JSOTSup 131 (Sheffield: Sheffield Academic Press, 1991), 279.

42. Driver and Neubauer, *The Fifty-Third Chapter of Isaiah*, 192 (italics removed).

43. Wolfgang M. W. Roth, 'The Anonymity of the Suffering Servant', *JBL* 83 (1964): 179 (emphasis original).

44. See Driver and Neubauer, *The Fifty-Third Chapter of Isaiah*, 153, 287–8.

45. For example, see Ronald E. Clements, 'Isaiah 53 and the Restoration of Israel', in Bellinger and Farmer, *Jesus and the Suffering Servant*, 47–54.

46. Although Sellin abandoned this theory, it influenced Sigmund Freud's work. See Sigmund Freud, *Moses and Monotheism*, trans. Katherine Jones (New York: Vintage, 1939), 42–4.

47. Baltzer, *Deutero-Isaiah*, 20–21; ; cf. *idem*, 'The Book of Isaiah', *HTR* 103 (2010): 267-8.

48. C. Chavesse, 'The Suffering Servant and Moses', *CQR* 165 (1964): 152–63.

49. Gerhard von Rad, *Old Testament Theology*, vol. 2: *The Theology of Israel's Prophetic Traditions*, trans. D. M. G. Stalker (London: Oliver and Boyd, 1965), 257.

50. See this chapter's epigram, which comes from von Rad, *Old Testament Theology*, vol. 2, 258.

51. von Rad, *Old Testament Theology*, vol. 2, 259.

52. Christopher R. Seitz, 'The Book of Isaiah 40–66: Introduction, Commentary, and Reflections', *NIB* 6: 464.

53. Gordon P. Hugenberger, 'The Servant of the Lord in the "Servant Songs" of Isaiah: A Second Moses Figure', in Richard Hess, Philip E. Satterthwaite, and Gordon Wenham (eds), *The Lord's Anointed: Interpretation of Old Testament Messianic Texts* (Grand Rapids: Baker, 1995), 129–38.

54. On allusions to Jeremiah in Isaiah 53, see Benjamin Sommer, *A Prophet Reads Scripture: Allusion in Isaiah 40–66* (Stanford: Stanford University Press, 1998), 64–6, 93–6.

55. Bernhard Duhm, *Die Theologie der Propheten als Grundlage für die innere Entwicklungsgeschichte der israelitischen Religion* (Bonn: Marcus, 1875), 287–92.

56. See the references provided in Patricia Tull Willey, *Remember the Former Things: The Recollection of Previous Texts in Second Isaiah*, SBLDS 161 (Atlanta: Society of Biblical Literature, 1997), 193 n. 16.

57. Driver and Neubauer, *The Fifty-Third Chapter of Isaiah*, 153–4.

58. On Grotius, Collins, and Bunsen, see North, *The Suffering Servant in Deutero-Isaiah*, 26–7, 41.

59. Brevard S. Childs, *Isaiah: A Commentary*, OTL (Louisville: Westminster John Knox, 2001), 414.

60. Childs, *Isaiah: A Commentary*, 417.

61. Childs, *Isaiah: A Commentary*, 414, 417. Beyond Childs, we find many other scholars who apply this imagery to subjects far beyond people with disabilities. For example, rather than an individual or group, James M. Ward writes that the servant 'is an office that anyone can fill'. See James M. Ward, 'The Servant Songs in Isaiah', *RevExp* 65 (1968): 141.

62. The phrase 'under the weight of your hand' (or 'from before your hand') in Jer 15:17 may imply a divinely induced physical condition as the phrase 'hand of the LORD' sometimes does (Exod 9:3; 1 Sam 5:6, 9). See J. J. M. Roberts, 'Hand of Yahweh', *VT* 21 (1971): 244–51. Yet this interpretation of Jer 15:17 appears unlikely because of the surrounding context of the verse.

63. Childs, *Isaiah*, 414.

64. There may have been female prophets within the Isaianic tradition (cf. Isa 8:3).

65. See North, *The Suffering Servant in Deutero-Isaiah*, 75.

66. Sigmund Mowinckel, *Der Knecht Jahwäs* (Giessen: Alfred Töpelmann, 1921).

67. Joseph Blenkinsopp, *Isaiah 40–55: A New Translation with Introduction and Commentary*, AB 19A (New York: Doubleday, 2000), 356.

68. Budde, 'The So-Called "Ebed-Yahweh Songs," and the Meaning of the Term "Servant of Yahweh" in Isaiah, Chaps. 40–55'.

69. For a concise review, see North, *The Suffering Servant in Deutero-Isaiah*, 17–20, 28–31, 57–62, 103–19.

70. Driver and Neubauer, *The Fifty-Third Chapter of Isaiah*, 49.

71. Harry M. Orlinsky, 'The So-Called "Servant of the Lord" and "Suffering Servant" in Second Isaiah', in *Studies on the Second Part of the Book of Isaiah*, VTSup 14 (Leiden: E. J. Brill, 1967), 18.

72. See Jill Middlemas, 'Did Second Isaiah Write Lamentations III?', *VT* 56 (2006): 523, with citations.

73. Hägglund, *Isaiah 53 in the Light of Homecoming after Exile*, 53–4.

74. I would like to thank Hector Avalos for bringing Amos 9:5 to my attention.

75. Tryggve N. D. Mettinger, *A Farewell to the Servant Songs: A Critical Examination of an Exegetical Axiom*, trans. Frederick H. Cryer (Lund: CWK Gleerup, 1983), 40.

76. Mettinger, *A Farewell to the Servant Songs*, 41.

77. Mettinger, *A Farewell to the Servant Songs*, 40.

78. Mettinger's primary example of suffering in this passage is 51:7, which reads, 'Listen to me, you who know righteousness, you people who have my teaching in your hearts; do not fear the reproach of others, and do not be dismayed when they revile you.' See Mettinger, *A Farewell to the Servant Songs*, 40. While a related form of the Hebrew word 'righteous' appears in Isa 53:11, the language of suffering in this verse ('reproach' and 'revile') describes cities and peoples elsewhere in Second Isaiah (cf. Isa 43:28; 47:3; 54:4), but has nothing to do with any vocabulary or disability imagery in Isaiah 53.

79. Barré, 'Textual and Rhetorical-critical Observations on the Last Servant Song (Isaiah 52:13–53:12)', 13.

80. Hägglund, *Isaiah 53 in the Light of Homecoming after Exile*, 27; Mettinger, *A Farewell to the Servant Songs*, 41–2; cf. Zoltán Kustár, *'Durch seine Wunden sind wir geheilt': eine Untersuchung zur Metaphorik von Israels Krankheit und Heilung im Jesajabuch*, BWANT 154 (Stuttgart: Kohlhammer, 2002), 180.

81. For a helpful discussion of the use of disability imagery in these prophetic texts, see Saul M. Olyan, *Disability in the Hebrew Bible: Interpreting Mental and Physical Differences* (New York: Cambridge University Press, 2008), 78–92.

82. Rebecca Raphael, *Biblical Corpora: Representations of Disability in Hebrew Biblical Literature*, LHBOTS 445 (New York: T & T Clark, 2008), 129, 130.

83. I would like to thank Hector Avalos for bringing the 'Uncle Sam' example to my attention.

84. Leland Edward Wilshire, 'The Servant-City: A New Interpretation of the "Servant of the Lord" in the Servant Songs of Deutero-Isaiah', *JBL* 94 (1975): 358.

85. Christopher R. Seitz, *Zion's Final Destiny: The Development of the Book of Isaiah* (Minneapolis: Fortress, 1991), 203–4.

86. Wilshire, 'The Servant-City', 359. F. W. Dobbs-Allsopp argues that Isaiah 54 reflects an Israelite 'city-lament'. He compares this Israelite lament genre to examples of Mesopotamian 'city-laments', including the 'Lamentation over the Destruction of Ur'. For his specific comparison between Isaiah 54 and the Mesopotamian 'Nipper Lament', see F. W. Dobbs-Allsopp, *Weep, O daughter of Zion: A Study of the City-Lament Genre in the Hebrew Bible* (Rome: Editrice Pontificio Istituto Biblico, 1993), 150–1.

87. Wilshire, 'The Servant-City', 365.

88. Wilshire, 'The Servant-City', 366.

89. Seitz, *Zion's Final Destiny*, 204.

CONCLUSION

1. David J. A. Clines, *I, He, We, and They: A Literary Approach to Isaiah 53*, JSOTSup 1 (Sheffield: JSOT Press, 1976), 25.
2. Clines, *I, He, We, and They*, 60, 62.
3. See Robert McRuer, *Crip Theory: Cultural Signs of Queerness and Disability* (New York: New York University Press, 2006), 2–3, 6–10, 28–32.
4. For a detailed study of the literary relationship of First and Second Isaiah as well as an argument that Second Isaiah edited an edition of First Isaiah for inclusion with Isaiah 40–55, see Hugh G. M. Williamson, *The Book Called Isaiah: Deutero-Isaiah's Role in Composition and Redaction* (Oxford: Oxford University Press, 1994).
5. See Jon D. Levenson, *Sinai and Zion: An Entry into the Jewish Bible* (San Francisco: Harper San Francisco, 1985), 137; William M. Schniedewind, *Society and the Promise to David: The Reception History of 2 Samuel 7:1–17* (New York: Oxford University Press, 1999), 115–16. For a detailed study of the 'democratization' of the Zion or Davidic theology, see Timo Veijola, *Verheissung in der Krise: Studien zur Literatur und Theologie der Exilszeit anhand des 89. Psalms* (Helsinki: Suomalainen Tiedeakatemia, 1982), 133–75.
6. On Zion theology, see the discussions and citations in Levenson, *Sinai and Zion*, 89–176; Benjamin Ollenburger, *Zion: The City of the Great King*, JSOTSup 41 (Sheffield: Sheffield Academic Press, 1987); Tryggve N. D. Mettinger, *The Dethronement of Sabaoth: Studies in the Shem and Kabod Theologies* (Uppsala: Gleerup, 1982); J. J. M. Roberts, 'The Davidic Origin of the Zion Tradition', *JBL* 92 (1973): 329–44; *idem*, 'Zion in the Theology of the Davidic-Solomonic Empire', in Tomoo Ishida (ed.), *Studies in the Period of David and Solomon* (Winona Lake, IN: Eisenbrauns, 1982), 93–108; *idem*, 'The Enthronement of Yhwh and David: The Abiding Theological Significance of Kingship Language of the Psalms', *CBQ* 64 (2002): 675–86. The LORD's protection of the Davidic dynasty and Jerusalem has parallels in the imperial ideologies of the god Marduk, the king Hammurabi, and the city Babylon as well as the deity Inanna, the king Sargon and the city Akkad. See J. J. M. Roberts, 'Solomon's Jerusalem and the Zion Tradition', in Andrew Vaughn and Ann Killebrew (eds), *Jerusalem in Bible and Archeology: The First Temple Period*, SBLSynS 18 (Atlanta: Society of Biblical Literature, 2003), 163–70. Some scholars date this Zion theology as late as the fifth or fourth century BCE. For example, see Gunter Wanke, *Die Ziontheologie der Korachiten in ihrem Zusammenhang,*

BZAW 97 (Berlin: Alfred Töpelmann, 1966). Yet the parallels with Babylonian and Assyrian material as well as the evidence and critiques provided in the literature above call this dating into question. It seems reasonable to date the origins of Zion theology to the pre-exilic period.

7. Tryggve N. D. Mettinger, *A Farewell to the Servant Songs: A Critical Examination of an Exegetical Axiom*, trans. Frederick H. Cryer (Lund: CWK Gleerup, 1983), 44. Cf. Hugh G. M. Williamson, *Variations on a Theme: King, Messiah and Servant in the Book of Isaiah* (Carlisle: Paternoster, 1998), 166.

8. Benjamin Sommer, *A Prophet Reads Scripture: Allusion in Isaiah 40–66* (Stanford: Stanford University Press, 1998), 96.

9. For example, see Brevard S. Childs, *Isaiah: A Commentary*, OTL (Louisville: Westminster John Knox, 2001), 422–3; Stephen L. Cook, *Conversations with Scripture: 2 Isaiah* (Harrisburg: Morehouse Publishing, 2008), 69–71, 93–101; Christopher R. Seitz, 'The Book of Isaiah 40–66: Introduction, Commentary, and Reflections', *NIB* 6.468–70; Williamson, *Variations on a Theme*, 113–66.

Works Cited

Ackerman, Susan. 'The Blind, the Lame, and the Barren shall not come into the House', in Candida Moss and Jeremy Schipper (eds), *Disability Studies and Biblical Literature*. New York: Palgrave Macmillan, forthcoming.

Ådna, Jostein. 'The Servant of Isaiah 53 as Triumphant and Interceding Messiah: The Reception of Isaiah 52:13–53:12 in the Targum of Isaiah with Special Attention to the Concept of Messiah', in Janowski and Stuhlmacher (eds), *The Suffering Servant: Isaiah 53 in Jewish and Christian Sources*. Trans. Daniel P. Bailey. Grand Rapids, MI: William B Eerdmans, 2004, pp. 89–224.

Americans with Disabilities Act of 1990, S. 933, section 3, paragraph 2. Available online at http://caselaw.lp.findlaw.com/casecode/uscodes/42/chapters/126/toc.html (accessed 5 February 2011).

Annus, Amar and Alan Lenzi. *Ludlul Bēl Nēmeqi*. State Archives of Assyria Cuneiform Texts 8 Helsinki: The Neo-Assyrian Text Corpus Project, 2010.

Assmann, Jan. *Moses the Egyptian: The Memory of Egypt in Western Monotheism*. Cambridge, MA: Harvard University Press, 1997.

Avalos, Hector. *Illness and Health Care in the Ancient Near East: The Role of the Temple in Greece, Mesopotamia, and Israel*. HSM 54. Atlanta, GA: Scholars, 1995.

Avalos, Hector, Sarah Melcher, and Jeremy Schipper (eds). *This Abled Body: Rethinking Disability and Biblical Studies*, Semeia Studies 55. Atlanta, GA: Society of Biblical Literature, 2007.

Baden, Joel S. 'The Nature of Barrenness in the Hebrew Bible', in Candida Moss and Jeremy Schipper (eds), *Disability Studies and Biblical Literature*. New York: Palgrave Macmillan, forthcoming.

Baden, Joel S. and Candida R. Moss, 'The Origin and Interpretation of sara'at in Leviticus 13-14', *JBL* (forthcoming).

Bailey, Daniel P. 'Appendix: Isaiah 53 in Codex A Text of 1 Clement 16:3–14', in Janowski and Stuhlmacher (eds), *The Suffering Servant*, pp. 321–3.

——. '"Our Suffering and Crucified Messiah" (Dial. 111.2): Justin Martyr's Allusions to Isaiah 53 in His Dialogue with Trypho with Special Reference to the New Edition of M. Marcovich', in Janowski and Stuhlmacher (eds), *The Suffering Servant*, pp. 324–417.

Works Cited

——. 'Concepts of *Stellvertretung* in the Interpretation of Isaiah 53', in William H. Bellinger and William R. Farmer (eds), *Jesus and the Suffering Servant: Isaiah 53 and Christian Origins*. Harrisburg, PA: Trinity, 1998, pp. 223–50.

Baltzer, Klaus. *Deutero-Isaiah: A Commentary on Isaiah 40–55*. Hermeneia. Trans. Margaret Kohl. Minneapolis, MN: Fortress, 2001.

——. 'The Book of Isaiah', *HTR* 103 (2010): 261–70.

Barnes, Colin, Len Barton, and Michael Oliver (eds). *Disability Studies Today*. Cambridge: Polity, 2002.

Barré, Michael L. S. S., 'Textual and Rhetorical-Critical Observations on the Last Servant Song (Isaiah 52:13–53:12)'. *CBQ* 62 (2000): 1–27.

Barstad, Hans M. 'The Future of the "Servant Songs": Some Reflections on the Relationship of Biblical Scholarship to its own Tradition', in Samuel E. Balentine and John Barton (eds), *Language, Theology, and the Bible: Essays in Honour of James Barr*. Oxford: Clarendon, 1994, pp. 261–70.

Barthélemy, Dominique. *Critique textuelle de l'Ancien Testament*, 4 vols. Göttingen: Vandenhoeck & Ruprecht, 1982–2005.

Begrich, Joachim. *Studien zu Deuterojesaja*. München: C. Kaiser, 1963.

Bellinger, William H. and William R. Farmer (eds). *Jesus and the Suffering Servant: Isaiah 53 and Christian Origins*. Harrisburg, PA: Trinity, 1998.

Biggs, Robert D. *Šà.zi.ga, Ancient Mesopotamian Potency Incantations*. Locust Valley, NY: J. J. Augustin, 1967.

Bingham, D. Jeffrey. 'Justin and Isaiah 53'. *VC* 53 (2000): 248–61.

Blenkinsopp, Joseph. *Opening the Sealed Book: Interpretations of the Book of Isaiah in Late Antiquity*. Grand Rapids, MI: William B. Eerdmans, 2006.

——. *Isaiah 40–55: A New Translation with Introduction and Commentary*. AB 19A. New York: Doubleday, 2000.

Bowie, David. 'Ziggy Stardust'. *The Rise and Fall of Ziggy Stardust and the Spiders from Mars*. RCA Records, 1972.

Brueggemann, Brenda. 'On (Almost) Passing', in Lennard J. Davis (ed.), *The Disability Studies Reader*. 3rd edn. New York: Routledge, 2010, pp. 209–19.

Budde, Karl. 'The So-Called "Ebed-Yahweh Songs," and the Meaning of the Term "Servant of Yahweh" in Isaiah, Chaps. 40–55'. *AJT* 3 (1899): 499–540.

Chavesse, C. 'The Suffering Servant and Moses'. *CQR* 165 (1964): 152–63.

Childs, Brevard S. *The Struggle to Understand Isaiah as Christian Scripture*. Grand Rapids, MI: William B. Eerdmans, 2004.

——. *Isaiah: A Commentary*. OTL. Louisville, KY: Westminster John Knox, 2001.

——. *Introduction to the Old Testament as Scripture*. Philadelphia: Fortress, 1979.

Chilton, Bruce D. *The Isaiah Targum: Introduction, Translation, Apparatus and Notes.* ArBib 11. Wilmington, NC: Michael Glazier, 1987.

Clare, Eli. *Exile and Pride: Disability, Queerness, and Liberation.* Cambridge: South End, 1999.

Clements, Ronald E. 'Isaiah 53 and the Restoration of Israel', in Bellinger and Farmer (eds), *Jesus and the Suffering Servant*, pp. 39–54.

Clines, David J. A. *I, He, We, and They: A Literary Approach to Isaiah 53.* JSOTSup 1. Sheffield: JSOT Press, 1976.

Collins, Adela Yarbro. *Mark: A Commentary.* Hermeneia. Minneapolis, MN: Fortress, 2007.

Collins, John J. *Introduction to the Hebrew Bible.* Minneapolis, MN: Fortress, 2004.

——. 'Teacher and Servant'. *RHPR* 80 (2000): 37–50.

Cook, Stephen L. *Conversations with Scripture: 2 Isaiah.* Harrisburg, PA: Morehouse Publishing, 2008.

Cooper, Alan. 'The Suffering Servant and Job: A View from the Sixteenth Century', in Clairia Mathews McGillis and Patricia K. Tull (eds), *'As Those Who are Taught': The Reception of Isaiah from the LXX to the SBL.* SBLSymS 27. Atlanta, GA: Society of Biblical Literature, 2006, pp. 189–200.

Cruse, Colin G. 'The Servant Songs: Interpretative Trends Since C. K. North'. *Studia Biblica et Theologica* 8 (1978): 3–27.

Davies, Andrew. 'Oratorio as Exegesis: The Use of the Book of Isaiah in Handel's Messiah'. *BibInt* 15 (2007): 464–84.

Davis, Lennard J. *Bending Over Backwards: Disability, Dismodernism and Other Difficult Positions.* New York: New York University Press, 2002.

——. *Enforcing Normalcy: Disability, Deafness, and the Body.* New York: Verso, 1995.

Dobbs-Allsopp, F. W. *Weep, O Daughter of Zion: A Study of the City-Lament Genre in the Hebrew Bible.* Rome: Editrice Pontificio Istituto Biblico, 1993.

Dorman, Johanna. *The Blemished Body: Deformity and Disability in the Qumran Scrolls.* Groningen: Rijksuniversiteit, 2007.

Driver, G. R. 'Isaiah 52:13–53:12: The Servant of the Lord', in Matthew Black and Georg Fohrer (eds), *In Memoriam Paul Kahle.* BZAW 103. Berlin: A. Töpelmann, 1968, pp. 90–105.

Driver, Samuel R. and Adolf Neubauer. *The Fifty-Third Chapter of Isaiah according to the Jewish Interpreters.* Oxford and London: James Parker and Company, 1877.

Duhm, Bernhard. *Das Buch Jesaia übersetzt und erklärt.* Göttingen: Vandenhoeck & Ruprecht, 1922.

——. *Die Theologie der Propheten als Grundlage für die innere Entwicklungsgeschichte der israelitischen Religion.* Bonn: Marcus, 1875.

Eiesland, Nancy L. *The Disabled God: Toward a Liberatory Theology of Disability.* Nashville, TN: Abingdon, 1994.

Elliger, Karl. *Deuterojesaja in seinem verhältnis zu Tritojeseja.* Stuttgart: W. Kohlhammer Verlag, 1933.

Elliot, Mark W. (ed.). *Isaiah 40–66.* ACCS 11. Downers Grove, IL: InterVarsity, 2007.

Ellison, Rosemary. 'Some Thoughts on the Diet of Mesopotamia from c. 3000–600 BCE'. *Iraq* 45 (1983): 146–50.

——. 'Diet in Mesopotamia: The Evidence of the Barley Ration Texts (c. 3000–1400 BCE). *Iraq* 43 (1981): 35–45.

Engell, Ivan. 'The 'Ebed Yahweh Songs and the Suffering Messiah in Deutero-Isaiah'. *BJRL* 31 (1948): 54–93.

Eshel, Esther. '4Q471b: A Self-Glorification Hymn'. *RevQ* 17 (1996): 175–203.

Euler, Karl Friedrich. *Die verkündigung vom leidenden Gottesknecht aud Jes 53 in der griechischen Bibel.* Berlin: W. Kohlhammer, 1934.

Freud, Sigmund. *Moses and Monotheism.* Trans. Katherine Jones. New York: Vintage, 1939.

García Martínez, Florentino and Eibert J. C. Tigchelaar (eds). *The Dead Sea Scrolls: Study Edition,* 2 vols. Leiden: Brill, 1997–8.

Garland-Thomson, Rosemarie. *Staring: How We Look.* New York: Oxford University Press, 2009.

——. *Extraordinary Bodies: Figuring Physical Disability in American Culture and Literature.* New York: Columbia University Press, 1997.

Gerleman, Gillis. *Studien zur alttestamentlichen Theologie.* Heidelberg: Schneider, 1980.

Ginsberg, Harold L. 'The Oldest Interpretation of the Suffering Servant'. *VT* 3 (1953): 400–4.

Ginzberg, Louis. *The Legends of the Jews,* 7 vols. Trans. Henrietta Szold and Paul Radin. Baltimore: The Johns Hopkins University Press, 1998.

Goldingay, John and David Payne. *A Critical and Exegetical Commentary on Isaiah 40–55,* 2 vols. ICC. New York: T & T Clark International, 2006.

Goulder, Michael D. 'Behold My Servant Jehoiachin'. *VT* 52 (2002): 175–90.

Gunkel, Hermann. *Introduction to the Psalms: The Genres of the Religious Lyric of Israel.* Completed by Joachim Begrich. Trans. James D. Nogalski. Macon, GA: Mercer University Press, 1998.

——. *The Psalms: A Form-Critical Introduction.* Trans. Thomas M. Horner. Philadelphia: Fortress, 1967.

Gunn, David M. 'Samson of Sorrows: An Isaianic Gloss on Judges 13–16', in Danna Nolan Fewell (ed.), *Reading Between Texts: Intertextuality and the Hebrew Bible.* Louisville, KY: Westminster John Knox, 1992, pp. 225–53.

Haag, Ernst. 'Die Botschaft vom Gottesknecht. Ein Weg zur Überwindung der Gewalt', in Norbert Lohfink (ed.), *Gewalt und Gewaltlosigkeit im Alten Testament*. Freiburg: Herder, 1983, pp. 159–213.

Haag, Herbert. *Der Gottesknecht bei Deuterojesaja*. Darmstadt: Wissenschaftliche, 1985.

Hägglund, Fredrick. *Isaiah 53 in the Light of Homecoming after Exile*. FAT 31. Tübingen: Mohr-Siebeck, 2008.

Hanson, Paul D. *Isaiah 40–66*. Interpretation. Louisville, KY: Westminster John Knox, 1995.

Harrison, R. K. 'Blindness'. *IDB* 1:448–9.

Hays, Richard B. *Echoes of Scripture in the Letters of Paul*. New Haven: Yale University Press, 1993.

Heessel, Nils. *Babylonisch-assyriche Diagnostik*. AOAT 43; Münster: Ugarit-Verlag, 2000.

Hengel Martin with Daniel P. Bailey. 'The Effective History of Isaiah 53 in the Pre-Christian Period', in Janowski and Stuhlmacher (eds), *The Suffering Servant*, pp. 75–146.

Himmelfarb, Martha. 'Sefer Zerubbabel', in David Stern and Mark J. Mirsky (eds), *Rabbinic Fantasies: Imaginative Narratives from Classical Hebrew Literature*. New Haven: Yale University Press, 1990, pp. 67–90.

Holden, Lynn. *Forms of Deformity*. JSOTSup 131. Sheffield: Sheffield Academic Press, 1991.

Holladay, William L. *Isaiah: Scroll of a Prophetic Heritage*. Grand Rapids, MI: William B. Eerdmans, 1978.

Hooker, Morna D. *Jesus and the Servant: The Influence of the Servant Concept of Deutero-Isaiah in the New Testament*. London: SPCK, 1959.

——. 'Did the Use of Isaiah 53 to Interpret His Mission Begin with Jesus?', in Bellinger and Farmer (eds), *Jesus and the Suffering Servant*, pp. 88–103.

——. 'Response to Mikeal Parsons'. in Bellinger and Farmer (eds), *Jesus and the Suffering Servant*, pp. 120–4.

Hugenberger, Gordon P. 'The Servant of the Lord in the "Servant Songs" of Isaiah: A Second Moses Figure', in Richard Hess, Philip E. Satterthwaite, and Gordon Wenham (eds), *The Lord's Anointed: Interpretation of Old Testament Messianic Texts*. Grand Rapids, MI: Baker Academic, 1995, pp. 105–40.

Hüllstrung, Wolfgang and Gerlinde Feine updated by Daniel P. Bailey. 'A Classified Bibliography on Isaiah 53', in Janowski and Stuhlmacher (eds), *The Suffering Servant*, pp. 462–92.

Itkonen, Lauri. *Deuterojesaja (Jes. 40–55) metrisch untersucht*. Helsinki: Finnischen Literatur-Gesellschaft, 1916.

Janowski, Bernd. *Stellvertretung: alttestamentliche Studien zu einem theologischen Grundbegriff.* Stuttgart: Verlag Katholisches Bibelwerk, 1997.

———. 'He Bore Our Sins: Isaiah 53 and the Drama of Taking Another's Place', in Janowski and Stuhlmacher (eds), *The Suffering Servant*, pp. 48–74.

Janowski, Bernd and Peter Stuhlmacher, eds. *The Suffering Servant: Isaiah 53 in Jewish and Christian Sources.* Trans. Daniel P. Bailey. Grand Rapids, MI: William B. Eerdmans, 2004.

Joachimsen, Kristin. 'Steck's Five Stories of the Servant in Isaiah lii 13–liii 12, and Beyond'. *VT* 57 (2007): 208–28.

Jobes, Karen H. and Moisés Silva. *Invitation to the Septuagint.* Grand Rapids, MI: Baker Academic, 2000.

Jones, Richard N. and David P. Wright, 'Leprosy'. *ABD* 4.277–82.

Juel, Donald. *Messianic Exegesis: Christological Interpretation of the Old Testament in Early Christianity.* Minneapolis, MN: Fortress, 1988.

Junior, Nyasha and Jeremy Schipper. 'Mosaic Disability and Identity in Exodus 4:10; 6:12, 30'. *BibInt* 16 (2008): 428–41.

Kaiser, Otto. *Der königliche Knecht; eine traditionsgeschichtlich-exegetische Studie über die Ebed-Jahwe-Lieder bei Deuterojesaja.* Göttingen: Vandenhoeck & Ruprecht, 1959.

Kinnier Wilson, J. V. 'Leprosy in Ancient Mesopotamia'. *RA* 60 (1966): 47–58.

Klawans, Jonathan. *Impurity and Sin in Ancient Judaism.* New York: Oxford University Press, 2000.

Köcher, Franz. *Die babylonisch-assyrische Medizin in Texten und Untersuchungen,* 6 vols. Berlin: Walter de Gruyter, 1963–80.

Knohl, Israel. *The Messiah before Jesus: The Suffering Servant of the Dead Sea Scrolls.* Trans. David Maisel. Berkeley: University of California Press, 2000.

———. 'The Suffering Servant: From Isaiah to the Dead Sea Scrolls', in Deborah A. Green and Laura S. Lieber (eds), *Scriptural Exegesis: The Shapes of Culture and the Religious Imagination: Essays in Honour of Michael Fishbane.* Oxford: Oxford University Press, 2009, pp. 89–104.

Kraetzschmar, Richard. *Das Buch Ezechiel übersetzt und erklärt.* Göttingen: Vandenhoeck & Ruprecht, 1900.

Kratz, Reinhard Gregor. *Kyros im Deuterojesaja-Buch: Redaktionsgeschichtliche Untersuchungen zu Entstehung und Theologie von Jes 40–55.* FAT 1. Tübingen: Mohr-Siebeck, 1991.

Kustár, Zoltán. *'Durch seine Wunden sind wir geheilt': eine Untersuchung zur Metaphorik von Israels Krankheit und Heilung im Jesajabuch.* BWANT 154. Stuttgart: W. Kohlhammer, 2002.

Laato, Antti. *The Servant of YHWH and Cyrus: A Reinterpretation of the Exilic Messianic Programme of Isaiah 40–55*. ConBOT 35. Stockholm: Almqvist & Wiksell, 1992.

Labat, René. *Traité akkadien de diagnostics et prognostics médicaux*, 2 vols. Paris: Académie Internationale d'Histoire des Sciences, 1951.

Lester, G. Brooke. 'Daniel Evokes Isaiah: The Rule of the Nations in Apocalyptic Allusion-Narrative'. PhD dissertation, Princeton Theological Seminary. Princeton, 2007.

Leunis Koole, Jan. *Isaiah, Part III*. Historical Commentary on the Old Testament. Kampen: Kok Pharos, 1997.

Levenson, Jon D. *Resurrection and the Restoration of Israel: The Ultimate Victory of the God of Life*. New Haven: Yale University Press, 2006.

——. *Sinai and Zion: An Entry into the Jewish Bible*. San Francisco: Harper San Francisco, 1985.

Levison, John R. and Priscilla Pope-Levison (eds). *Return to Babel: Global Perspectives on the Bible*. Louisville, KY: Westminster John Knox, 1999.

Lichtheim, Miriam. *Ancient Egyptian Literature*, 3 vols. Berkeley: University of California Press, 1973.

Linafelt, Tod. *Surviving Lamentations: Catastrophe, Lament, and Protest in the Afterlife of a Biblical Book*. Chicago: University of Chicago Press, 2000.

Lindblom, Johannes. *The Servant Songs in Deutero-Isaiah: A New Attempt to Solve an Old Problem*. Lund: CWK Gleerup, 1951.

Lumbala, François Kabasele. 'Isaiah 52:13–53:12: An African Perspective', in Levinson and Pope-Levison (eds), *Return to Babel*, pp. 101–6.

Luz, Ulrich. *Matthew 8–20: A Commentary*, 3 vols. Hermeneia. Trans. James E. Crouch. Minneapolis, MN: Fortress Press, 2001.

MacDonald, Nathan. *What Did the Ancient Israelites Eat?: Diet in Biblical Times*. Grand Rapids, MI: William B. Eerdmans, 2008.

Magdalene, F. Rachel. *On the Scales of Righteousness: Neo-Babylonian Trial Law and the Book of Job*. BJS 48. Atlanta, GA: Society of Biblical Literature, 2007.

——. 'The ANE Legal Origins of Impairment as Theological Disability and the Book of Job'. *PRSt* 34 (2007): 23–60.

Marcus, David. 'Some Antiphrastic Euphemisms for a Blind Person in Akkadian and Other Semitic Languages'. *JAOS* 100 (1980): 307–10.

Markschies, Christoph. 'Jesus Christ as a Man before God: Two Interpretative Models for Isaiah 53 in the Patristic Literature and Their Development', in Janowski and Stuhlmacher (eds), *The Suffering Servant*, pp. 225–323.

Marrow, James H. *Passion Iconography in Northern European Art of the Late Middle Ages and Early Renaissance: A Study of the Transformation of Sacred Metaphor into Descriptive Narrative.* Kortrijk: Van Ghemmert, 1979.

McRuer, Robert. *Crip Theory: Cultural Signs of Queerness and Disability.* New York: New York University Press, 2006.

Melugin, Roy F. *The Formation of Isaiah 40–55.* BZAW 141. Berlin: Walter de Gruyter, 1976.

Menten, Maarten J. J. 'The Source of the Quotation of Isaiah 53:4 in Matthew 8:17'. *NovT* 39 (1997): 313–27.

Metallica. 'Leper Messiah'. *Master of Puppets.* Elektra Records, 1986.

Mettinger, Tryggve N. D. *A Farewell to the Servant Songs: A Critical Examination of an Exegetical Axiom.* Trans. Frederick H. Cryer. Lund: CWK Gleerup, 1983.

——. *The Dethronement of Sabaoth: Studies in the Shem and Kabod Theologies.* Uppsala: Gleerup, 1982.

Middlemas, Jill. 'Did Second Isaiah Write Lamentations III?' *VT* 56 (2006): 506–25.

Milgrom, Jacob. *Leviticus 1–16: A New Translation with Introduction and Commentary.* AB 3. New York: Doubleday, 1991.

Moon, Cyris Heesuk. 'Isaiah 52:13–53:12: An Asian Perspective', in Levinson and Pope-Levison (eds), *Return to Babel*, pp. 107–13.

Morris, Jenny. *Pride against Prejudice: Transforming Attitudes to Disability.* London: The Women's Press, 1991.

Mowinckel, Sigmund. *Der Knecht Jahwäs.* Giessen: Alfred Töpelmann, 1921.

Muilenburg, James. 'Isaiah, Chapters 40–66', in G. A. Buttrick (ed.), *The Interpreter's Bible.* New York and Nashville, TN: Abingdon, 1956.

North, Christopher R. *The Suffering Servant in Deutero-Isaiah: A Historical and Critical Study.* 2nd edn. London: Oxford University Press, 1956.

Nussbaum, Martha C. *Frontiers of Justice: Disability, Nationality, Species Membership.* Cambridge, MA: Harvard University Press, 2006.

O'Kane, Martin. 'Picturing "The Man of Sorrows": The Passion-Filled Afterlives of a Biblical Icon'. *RelArts* 9 (2005): 62–100.

Ollenburger, Benjamin. *Zion: The City of the Great King.* JSOTSup 41. Sheffield: Sheffield Academic Press, 1987.

Olyan, Saul M. *Disability in the Hebrew Bible: Interpreting Mental and Physical Differences.* New York: Cambridge University Press, 2008.

——. 'The Ascription of Physical Disability as a Stigmatizing Strategy in Biblical Iconic Polemics'. *JHS* 9, article 14 (2009): 1–15, online: www.arts.ualberta.ca/JHS/Articles/article_116.pdf (accessed 14 February 2011).

Orlinksky, Harry M. 'The So-Called "Servant of the Lord" and "Suffering Servant" in Second Isaiah', in *Studies on the Second Part of the Book of Isaiah*. VTSup 14. Leiden: E. J. Brill, 1967, pp. 1–133.

Oswalt, John N. *The Book of Isaiah: Chapters 40–66*. NICOT. Grand Rapids, MI: William B. Eerdmans, 1998.

Parry, Donald W. and Elisha Qimron (eds). *The Great Isaiah Scroll (1QIsaᵃ): A New Edition*. Studies on the Texts of the Desert of Judah 32. Lieden: Brill, 1999.

Parsons, Mikael C. *Body and Character in Luke and Acts: The Subversion of Physiognomy in Early Christianity*. Grand Rapids, MI: Baker Academic, 2006.

——. 'Isaiah 53 in Acts 8: A Reply to Morna Hooker', in Bellinger and Farmer (eds), *Jesus and the Suffering Servant*, pp. 104–19.

Paul, Shalom M. *Isaiah 40–66: Introduction and Commentary*, 2 vols. Mikra Leyisrael. Jerusalem: Magnes, 2008 (Hebrew).

Pixley, Jorge. 'Isaiah 52:13–53:12: A Latin American Perspective', in Levinson and Pope-Levinson (eds), *Return to Babel: Global Perspectives on the Bible*, pp. 93–100.

Raphael, Rebecca. *Biblical Corpora: Representations of Disability in Hebrew Biblical Literature*. LHBOTS 445. New York: T & T Clark, 2008.

——. 'Things Too Wonderful: A Disabled Reading of Job'. *PRSt* 31 (2004): 399–424.

Reventlow, Henning Graf. 'Basic Issues in the Interpretation of Isaiah 53', in Bellinger and Farmer (eds), *Jesus and the Suffering Servant*, pp. 23–38.

Reynolds, Frances (ed.). *The Babylonian Correspondence of Esarhaddon and Letters to Assurbanipal and Sin-Šarru-Iškun from Northern and Central Babylonia*. SAA 18. Helsinki: Helsinki University Press, 2003.

Ringgren, Helmer. *The Messiah in the Old Testament*. Studies in Biblical Theology 18. London: SCM Press, 1956.

Roberts, J. J. M. 'Solomon's Jerusalem and the Zion Tradition', in Andrew Vaughn and Ann Killebrew (eds), *Jerusalem in Bible and Archeology: The First Temple Period*. SBLSynS 18. Atlanta, GA: Society of Biblical Literature, 2003, pp. 163–70.

——. 'The Enthronement of Yhwh and David: The Abiding Theological Significance of Kingship Language of the Psalms'. *CBQ* 64 (2002): 675–86.

——. 'Zion in the Theology of the Davidic–Solomonic Empire', in Tomoo Ishida (ed.), *Studies in the Period of David and Solomon*. Winona Lake, IN: Eisenbrauns, 1982, pp. 93–108.

——. 'The Davidic Origin of the Zion Tradition'. *JBL* 92 (1973): 329–44.

——. 'Hand of Yahweh'. *VT* 21 (1971): 244–51.

Roth, Wolfgang M. W. 'The Anonymity of the Suffering Servant'. *JBL* 83 (1964): 171–9.

Rowley, Harold Henry. 'The Servant of the Lord', in Harold Henry Rowley, *The Servant of the Lord and Other Essays on the Old Testament*. London: Lutterworth, 1952, pp. 1–57.

Samuels, Ellen. 'My Body, My Closet: Invisible Disability and the Limits of Coming-Out Discourse'. *Gay Lesbian Quarterly* 9 (2003): 233–55.

Sapp, David A. 'The LXX. 1QIsa, and MT Versions of Isaiah 53 and the Christian Doctrine of Atonement', in Bellinger and Farmer (eds), *Jesus and the Suffering Servant*, pp. 170–92.

Sawyer, John F. A. *The Fifth Gospel: Isaiah in the History of Christianity*. Cambridge: Cambridge University Press, 1996.

——. *Prophecy and the Biblical Prophets*. Oxford: Oxford University Press, 1993.

Scharbert, Josef. 'Stellvertretendes Sühneleiden in den Ebed-Jahwe-Lieder und in altorientalischen Ritualtexten'. *BZ* (1958): 190–213.

Schipper, Jeremy. *Disability Studies and the Hebrew Bible: Figuring Mephibosheth in the David Story*. LHBOTS 441. New York: T & T Clark, 2006.

——. 'Embodying Deuteronomistic Theology in 1 Kings 15:22–24', in Tamar Kamionkowski and Wonil Kim (eds), *Bodies, Embodiment and Theology of the Hebrew Bible*. LHBOTS 465. New York: T & T Clark, 2010, pp. 77–89.

——. 'Healing and Silence in the Epilogue of Job'. *Word and World* 30 (2010): 16–22.

——. 'Deuteronomy 24:5 and King Asa's Foot Disease in 1 Kings 15:23b'. *JBL* 128 (2009): 643–8.

——. 'Disabling Israelite Leadership: 2 Samuel 6:23 and Other Images of Disability in the Deuteronomistic History', in Avalos, Melcher, and Schipper (eds), *This Abled Body*, pp. 103–13.

Schniedewind, William M. *Society and the Promise to David: The Reception History of 2 Samuel 7:1–17*. New York: Oxford University Press, 1999.

Scurlock, JoAnn. *Magico-Medical Means of Treating Ghost-Induced Illnesses in Ancient Mesopotamia*. Ancient Magic and Divination 3. Leiden: Brill, 2006.

Scurlock, JoAnn and Burton R. Anderson. *Diagnoses of Assyrian and Babylonian Medicine: Ancient Sources, Translations, and Modern Medical Analyses*. Urbana, IL: University of Illinois Press, 2005.

Seitz, Christopher R. *Zion's Final Destiny: The Development of the Book of Isaiah*. Minneapolis, MN: Fortress, 1991.

——. 'The Book of Isaiah 40–66: Introduction, Commentary, and Reflections'. *NIB* 6: 307–552.

Sellin, Ernst. *Mose und seine Bedeutung für die israelitisch-jüdische Religionsgeschichte*. Leipzig: Deichert, 1922.

——. *Studien zur Entstehungsgeschichte der jüdischen Gemeinde nach dem babylonischen Exil. I. Der Knecht Gottes bei Deuterojesaja*. Leipzig: Deichert, 1901.

Siebers, Tobin. *Disability Aesthetics*. Ann Arbor: University of Michigan Press, 2010.

——. *Disability Theory*. Ann Arbor: University of Michigan Press, 2008.

Skinner, John. *The Book of the Prophet Isaiah: Chapters XL–LXVI*. CBC. Cambridge: Cambridge University Press, 1954.

Snyder, Sharon L. and David T. Mitchell, *Cultural Locations of Disability*. Chicago: University of Chicago Press, 2006.

——. *Narrative Prosthesis: Disability and the Dependencies of Discourse*. Ann Arbor: University of Michigan Press, 2000.

——. 'Disability Studies and the Double Bind of Representation', in Sharon L. Snyder and David T. Mitchell (eds), *The Body and Physical Difference: Discourses on Disability*. Ann Arbor: University of Michigan Press, 1997, pp. 1–31.

Soggin, Jan Alberto. 'Tod und Auferstehung des leidendes Gottes-Knechtes: Jesaja 53, 8–10'. *ZAW* 85 (1975): 346–55.

Sommer, Benjamin. *A Prophet Reads Scripture: Allusion in Isaiah 40–66*. Stanford, CA: Stanford University Press, 1998.

Spieckermann, Hermann. 'The Conception and Prehistory of the Idea of Vicarious Suffering in the Old Testament', in Janowski and Stuhlmacher (eds), *The Suffering Servant*, pp. 1–47.

Steck, Odil Hannes. *Gottesknecht und Zion: Gesammelte Aufsätze zu Deuterojesaja*. FAT 4. Tübingen: Mohr-Siebeck, 1992.

Stoddard Holmes, Martha. *Fictions of Affliction: Physical Disability in Victorian Culture*. Ann Arbor: University of Michigan Press, 2004.

Stratton, Beverly J. 'Engaging Metaphors: Suffering with Zion and the Servant in Isaiah 52–53', in Stephen E. Fowl (ed.), *The Theological Interpretation of Scripture: Classic and Contemporary Readings*. Cambridge: Blackwell, 1997, pp. 219–37.

Sweeney, Marvin. 'The Book of Isaiah in Recent Research'. *Currents in Research: Biblical Studies* 1 (1993): 141–62.

Tate, Marvin E. 'The Book of Isaiah in Recent Study', in James W. Watts and Paul R. House (eds), *Forming Prophetic Literature: Essays on Isaiah and the Twelve in Honor of John D. W. Watts*. JSOTSup 235. Sheffield: Sheffield Academic Press, 1996, pp. 22–56.

Thomas, D. Winton. 'A Consideration of Isaiah liii in the Light of Recent Textual and Philological Study'. *Ephemerides Theologicae Lovanienses* 44 (1968): 79–86.

——. 'A Consideration of Some Unusual Ways of Expressing the Superlative in Hebrew'. *VT* 18 (1953): 209–44.

Tigay, Jeffery. ' "Heavy of Mouth" and "Heavy of Tongue": On Moses' Speech Difficulty'. *BASOR* 231 (1978): 57–67.

Tremain, Shelley (ed.). *Foucault and the Government of Disability*. Ann Arbor: University of Michigan Press, 2005.

Troxel, Ronald L. *LXX-Isaiah as Translation and Interpretation: The Strategies of the Translator of the Septuagint of Isaiah*. JSJTSup 124. Leiden: Brill, 2008.

Tull Willey, Patricia. *Remember the Former Things: The Recollection of Previous Texts in Second Isaiah*. SBLDS 161. Atlanta, GA: Society of Biblical Literature, 1997.

Veijola, Timo. *Verheissung in der Krise: Studien zur Literatur und Theologie der Exilszeit anhand des 89. Psalms*. Helsinki: Suomalainen Tiedeakatemia, 1982.

von Rad, Gerhard. *Old Testament Theology, Volume II: The Theology of Israel's Prophetic Traditions*. Trans. D. M. G. Stalker. London: Oliver and Boyd, 1965.

Wagner, J. Ross. *Heralds of the Good News: Isaiah and Paul in Concert*. NovTSup 101. Leiden: Brill, 2002.

Waltke, Bruce K. and Michael O'Connor. *An Introduction to Biblical Hebrew Syntax*. Winona Lake, IN: Eisenbrauns, 1990.

Walls, Neal H. 'The Origins of the Disabled Body: Disability in Ancient Mesopotamia', in Avalos, Melcher, and Schipper (eds), *This Abled Body*, pp. 13–30.

Walton, John H. 'The Imagery of the Substitute King Ritual in Isaiah's Fourth Servant Song'. *JBL* 122 (2003): 734–43.

Wanke, Gunter. *Die Ziontheologie der Korachiten in ihrem Zusammenhang*. BZAW 97. Berlin: Alfred Töpelmann, 1966.

Ward, James M. 'The Servant Songs in Isaiah'. *RevExp* 65 (1968): 133–46.

Watts, John D. W. *Isaiah 34–66*. Revised edn. WBC 25. Nashville, TN: Nelson Reference & Electronic, 2005.

Wells, Calvin. *Bones, Bodies, and Disease: Evidence of Disease and Abnormality in Early Man*. New York: Frederick A. Praeger, 1964.

Wendell, Susan. *The Rejected Body: Feminist Philosophical Reflections on Disability*. New York: Routledge, 1996.

Westermann, Claus. *Isaiah 40–66: A Commentary*. OTL. Trans. David M. G. Stalker. Philadelphia: Westminster, 1969.

Wilshire, Leland Edward. 'The Servant-City: A New Interpretation of the "Servant of the Lord" in the Servant Songs of Deutero-Isaiah'. *JBL* 94 (1975): 356–67.

Whitehouse, Walter M. 'Radiologic Findings in the Royal Mummies', in James Harris and Edward Wente (eds), *An X-Ray Atlas of the Royal Mummies*. Chicago: University of Chicago Press, 1980, pp. 286–327.

Whybray, Roger N. *Thanksgiving for a Liberated Prophet: An Interpretation of Isaiah Chapter 53*. JSOTSup 4. Sheffield: JSOT Press, 1978.

Wilken, Robert Louis (ed.). *Isaiah: Interpreted by Early Christian and Medieval Commentators*. The Church's Bible. Grand Rapids, MI: William B. Eerdmans, 2007.

Williamson, Hugh G. M. *The Book Called Isaiah: Deutero-Isaiah's Role in Composition and Redaction*. Oxford: Oxford University Press, 1994.

——. *Variations on a Theme: King, Messiah and Servant in the Book of Isaiah*. Carlisle: Paternoster, 1998.

Wiseman, D. J. 'A New Text of the Babylonian Poem of the Righteous Sufferer'. *Anatolian Studies* 30 (1980): 101–07.

Wolff, Hans Walter. *Jesaja 53 im Urchristentum*. Introduction by Peter Stuhlmacher. Giessen: Brunnen Verlag, 1984.

——. 'Wer ist der Gottesknecht in Jesaja 53?' *EvT* 22 (1962): 338–42.

Wright, David P. 'Unclean and Clean (OT)'. *ABD* 6: 729–41.

——. 'The Spectrum of Priestly Impurity', in Gary A. Anderson and Saul M. Olyan (eds), *Priesthood and Cult in Ancient Israel*. JSOTSup 125. Sheffield: JSOT Press, 1991, pp. 150–81.

Wynn, Kerry. 'The Normate Hermeneutic and Interpretations of Disability in Yahwistic Narratives', in Avalos, Melcher, and Schipper (eds), *This Abled Body*, pp. 91–101.

Zimmerli, Walther. 'Zur Vorgeschichte von Jes 53', in *Studien zur alttestamentlichen Theologie und Prophetie*. München: Kaiser, 1974, pp. 213–21.

Zimmerli, Walther and Joachim Jeremias. *The Servant of God*. SBT 20. Trans. Harold Knight. London: SCM Press, 1957.

Index to Biblical and Other Ancient Texts